D0806333

A SECOND
FEDERALIST

Selected from the Annals of Congress

by CHARLES S. HYNEMAN
INDIANA UNIVERSITY

and GEORGE W. CAREY
GEORGETOWN UNIVERSITY

A SECOND
FEDERALIST
Congress creates a government

724675

UNIVERSITY OF SOUTH CAROLINA PRESS
Columbia, South Carolina

Copyright © 1967
by Meredith Publishing Company

First edition (paperback) published 1967 by
Appleton-Century-Crofts, Division
of Meredith Publishing Company, New York, N.Y.

This edition published 1970 by
the University of South Carolina Press,
Columbia, S.C. Reprinted by
special arrangement with Appleton-Century-Crofts,
Educational Division, Meredith Corporation.

Standard Book Number: 87249-173-0

Library of Congress Catalog Card Number: 74-119334

Manufactured by Edwards Brothers, Inc.

In lieu of dedication

The editors of this volume name here those members of Congress during the early years who most excited their admiration for quality of thought, forthrightness of expression, and display of rectitude in reconciling personal position with a commitment to decision by majority.

FISHER AMES OF MASSACHUSETTS
JAMES A. BAYARD OF DELAWARE
JOHN C. CALHOUN OF SOUTH CAROLINA
WILLIAM GASTON OF NORTH CAROLINA
ROBERT GOODLOE HARPER OF SOUTH CAROLINA
BENJAMIN HUGER OF SOUTH CAROLINA
JAMES MADISON OF VIRGINIA
CHARLES PINCKNEY OF SOUTH CAROLINA
JOSIAH QUINCY OF MASSACHUSETTS
ROGER SHERMAN OF CONNECTICUT
WILLIAM L. SMITH OF SOUTH CAROLINA
HENRY ST. GEORGE TUCKER OF VIRGINIA

PREFACE

All of the materials presented in this volume, other than the notes prepared by the editors, were taken from the *Annals of Congress*.

The *Annals* is a record of what was said and what was done by Congress during the first four decades under the Constitution of 1787. It is a counterpart of the *Congressional Record*, which records debates and actions of Congress today. But the *Annals* differs from the *Congressional Record* in at least three important respects: the debates in Congress today are taken down by official reporters who answer to the two chambers for the completeness and the accuracy of their reporting; all speeches made on the floors of the two chambers are recorded in shorthand by the reporter; and all speeches, questions and answers, and repartee appear in the *Congressional Record* verbatim. Exceptions to the last two points are minor and unimportant.

On each of these three points, the *Annals of Congress* is significantly different. Neither house of Congress designated an official reporter until long after the period covered by the *Annals*. The reporting was by newspapermen who took down the speeches and noted the actions which they thought would be of interest to their readers, or by other printers who reported what they thought they had a market for in special publications. These early reporters took no account of much of the debate that occurred in the House of Representatives, and they were not allowed to hear the debates in the Senate during the first several sessions of Congress. Finally, the reporting was generally not verbatim; paragraphs and sometimes the entire speech appear to be in the speaker's own words, but usually the *Annals* supplies us with a third person account of what the speaker said. A compilation of these reports, believed to be the most complete and accurate accounts of what was actually said, was put together in 1834 by a leading publishing house, Gales and Seaton, and issued in forty-two volumes. They cover all the sessions of Congress from the opening of the first through the first session of the Eighteenth Congress (adjourned May 27, 1824). This is the *Annals of Congress*, from which all the selections in this volume were taken.

We cannot confidently evaluate the accuracy of the reporting in the *Annals*, for about all we know to have been said is what the reporters have told us. There was some complaint about the reporting by Congressmen, but there was also high praise. A resolution introduced in the House of Representatives late in its first session averred that "glaring deviations from the truth" had been made, including distorting of remarks and imputing to members of Congress statements which they had not made. The resolution proposed to terminate the privileges that the House had given to the reporters, including the right to sit on the floor near the Speaker's table. The resolution was not adopted, but the report of what was said for and against it indicates that there was solid factual support for the charges that it carried. James Madison, for instance, said that he had seen in the newspapers "very great misconceptions of what fell from him." Expressions of dissatisfaction with the reporting are noted from time to time in the *Annals* over a period of several years. But successive proposals to authorize the appointment of an official reporter failed to carry. If the reporting was far from perfect in the views of Congressmen, it at least was tolerable. And it is certain that part of the time, some of the Congressmen were highly pleased with the product. In 1796, for instance, Representative John Swanwick praised the editor of a newspaper who had "not only done everything in his power to obtain the debates of the House at full length, but had frequently advertised that if errors were committed by his reporters, they should on application be instantly rectified."

Awareness of imperfections in the original reporting of speeches made it easy for the editors, in preparing the volume now in hand, to decide to modernize punctuation, to separate lines of print into sentences and paragraphs, and occasionally to insert words to clarify meaning. In all cases there was scrupulous concern to lay before the reader what the speaker is thought to have said. In many instances only part of a speech is reprinted. An ellipsis preceding the quoted remarks indicates that one or more full paragraphs of the speech precede the part quoted. An ellipsis following the quoted remarks indicates that one or more full paragraphs of the speech follow the part quoted. An ellipsis between paragraphs indicates that one or more full paragraphs of a speech are omitted. In selections including the remarks of two or more men, an ellipsis following the name of a speaker indicates that the gentleman's opening remarks are omitted. Numbers in italics mark the transition from one page of the *Annals* to the next. They are provided for those who may wish to quote from this book, citing pages in the *Annals*. But those who would, in their own publications, quote from this printing, will be wise to check any of the items with the original print in the *Annals of Congress*.

We can speak with more certainty about the comprehensiveness of the reporting than about its accuracy. In no session of the eighteen Congresses embraced by the *Annals* were all of the speeches reported for the House of Representatives. As time went on, more and more of the remarks on the floor were taken down and put into print for our examination today. The record for the House of Representatives during the six months it sat in its first session fills 828 column-pages in the *Annals;* an equal number of days in the last session reported fills 2123 column-pages. Throughout the period, reporting in the third person abounds, but in reports of the later sessions more and more of the remarks are presented in the first person, in many instances giving strong reason to believe that the entire speech was recorded verbatim. Yet, in spite of the steady extension of coverage, one encounters throughout the period some abbreviated reports. In 1816: "Mr. Randolph had spoken before in this debate, but the length of his first speech, which continued three days, and which it would take more than a week to write off from the reporter's brief notes, prevents its publication. The remarks which follow were [by Mr. Randolph] in reply to Mr. Calhoun." In 1823: "This motion gave rise to a debate of something like an hour. It was supported by Mr. Sterling, and opposed by Mr. W. Smith, of Virginia, and Mr. Campbell, of Ohio."

The Senate refused, in its first session, to open its doors to the general public or to reporters and continued this policy of exclusion until the close of the Third Congress. The reason for this aloofness from the public, apparently, was a belief that the Senate represented the states rather than the general population. This view was opposed by a minority of the Senators, however, and their continued effort to open the doors finally met success. The public was allowed to hear discussion of a contested seat (whether Albert Gallatin of Pennsylvania had lived the required number of years in the United States) during the Third Congress. With the opening of the Fourth Congress on March 4, 1795, reporting of the debates in the Senate became a regular occurrence. It was several years, however, before the Senate debates were recorded as fully as those of the House. The reporters and their readers no doubt agreed with the Congressmen that the members of the House of Representatives were the true representatives of the people and the Senators only remotely so. Only thirteen of the seventy-nine numbered selections in this book present speeches that were made in the Senate.

The selection of materials for inclusion in this volume was guided by one principle. The editors searched for the best thought expressed on issues that were of critical importance in fixing the character of the American political system. If there were deviations from the rule, the most frequent were to yield a bit on the quality of the argument in order to make a place for the best that could be found on an unusually important issue. Some of the debate in chapter 11 on the Bill of Rights illustrates; remarks which cannot be defended as thoughtful analysis are included in that chapter because of the great importance which many people today attach to the origin of constitutional guarantees of personal freedom. Less frequent was the decision to include a speech because it made what seems today a novel proposition (as was more than once the case with Representative James Jackson). Still another departure from strict principle was the inclusion of remarks that provide a historical background helpful for a better understanding of those statements that more fully meet the test of "best thought" on an issue of critical importance. One of the truly great speeches of the early period, only a small part of which is included here (that of Representative Benjamin Huger in selection 2.4), relied largely on a recital of past events to establish the distinctive character of our federal system. If "best thought" means "best reasoning," then several paragraphs of Mr. Huger's speech are in this volume because they give us his view of history rather than a display of analytic power.

The selection was a taxing and chastening process. Taxing because decisions to include or not to include often required a choice among statements at the margin of equal attractiveness to the editors. Chastening because one is forced to ponder his right to make the judgment when he says to Henry Clay, or Albert Gallatin, or John Quincy Adams, What you have said does not match, for quality of thought, the remarks of some of your colleagues who failed to win your high place in history. Clay must yield to Barbour on interpretation of the tenth amendment; Gallatin must give place to Harper on the treaty power; and nothing that John Quincy Adams said, on any subject, ranks higher in quality than the best thought of one or more of his colleagues.

A plain implication of the foregoing remarks is that the selection of items for inclusion eliminated many that are worthy of study today. In the judgment of the editors, the debates in Congress during its first forty years provide the materials for a book twice the size of this one, with every page in it of enduring value for students of government and politics. The speeches that are presented in this compilation are the result of an effort to pick the best from a great treasury of riches. The reader can judge for himself whether they present challenges to thought which entitle them to be offered as essays for A Second Federalist.

C.S.H.
G.W.C.

ACKNOWLEDGMENTS

It gives us great pleasure to express here our gratitude to the following persons for assistance which eased the task of preparing this volume:

To Mr. William Baroody and American Enterprise Institute; Mr. Richard A. Ware and Relm Foundation; Mr. William Benton and Encyclopedia Britannica; and Mr. Max Kampelman. Their generosity made it possible for each of us to withdraw from some of our other duties while this volume was being brought to completion.

To Karl O'Lessker of the faculty of Wabash College and Charles McCall of the faculty of Indiana University for a careful reading of the compiled materials and advice in making final selections of material to be included; and to George Graham of the faculty of Vanderbilt University for a running commentary on the fundamentals of political life which greatly improved our understanding.

For assistance in reproduction of printed pages and preparation of manuscript, to Miss Helen Lightfoot, Mrs. Eleanor Lasley, Mrs. Marilyn Coate, Mrs. Sandra Schweiger, and Mrs. Judy Stewart of the Indiana University Library; Mrs. Darlyne Sowder, Miss Linda May, and Mrs. Judy Kelp of the Indiana University Department of Government; Mr. Richard D. Martin of Bloomington, Indiana; and Mr. and Mrs. Ira Bitz of Washington, D.C.

Finally, for careful proofreading, to Lily Cabbadge, Judy Cameron, and Diane Liebenow, students attracted by an appropriate hire; Richard Charles Hyneman, a wayfarer snared in passing; and Frances Tourner Hyneman, once again victimized by her permanent entrapment.

C.S.H.
G.W.C.

CONTENTS

Preface   vii

Acknowledgments   xiii

An Overview   1

I. A NEW NATION AND THE CONSTITUTION

Introduction   7

1. The New American System   13

A New Constitution for a New Nation   13
A More Perfect Union   16
A Right of Self-Government   21
A Free and Enlightened Nation   24

2. The Constitution   35

Character and Purpose   35
Compact of States or Act of the People?   38
Constitutional Amendment: To Change or Preserve?   47
Constitutional Amendment: To Interweave or
  Append?   52

II. CONSTITUTIONAL INTERPRETATION AND
  ENFORCEMENT

Introduction   57

3. **The Constitution: Interpretation and Enforcement**   63

Legislative Interpretation   63
Popular Resistance   72
Nullification, Rebellion, and Secession   76
Judicial Review   84

4. **The Federal Structure**   93

The Distribution of Governmental Authority   93
The Location of Power over Government   97
Large States vs. Small States   103

5. **Delegated and Reserved Powers**   114

General Welfare and the Spending Power   114
Loose vs. Strict Construction   123

III. **SEPARATION OF POWERS**

Introduction   137

6. **Separation of Powers and the Legislative Branch**   143

Principles: Separation of Powers and Checks
    and Balances   143
The Primacy of Legislative Power   148
Frontiers of Legislative Power: Appropriations   151
Frontiers of Legislative Power: Treaties   159

7. **The President and the Executive Branch**   163

The Executive Power and Presidential Responsibility   163
Executive Leadership, Influence, and Domination   172
Limits of the President's Authority   179

8. **The Judiciary**   183

The Judicial Department   183
A Federal Judicial System   186
The Independence of the Judiciary   191

IV. REPUBLICAN GOVERNMENT

Introduction   205

9. Foundations of Popular Government   211

The Republican Character   211
Popular Elections and Public Information   214
Political Organization: Clubs, Factions, Parties   223

10. Representation   236

Popular Instruction of Legislators: A Constitutional
  Right?   236
Instruction of Legislators Reargued: The Voice of
  the People   239
Efficacy of Representation: Majority Rule and
  Minority Opposition   250

11. The Adoption of a Bill of Rights   258

12. Loyalty, Sedition, and Personal Freedom   282

Debate on the Sedition Act of 1798   282
Limits of Opposition: The Issue of Moral Treason   297

Appendix: Biographical Sketches   305

AN OVERVIEW

Let us, at the outset, indicate both the nature of our approach and the reasons why we feel a collection of this character represents a contribution to our knowledge of the American political system.

In at least two significant ways, the ratification of the Constitution marked the beginnings of a new American nation: This event signified the establishment of a new political system and represented a deliberate effort to establish a responsive and popularly controlled government. At the present time, we hardly need dwell on the success of the Constitution in establishing an effective government. Yet a matter continually explored by careful students but never satisfactorily explained is, "What accounts for our great success in displaying to the world a new design in republican government?"

We know that some nations have tried to duplicate the American experience and have failed dismally, even when it appeared that economic, social, and political conditions were even more favorable than those confronting the founders of our system. Conversely, other nations, under seemingly adverse conditions, have successfully incorporated certain principles derived from the American experience —federalism, separation of powers, checks and balances, judicial review, and "limited government" being among the most prominent. All of this, however, merely adds to the "mystery" of the American experience, for by holding all seemingly relevant variables constant, as best we can, there seems to be no single or easy explanation for our success in the art of self-government.

This collection, then, was born out of a conviction that a fuller awareness and understanding of the beliefs, problems, and controversies of the formative years of our republic would better enable us to explain and appreciate the growth and development of American political institutions. Even a more deeply held conviction, however, was that greater insight into the reasons for the success of the American republic could be obtained through a study of this early period, when the tasks of giving meaning, form, shape, and substance to the Constitution were of greater urgency and importance than at any other point in our history. These convictions, in turn, are based on an assumption, somewhat at variance from those underlying other enterprises intended to explain the American political evolution; namely, the course of our development as a self-governing nation can, in large measure, be attributed to the deliberative processes established and provided for by the Constitution itself. In this, our approach varies, at least in emphasis, from those that have dwelt upon other factors, principally social and economic, as determinants of the direction of our political and national growth.

From the early congressional debates, as reported in the *Annals of Congress* (1789-1824), we have sought to gather the best thought available on those matters most relevant to our constitutional development. (See the Preface for fuller discussions of our basis of selection and of the reliability and accuracy of the reporting during this period.) For an understanding of the objectives and the determinations that fixed the character of our early Constitution making, these debates would certainly seem to be the richest source of material we could possibly hope to find. There are several reasons why this is so, a few of the most obvious being these: First, then as now, Congress was a national forum in which differing views that had at least a modicum of popular support could gain a hearing under conditions and circumstances that would allow for free debate and exchange of ideas. The President, quite obviously, could speak only as one man; and though he might have represented a distillation of American opinion, we are still left to wonder what might have been the thoughts and opinions he had "distilled" in his pronouncements. The Supreme Court, relatively insignificant during the early years, did not confront the range of problems facing Congress, nor would its very procedures allow for the revealing debates and exchanges to be found in the congressional debates. Second, and a related point, Congress, then as now, was an arena in which, as the following chapters will show, the "combatants" were eager to do battle when they felt there was the slightest gain to be realized. In this environment no one could win cheap points or even apodictically advance propositions without at least the expectation of opposition from some quarter. Indeed, most revealing to those seeking to understand American development are, on the one hand, those statements or pronouncements that went unchallenged and, on the other, those arguments, as yet never successfully answered, advanced against what is now accepted constitutional interpretation. Third, the task of giving meaning and direction to our Constitution fell squarely on the shoulders of Congress. Congress during the period under study was the moving force in filling out the "constitutional skeleton." At precisely this point Congress made many binding decisions—we say "binding" partly because for very practical reasons they could not be "undone" and partly because they represented a "consensus" of opinion that is still very much with us—that have gained a status almost equal to that of the most specific constitutional provisions. Admittedly, the early Congresses did not solve or resolve all important conflicts or questions. By looking at the early debates, however, we can see, and better appreciate, the bases for those arguments that occurred at later periods in our history concerning the same critical questions (e.g., whether the Constitution is a "compact" or an "organic" act, the removal powers of the President, delegation of legislative authority to the President, the status of Supreme Court pronouncements on the meaning of the Constitution, and many others of equal importance). Fourth, then as now, the members of Congress were of such a caliber that the debates or discourses from this quarter most assuredly must have been of the highest quality to be found in that period of our history.

In a new and far different context from that in which we normally place them, we find James Madison, John C. Calhoun, Henry St. George Tucker, and, among others, John Taylor. In saying this, we by no means imply that other "lesser lights" did not make contributions that, by any standard, are equal or even superior to those of their more famous colleagues. (See the Appendix for brief biographical sketches of the participants.)

We have divided our materials into four major sections and twelve chapters. The introductory essays which precede each major section, hopefully, will make clear our reasons for organizing materials in the manner we have. Throughout the collection we have supplied explanatory notes where we felt them to be essential for an understanding of the material. If what follows advances the reader's understanding of the act of creation and the growth and development of the American political system, this work will have served its purpose.

part I

A NEW NATION AND THE CONSTITUTION

Introduction

The Constitution, as we shall see throughout these early congressional debates, can legitimately be viewed from many perspectives. However, few, if any, would question that, by altering basic power relationships between the states and national government and by erecting a national government drastically different from that the American people had known under the Articles of Confederation, it "founded" or established a new political order. Normally such "acts of founding" are considered to be among the most delicate and serious any people can undertake, the more so when they are initiated with a felt need to substantially alter or even abandon the existing political order. While the framers were quite aware of the importance and seriousness of their task, there are good reasons to believe that it was not as difficult as it might, at first glance, appear. Though the Philadelphia convention was, by any standard, a truly deliberative assembly of distinguished, practical, and mature individuals, its proceedings were marked by alacrity. The convention itself lasted for approximately three and a half months, and this, considering both the nature of the undertaking and the drastic changes in the political relationships, procedures, and institutions that were embodied in the Constitution, is somewhat remarkable. Furthermore, even when we allow for the fact that those actively pushing for the adoption of the Constitution were extremely shrewd strategists and tacticians, we cannot escape surprise at the rapidity with which the state conventions ratified it. In less than a year after the convention's adjournment, with the ratifications of Virginia and New York, the new political order, for all intents and purposes, was a reality.

Because the Constitutional Convention is usually discussed in terms of conflicts and compromises, we often tend to overlook the extent and depth of agreement that must have necessarily existed to establish a new political system in so short a time. We do know for certain that discontent with the government established by the Articles led most political leaders to conclude that some changes in the existing system were necessary. The resolution authorizing a convention to meet for the "sole and express purpose of revising the Articles," passed by the Congress under the Articles, is in itself sufficient testimony of this. Of course, in the early stages of deliberation the delegates did have different opinions about the extent of change required by the circumstances; but significantly, after Randolph's presentation of the Virginia Plan, which involved complete abandonment of the Articles, no one contended that the consideration or even the adoption of this or any similar plan exceeded the legitimate authority of the convention.

So much seems clear: The delegates approached their task determined to establish a government with sufficient powers to accomplish certain highly desired ends or objectives and with the tacit understanding that something more than mere revision of the Articles would be necessary for this purpose. Washington's letter transmitting the proposed Constitution to the President of Congress acknowledges this very fact.

The friends of our country have long seen and desired that the power of making war, peace, and treaties, that of levying money, and regulating commerce, and the correspondent executive and judicial authorities, should be fully and effectually vested in the General Government of the Union; but the impropriety of delegating such extensive trust to one body of men is evident—hence results the necessity of a different organization.

Moreover, this common belief and its basis were fully articulated by the proponents of the Constitution in answering those who contended that the convention had gone beyond its legitimate authority. Madison, in *Federalist* number forty, reiterates the position and line of argument adopted by others in state ratifying convention debates:

Suppose, then, that the expressions defining the authority of the convention were irreconcilably at variance with each other; that a *national* and *adequate government* could not possibly, in the judgment of the convention, be effected by *alterations* and *provisions* in the *articles of confederation;* which part of the definition ought to have been embraced, and which rejected? Which was the more important, which the less important part? Which the end; which the means?

These are clearly rhetorical questions, for the answers given by Madison and the overwhelming majority of the delegates at the Philadelphia convention are clear and unambiguous.

Crucial, then, for an understanding and appreciation of our constitutional development, both during the formative years and after, is an awareness of the goals that the framers sought to achieve through the new and greatly strengthened national government. Many sources—the convention debates, the proceedings of the state ratifying conventions, the Preamble of the Constitution, *The Federalist,* and, among others, the very nature of the powers delegated to the national government by the Constitution—give us a fairly clear picture of the founders' purposes. We do know for certain that among their chief concerns was the establishment of a national government possessing sufficient powers to provide for the common defense and a more effective direction of foreign relations, to establish—when the circumstances seemed to require—uniform rules for the regulation of commerce, both foreign and domestic, to settle disputes that would arise between the states, to guarantee adequate revenues for the national government, and to secure the people from domestic insurrections. In addition, they sought to achieve these goals through a governmental system that would allow for a high degree of popular control.

Beyond any doubt, the Constitution was, during the period which produced the debates we report in this book, on trial. Representative Jackson in the very first session of Congress states this in the following picturesque terms:

Our Constitution . . . is like a vessel just launched, and lying at the wharf; she is untried, you can hardly discover any one of her properties. It is not known how she will answer her helm, or lay her course; whether she will bear with safety the precious freight to be deposited in her hold.

While this statement reflects the prevailing attitudes of this period—that is, uncertainty as to the efficacy of the Constitution—it certainly suggests agreement on the goals and purposes for which the new government was designed. To be sure, many of the statements set forth below (particularly in selections 1.1 through 1.5) indicate this. It is equally true that these debates reveal important areas of disagreement over matters relating to the objectives and nature of the Constitution. (Chapter 2, for example, points up some of these areas.) Therefore, for a fuller understanding of subsequent constitutional development, we must ask, What accounts for both this agreement and disagreement? To answer this we can only recur to Jackson's metaphor and ask what must have been a paramount question in those early years, Does the constitutional machinery actually operate to fulfill its purposes and objectives? In asking this, we see at once that a further and highly crucial question must be answered: Beyond those clearly spelled out and generally acknowledged, what were the purposes and objectives of the Constitution? A consideration of this question, in turn, leads us directly to a likely explanation for the differences of opinion we encounter in these debates: The Constitution, especially during this "trial" period, when there simply were no established and recognized precedents for constitutional interpretation, could be viewed to embody many objectives and principles beyond and even more fundamental than those that had been fully articulated and generally recognized and accepted. To make matters worse, these constitutional interpretations, in going beyond the express provisions of the Constitution to broader theoretical explanations of the motives, attitudes, purposes, and beliefs of the founders, served to stimulate controversy and debate, because reasonable men not only could find grounds to question existing explanations but also could formulate conflicting interpretations that were equally consistent and plausible.

Many of the questions raised in the debates that follow illustrate this. What assumptions about the nature of the American people are reflected in the Constitution? What implicit principles are contained in the Constitution regarding the resolution or compromise of political conflict? Is, for example, the Constitution to be considered a compact between the states or as an act of the people? To what extent and in what ways, when contending parties differ over the proper interpretation of a particular constitutional provision, is it legitimate to resolve such disputes by reference to the intentions of the framers? Or, when should definite resolution be sought through constitutional amendments? Such questions of necessity involve interpretations and views of the Constitution that go well beyond its express provisions.

These and similar concerns, in one form or another, have recurred throughout our constitutional history. But the debates in part 1 (chapters 1 and 2) are, so to speak, "strategically" significant for an appreciation of our constitutional growth and stability because, in more ways than one, they serve to both focus and provide general boundaries for subsequent controversies of similar nature.

To begin with, the general agreement that we have noted concerning the purposes of union must have operated to limit the number of broader interpretations of the Constitution presented for consideration in Congress. Imagine, for just a moment, that there had not been such widespread agreement. Conceivably, then, interpretations or overall views of the Constitution could have been so varied and numerous as to preclude any decision on issues that involved these considerations. The national government would then perforce have come to a standstill at the very moment it had to act decisively to assure its survival. In any event, without basic agreement, we could certainly expect to find a greater variety of theoretical interpretations of the Constitution than we do.

We can stress this point in still another way: the participants in the early controversies were careful to interpret the constitutional language in such a manner as to render it consistent with one or more of the Constitution's acknowledged purposes. Clearly this did not serve to produce agreement among contending parties on specific issues, partly because men did differ about the relative priorities to assign to the relevant purposes when conflict or incompatibility between them was evident; but, in viewing these debates from a broader perspective, we can see how this process would serve to restrict significantly both the number and nature of permissible interpretations.

Beyond this, because precedents have been important in our constitutional development, we must view these debates, not so much from the angle of the specific decisions rendered in controversies involving these questions, but rather, as establishing and even legitimizing certain theoretical views of the Constitution that would be highly relevant in subsequent controversies. Indeed, the mere fact that these positions were set forth and seriously considered during the formative years by those closely associated with "the act of founding," both in point of time and otherwise, accounts in large part for the critical role they have played and continue to play in the resolution of major conflicts over "the true meaning," "spirit," or "essence" of the Constitution.

Another noteworthy aspect of these debates—and one that is related to our commentary above—is the attention accorded the potential dangers threatening national unity. Most of the selections that follow identify one or more such dangers. This emphasis was, for at least two prominent reasons, perfectly natural. First, the United States was at the time a young nation living under new rules aimed at producing greater unity and, until the new government could "take roots" by gaining the confidence and admiration of the people, its existence could be threatened from more than one quarter. We need only recall that the Constitution was originally superimposed on a number of politically distinct and sovereign states within a relatively short period after a prolonged war for independence from a leading world power. Second, as we have pointed out, agreement of some sort concerning the nature of the new system seemed essential for its survival, because within the limits or boundaries provided by these areas of agreement, men of goodwill could successfully resolve those conflicts that would inevitably arise within the nation. Yet many of the participants in the early debates implicitly recognized that unless sufficient care were taken, this consensus would be endangered.

Finally, what follows should be read with this thought continually in mind: Americans, for reasons not fully known to us, have enjoyed a stable government that has been able to operate effectively in the context of great social, economic, racial, religious, and political diversity. Hopefully the following chapters will provide the reader with some insight into the reasons for our relative success.

chapter 1

The new American system

A NEW CONSTITUTION FOR A NEW NATION

1.1 John Adams: "What other form of government can so well deserve our esteem and love?"*

. . .¹

Employed in the service of my country abroad during [the period of government under the Articles of Confederation], I first saw the Constitution of the United States in a foreign country. . . .

Returning to the bosom of my country after a painful separation from it for ten years, I had the honor to be elected to a station under the new order of things, and I have repeatedly laid myself under the most serious obligations to support the Constitution. The operation of it has equaled the most sanguine expectation of its friends, and from an habitual attention to it, satisfaction in its administration, and delight in its effects upon the peace, order, prosperity, and happiness of the nation I have acquired an habitual attachment to it and veneration for it.

---

* From the inaugural address of President Adams, March 4, 1797. *Annals,* 4th Congress, 2nd session, pp. 1583-1584.

¹ An ellipsis preceding the quoted remarks indicates that one or more full paragraphs of the speech precede the part quoted.

What other form of government, indeed, can so well deserve
our esteem and love?

. . . to a benevolent human mind there can be no spectacle presented by any nation more pleasing, more noble, majestic, or august,
than an assembly like that which has so often been seen in this and
the other Chamber of Congress, of a Government *1584*[2] in which
the Executive authority, as well as that of all the branches of the
Legislature, are exercised by citizens selected at regular periods by
their neighbors to make and execute laws for the general good. Can
anything essential, anything more than mere ornament and decora-
tion, be added to this by robes and diamonds? Can authority be
more amiable and respectable when it descends from accidents or
institutions established in remote antiquity than when it springs
fresh from the hearts and judgments of an honest and enlightened
people? For it is the people only that are represented. It is their
power and majesty that is reflected, and only for their good, in every
legitimate government, under whatever form it may appear. The
existence of such a government as ours for any length of time is a
full proof of a general dissemination of knowledge and virtue
throughout the whole body of the people. And what object or consideration more pleasing than this can be presented to the human
mind? If national pride is ever justifiable or excusable it is when it
springs, not from power or riches, grandeur or glory, but from conviction of national innocence, information, and benevolence.

In the midst of these pleasing ideas we should be unfaithful to
ourselves if we should ever lose sight of the danger to our liberties if
anything partial or extraneous should infect the purity of our free,
fair, virtuous, and independent elections. If an election is to be determined by a majority of a single vote, and that can be procured
by a party through artifice or corruption, the Government may be
the choice of a party for its own ends, not of the nation for the national good. If that solitary suffrage can be obtained by foreign nations by flattery or menaces, by fraud or violence, by terror, intrigue, or venality, the Government may not be the choice of the
American people, but of foreign nations. It may be foreign nations
who govern us, and not we, the people, who govern ourselves; and

---

[2] Numbers in italics mark the transition from one page of the *Annals* to
the next. They are provided for the student who may wish to quote from this
book, citing pages in the *Annals*.

candid men will acknowledge that in such cases choice would have little advantage to boast of over lot or chance.
. . .³

1.2   Richard B. Lee: "Every man is safe and there is none to make him afraid. To produce this effect was the intention of the Constitution."*

Mr. Chairman, while I agree with my colleague [Mr. Madison] that the first essays from which our Constitution arose had relation only to our trade; he will, I am sure, acknowledge that this was not the only object for which the grand Convention met, he will acknowledge that this is not the principal object contemplated by the Constitution.

. . . The people had more important objects in view. I do not think, therefore, that so much stress ought to be laid on this idea, as gentlemen have been inclined to bestow on it.

But, having been induced to go back to the period which gave birth to our Constitution, I shall be excused, if, before I return to the present subject, I take a review of the then existing circumstances of the United States. We had then a Government contemned abroad, and despised at home, incapable of commanding the respect of foreign nations or the obedience of our own citizens. Its credit was sunk abroad and at home. Debts were accumulating in Europe and in America. Our commerce was almost annihilated, our agriculture languished, paper tenders existed in some States, 262 the ties of confidence between man and man, and, consequently, the ties of morality were broken asunder; nay, animosities between the States began to prevail, instead of fraternal concord.

Such was the situation of the United States, and to remedy these evils was the Constitution made. Has it not produced the intended effects? That it has, I need only appeal to the feelings of every fellow-citizen who hears me. I should, therefore, unnecessarily take up the time of the Committee in enumerating the various blessings

³ An ellipsis following the quoted remarks indicates that one or more full paragraphs of the speech follow the part quoted.

* From a speech by the Representative from Virginia in the House of Representatives, January 21, 1794, on a series of resolutions proposing a policy relating to commerce with foreign nations. *Annals,* 3d Congress, 1st session, pp. 261-262.

which it has showered on our country. I will only mention the stimulus which our agriculture has received. In traveling through the various parts of the United States, I find fields, a few years ago waste and uncultivated, filled with inhabitants and covered with harvests; new habitations reared; contentment in every face; plenty on every board. Confidence is restored, and every man is safe under his own vine and his own fig tree, and there is none to make him afraid. To produce this effect, was the intention of the Constitution, and not solely to regulate our trade, and it has succeeded. . . .

. . .

A MORE PERFECT UNION

1.3   George Washington: "Every part of our country feels an immediate and particular interest in union."*

. . .

The unity of government which constitutes you one people is also now dear to you. It is justly so, for it is a main pillar in the edifice of your real independence, the support of your tranquility at home, your peace abroad, of your safety, of your prosperity, of that very liberty which you so highly prize. But as it is easy to foresee that from different causes and from different quarters much pains will be taken, many artifices employed, to weaken in your minds the conviction of this truth, as this is the point in your political fortress against which the batteries of internal and external enemies will be most constantly and actively (though often covertly and insidiously) directed, it is of infinite moment that you should properly estimate the immense value of your national union to your collective and individual happiness; that you should cherish a cordial, habitual, and immovable attachment to it; accustoming yourselves to think and speak of it as of the palladium of your political safety and prosperity; watching for its preservation with jealous anxiety; discountenancing whatever may suggest even a suspicion that it can in any

* From his Farewell Address near the close of his second presidential term, September 17, 1796. *Annals*, 4th Congress, 2nd session, pp. 2781-2783.

event be abandoned, and indignantly frowning upon the first dawning of every attempt to alienate any portion of our country from the rest or to enfeeble the sacred ties which now link together the various parts.

For this you have every inducement of sympathy and interest. Citizens by birth or choice of common country, that country has a right to concentrate your affections. The name of American, which belongs to you in your national capacity, must always exalt the just pride of patriotism more than any appellation derived from local discriminations. With slight shades of difference, you have the same religion, manners, habits, and political principles. You have in a common cause fought and triumphed together. The independence and liberty you possess are the work of joint councils and joint efforts, of common dangers, sufferings, and successes.

But these considerations, however powerfully they address themselves to your sensibility, are greatly outweighed by those which apply more immediately to your interest. Here every portion of our country finds the most commanding motives for carefully guarding and preserving the union of the whole.

The *North,* in an unrestrained intercourse with the *South,* protected by the equal laws of a common government, finds in the productions of the latter great additional resources of maritime and commercial enterprise and precious materials of manufacturing industry. The *South,* in the same intercourse, benefiting by the same agency of the *North,* sees its agriculture grow and its commerce expand. Turning partly into its own channels the seamen of the *North,* it finds its particular navigation invigorated; and while it contributes in different ways to nourish and increase the general mass of the national navigation, it looks forward to the protection of a maritime strength to which itself is unequally adapted. The *East,* in a like intercourse with the *West,* 2782 already finds, and in the progressive improvement of interior communications by land and water will more and more find, a valuable vent for the commodities which it brings from abroad or manufactures at home. The *West* derives from the *East* supplies requisite to its growth and comfort, and what is perhaps of still greater consequence, it must of necessity owe the secure enjoyment of indispensable *outlets* for its own productions to the weight, influence, and the future maritime strength of the Atlantic side of the Union, directed by an indissoluble community of in-

terest as *one nation*. Any other tenure by which the *West* can hold this essential advantage, whether derived from its own separate strength or from an apostate and unnatural connection with any foreign power, must be intrinsically precarious.
. . . 2783[4]

To the efficacy and permanency of your union a government for the whole is indispensable. No alliances, however strict, between the parts can be an adequate substitute. They must inevitably experience the infractions and interruptions which all alliances in all times have experienced. Sensible of this momentous truth, you have improved upon your first essay by the adoption of a Constitution of Government better calculated than your former for an intimate union and for the efficacious management of your common concerns. This Government, the offspring of our own choice, uninfluenced and unawed, adopted upon full investigation and mature deliberation, completely free in its principles, in the distribution of its powers, uniting security with energy, and containing within itself a provision for its own amendment, has a just claim to your confidence and your support. Respect for its authority, compliance with its laws, acquiescence in its measures are duties enjoined by the fundamental maxims of true liberty. The basis of our political systems is the right of the people to make and to alter their constitutions of government. But the constitution which at any time exists till changed by an explicit and authentic act of the whole people is sacredly obligatory upon all. The very idea of the power and the right of the people to establish government presupposes the duty of every individual to obey the established government.
. . .

1.4   Joseph Anderson: "By union of interest, we find that we are absolutely necessary to each other."*

. . .

I now approach, Mr. President, a more serious part of this sub-

---

[4] An ellipsis between paragraphs indicates that one or more full paragraphs of the speech are omitted.

* From a speech by the Senator from Tennessee in the Senate, December 1, 1808, relating to the embargo on shipping to and from American ports. *Annals,* 10th Congress, 2nd session, pp. 210-212.

ject, and I am extremely sorry it has been brought into the debate; but as it has, we must endeavor to meet it. We have been told that the embargo law is peculiarly oppressive and disagreeable to our brethren of the Eastern States, and that whenever the people dislike a law they will in some way or other get clear of it. We have also been told that if this law is not repealed, it will in all probability produce disunion.

This, Mr. President, is a very serious state of things if the gentlemen are correct; but, sir, in the warmth of argument our feelings sometimes gain an ascendency over our reason, and I hope this is the case with those gentlemen. I will not draw any comparison between the sufferings of our fellow-citizens of the East and those of any other section of the Union—we all experience them. But, sir, I have too much confidence in the patriotism of the people of those states to believe that they will have recourse to any illegal or violent measures to effect the removal of the law; and less do I believe that they will risk that high character which they so well acquired in contending for the rights of self-government, by using coercive means to destroy that fair fabric, which the united exertions of the whole people, the lives of our heroes, the wisdom of our statesmen, and the firmness and magnanimity of the great Washington have reared for this happy country.

And now for what would our fellow-citizens thus commit their characters and their best interests, 211 which no time or circumstances could restore? Why, say the gentlemen, to obtain a repeal of the embargo. Sir, it is impossible that men so enlightened should put so much at hazard to obtain the repeal of a law which by the common consent of the nation in a Constitutional way will no doubt ere long cease to exist. And, sir, I think it must be equally unfounded that our fellow-citizens of the East can for one moment seriously contemplate withdrawing from the federal Union. Our interest binds us too firmly together to admit of such a supposition. The Eastern and Western people are more strongly united by a common interest than is generally understood. We are entirely agricultural, and inhabit one of the most fertile countries on the globe. Our produce, which is already very great and rapidly increasing, will require a large supply of shipping to carry it to market; that shipping our Eastern brethren have hitherto principally supplied and will, we trust, continue to supply.

Thus, by this union of interest we find that we are absolutely necessary to each other. The Southern States also supply vast quantities of heavy produce which our Eastern brethren would always have a preference in carrying while we continued united. But should a separation take place (which I trust and hope no time or circumstances may produce), in that event we should be like two near friends engaged in a serious quarrel, which is always more bitter than between strangers. We should conceive that our Eastern brethren had withdrawn unjustly from us, had greatly sacrificed our interest as well as their own. And our attachment, by which we now feel most strongly bound to them, would, of course, become alienated, having no longer a community of interests to support it, which it must be acknowledged has, in a political point of view, great and decided influence. We should, of course, seek other means and other channels, by which to transport our commodities. The old Government would withal make such regulations with respect to commerce that our Eastern brethren (whose products are infinitely small in quantity compared with those of the middle, southern, and western sections of the Union) would lose an immense portion of those benefits which they now enjoy. And although they would injure us in point of physical strength, in proportion to their numbers to the whole force of the Union; yet, in so great a degree they must also injure themselves.

Our vast importance as a nation must sink with this division, neither portion of it must expect to have much weight in the scale of the political world, nothing would be left untried by the intriguing nations of the old world to establish and preserve as much as possible collisions of interests and discontents in our respective Governments. Viewed in all its bearings, it excites the most solemn consideration, one that fills the heart with the most melancholy sorrow; and under the view that I have presented, and the catalogue of evils that might be added, I think it impossible that our Eastern brethren can have one serious thought of involving themselves, their 212 wives and children, and their common country in all the horrors of anarchy and of civil war.

A RIGHT OF SELF-GOVERNMENT

1.5 Daniel Buck and William Vans Murray: "For what did America contend? It was to gain to ourselves the important right of self-government."*

Mr. Buck: . . .[5] But suffer me to solicit the attention of this House while I premise a few things, before I immediately apply my observations to the point in question. For what did America contend; for what did she endure the toils of war and sacrifice thousands of her citizens; for what did many members within these walls endure the same fatigues of war, stem the rage of battle, and shed their own precious blood? I believe every mind will accord with me when I say that it was to cast off the oppressive power of a nation which, being detached from us, usurped and arrogated to herself the right of dictating to us laws contrary to our will, while we had no voice in passing those laws through the medium of our Representatives; and to gain to ourselves the important right of self-government. Our success was equal to the magnitude of the object. We gained the glorious prize. Liberty and peace succeeded war. The ferocious and turbulent passions were lulled to rest. And, in 1787, free and united America, undisturbed by factions within, unawed by foes without, was seen exercising her cool, dispassionate reason, that divine gift of God to man, in concerting and framing a system to perpetuate to herself and posterity, the glorious prize she had won, the invaluable blessing of self-government, founded on the dispassionate will of the great body of the sovereign people.

Three great objects met her attention: first, rules to check the

* Remarks in the House of Representatives by Representatives Buck of Vermont and Murray of Maryland, in debate on a resolution requesting the President to present to the House documents relating to the negotiation of the Jay Treaty with Great Britain. Buck, March 7, 1796; Murray, March 23, 1796. *Annals*, 4th Congress, 1st session, p. 431 (Buck) and pp. 698-700 (Murray).

[5] An ellipsis following the name of the speaker indicates that the gentleman's opening remarks have been omitted.

licentious wickedness of individuals, and mark out their separate rights; second, intermediate judges to apply those rules; and, thirdly, negotiations, compacts, and Treaties, with foreign nations. It being impossible for the great body of the people to collect individually to perform those necessary functions, they frame a Constitution in which they express their will in respect to each; they constitute the Legislative, Executive, and Judiciary departments; mark out and assign to each their separate and distinct powers, and place them as three great organs through which the future will of the people is to be known in respect to those great functions.

The Constitution is then, emphatically, the expression of the will of the great body of the sovereign people, and while Government moves on conformably to it, we may with the utmost propriety say that the laws dictated by the will of the people reign and not men or kings, and this is in the strictest sense of the word self-government so far as it can apply to a nation; but if we depart from this basis, then may it be said that men reign and not the laws; the will of the people is then abandoned and the glorious rights for which we have contended sacrificed and lost. . . .

. . .

Mr. Murray: . . . It would be a little tiresome, but not superfluous, to take a glance of the two Governments: the Constitution of the United States, and the British Government. In the first, we find certain definite portions of power accurately meted out by the people in a written instrument to the respective branches of Government. We find the people explicitly recognized as capable of distributing their powers as best suited their opinion of their duties and interests as a nation. We find certain State capacities with certain portions of reserved sovereignty in the system. We find a Republican form to be administered upon written principles and maxims, not susceptible of being administered upon any other principles than those which are prescribed. We find the whole of the Government but the organs of the will of the nation. A man would naturally conclude that when powers were so very definitely measured, that one great object was, as much as possible, to exclude analogy as 699 the ground of assuming what was not expressly delegated and modified agreeably to the written paper; and that the same wisdom in the nation that digested such a system would demand of its public functionaries an exercise of the respective grants of power conformably strictly to the various portions deposited in their hands.

Look, on the contrary, at the British Government. He would agree that we had inherited and borrowed from that Constitution and their laws, a thousand profound maxims and principles that led to the improvements which we now enjoy.

But he insisted that we had improved upon them in the assignment of duties and grants of power; in the explicitness of those grants, by which contest among the branches was to be avoided. In looking at the British Constitution, he could see nothing of fixed right in their form of Government but the Monarchy. He saw in the King, rather than the people, the great reservoir from whence the power and privileges of the Lords and Commons, of justice and of honor, flowed in streams narrowed or enlarged at pleasure and according to the action and reaction of the Commons and the Peerage upon the King. In him he saw the Sovereign. In America, he saw in the collective capacity of the nation the sovereign, and Government, its established mode of action. The Commons in England grant supplies to the King. Here we grant supplies to fulfil the views and obligations of the people. Here an appropriation is less a grant of money than an act of duty to which the Constitution, that is the will of the nation, obliges us. There, supplies and grievances have been for centuries a measure of compromise and the mode by which the Commons have accumulated powers and checks against a throne. There, we see the powers of the Commons growing by absorption from the prerogative of the Crown. Here, we see in the powers of this House, not the spoils of contest, not the trophies of repeated victory over the other branches of the Government, but a specific quantum of trust placed in our hands to be exercised for the people agreeably to the Constitution. We ascend for our derivation of authority and strength to the fountain of all political power; they gain theirs by cutting away that royal reservoir that has been sucking in for ages by dark and now unexplorable channels, the authorities and powers of the nation. The Commons are called by the King, and may not be called by him more than once in three years. Their very existence depends upon their instrumentality in furnishing supplies to the King. The Lords are of his creation. The Commons, if refractory, can be dissolved, and an appeal thus be made to the nation. The Senate here is created by the people, and elected for only six years. Here the PRESIDENT cannot dissolve Congress, even if they chose to adopt a right of stopping the wheels of Government. *700* Theirs is a system in which jealousy must hold the balance between branches, some of which have at best but a precarious existence, and another branch, which is the only great substantive figure in their form of Government. In fact, the two Constitutions differ essentially. The branches here are elected for short periods by the people. The PRESIDENT is one organ constituted and elected by the people. The Senate are constituted and elected by the people. This House is elected by the people, not to struggle with each other, but to give action to the Constitution; and no right can be assumed by any one branch that gives a power of making the Constitution inactive or inefficient to its great ends. To overturn this Constitution is not merely to oppose it by violence. To refuse to act, to withhold an active discharge of the duties it enjoins upon the different branches, would as effectually prostrate it as open violence could do.

. . .

A FREE AND ENLIGHTENED NATION

1.6   Josiah Parker and Fisher Ames: "Out of four millions of people, scarcely any part of them could be classed upon the same ground with the rabble of Europe."*

[Note by the editors. A draft of an address by the House of Representatives to President Washington near the close of his last term of office contained this language: "The spectacle of a whole nation, the freest and most enlightened in the world . . . offering through its Representatives a tribute of unfeigned approbation of its first citizen . . ." Representative Parker moved to strike out the words "Freest and most enlightened."]

Mr. Parker said, when he made the motion he did not refer to any particular nation. He had neither France nor England in view.

---

* Remarks in the House of Representatives by Representatives Parker of Virginia and Ames of Massachusetts, December 15, 1796. *Annals*, 4th Congress, 2nd session, p. 1638 (Parker) and pp. 1641-1642 (Ames).

He did not wish to see us contrast our political situation with that of any other country. His objections to the words, he said, arose from our making the declaration ourselves. Our Government, he acknowledged was free; it was the best in his opinion anywhere. He wished to believe the people as enlightened as any other. He believed they were, and if they were not they had only themselves to blame. But however enlightened or free we were, in his opinion we were not the proper organs to declare it; . . .

. . .

Mr. Ames said, if any man were to call himself more free and enlightened than his fellows, it *1642* would be considered as arrogant self-praise. His very declaration would prove that he wanted sense as well as modesty. But a nation might be called so by a citizen of that nation without impropriety, because, in doing so, he bestows no praise of superiority on himself; he may be in fact, and may be sensible that he is less enlightened than the wise of other nations.

This sort of national eulogium may, no doubt, be fostered by vanity and grounded in mistake; it is sometimes just, it is certainly common, and not always either ridiculous or offensive. It did not say that France or England had not been remarkable for enlightened men; their literati are more numerous and distinguished than our own.

The character, with respect to this country, he said, was strictly true. Our countrymen, almost universally, possess some property and some pretensions of learning—two distinctions so remarkably in their favor as to vindicate the expression objected to. But go through France, Germany, and most countries of Europe and it will be found that, out of fifty millions of people, not more than two or three [millions] had any pretensions to knowledge, the rest being, comparatively with Americans, ignorant. In France, which contains twenty-five millions of people, only one [million] was calculated to be in any respect enlightened, and, perhaps, under the old system there was not a greater proportion possessed property; whilst in America, out of four millions of people scarcely any part of them could be classed upon the same ground with the rabble of Europe. That class called vulgar, canaille, rabble, so numerous there, does not exist here as a class, though our towns have many individuals of it. Look at the lazaroni of Naples; there are twenty thousand or more houseless people, wretched and in want! He asked whether, where men wanted everything and were in proportion of 29 to 1, it was possible they could be trusted with power? Wanting wisdom and morals, how would they use it? It was, therefore, that the iron hand of despotism was called in by the few who had anything, to preserve any kind of control over the many. This evil, as it truly was and which he did not propose to commend, rendered true liberty hopeless.

In America, out of four millions of people, the proportion which cannot read and write and who, having nothing, are interested in plunder and confusion and disposed for both, is small. In the Southern States, he knew there were people well-informed. He disclaimed all design of invidious comparison: the members from the South would be more capable of doing justice to their constituents. But in the Eastern States he was more particularly conversant and knew the people in them could generally read and write and were well-informed as to public affairs. In such a country, liberty is likely to be permanent. They are enlightened enough to be free. It is possible to plant it in such a soil, and reasonable to hope that it will take root and flourish long, as we see it does. But can liberty such as we understand and enjoy exist in societies where the few only have property and the many are both ignorant and licentious? . . .
. . .

1.7 Debate on Citizenship:*   "I look upon the privilege of an American Citizen to be an honorable one."

[Note by the editors. The following remarks were made in debate on a bill which became the first naturalization law of the United States. The bill provided that any free white person, after residing a year in the United States, might become a citizen of the United States by satisfying a magistrate that he intended to reside in this country, and by taking an oath of allegiance.]

* Representatives Thomas Hartley of Pennsylvania, John Page of Virginia, James Madison of Virginia, James Jackson of Georgia, and Aedanus Burke of South Carolina. Debate in the House of Representatives, February 3, 1790. *Annals,* 1st Congress, 2nd session, p. 1109 (Hartley); p. 1110 (Page); pp. 1111-1112 (Madison); p. 1114 (Jackson); pp. 1114-1115 (Page); pp. 1117-1118 (Burke).

Mr. Hartley said he had no doubt of the policy of admitting aliens to the rights of citizenship but he thought some security for their fidelity and allegiance was requisite besides the bare oath; that is, he thought an actual residence of such a length of time as would give a man an opportunity of esteeming the Government, from knowing its intrinsic value, was essentially necessary to assure us of a man's becoming a good citizen. The practice of almost every state in the Union countenanced a regulation of this nature; and perhaps it was owing to a wish of this kind, that the States had consented to give this power to the General Government. The terms of citizenship are made too cheap in some parts of the Union; to say that a man shall be admitted to all the privileges of a citizen without any residence at all, is what can hardly be expected.

. . .

Mr. Page was of opinion, that the policy of European nations and States respecting naturalization did not apply to the situation of the United States. Bigotry and superstition or a deep-rooted prejudice against the Government, laws, religion, or manners of neighboring nations had a weight in that policy which cannot exist here where a more liberal system ought to prevail. I think, said he, we shall be inconsistent with ourselves if, after boasting of having opened an asylum for the oppressed of all nations, and established a Government which is the admiration of the world, we make the terms of admission to the full enjoyment of that asylum so hard as is now proposed. It is nothing to us whether Jews or Roman Catholics settle amongst us; whether subjects of Kings or citizens of free States wish to reside in the United States. They will find it their interest to be good citizens, and neither their religious nor political opinions can injure us if we have good laws, well executed.

Mr. Madison: When we are considering the advantages that may result from an easy mode of naturalization, we ought also to consider the cautions necessary to guard against abuses. It is no doubt very desirable that we should hold out as many inducements as possible for the worthy part of mankind to come and settle amongst us and throw their fortunes into a common lot with ours. But why is this desirable? Not merely to swell the catalogue of people. No, sir, it is to increase the wealth and strength of the community; and those who acquire the rights of citizenship, without adding to the strength or wealth of the community, are not the people we are in want of. And what is proposed by the amendment is, that they shall take nothing more than an oath of fidelity and declare their intention to reside in the United States. Under such terms, it was well observed by my colleague, aliens might acquire the right of citizenship, and return to the country from which they came, and evade the laws intended to encourage the commerce and industry of the real citizens and inhabitants of America, enjoying at the same time all the advantages of citizens and aliens.

I should be exceedingly sorry, sir, that our rule of naturalization excluded a single person of good fame that really meant to incorporate himself into our society; on the other hand, I do not wish that any man should acquire the privilege but *1112* such as would be a real addition to the wealth or strength of the United States.

It may be a question of some nicety how far we can make our law to admit an alien to the right of citizenship step by step; but there is no doubt we may, and ought to require residence as an essential.

Mr. Jackson conceived the present subject to be of high importance to the respectability and character of the American name. The veneration he had for, and the attachment he had to, this country made him extremely anxious to preserve its good fame from injury. He hoped to see the title of a citizen of America as highly venerated and respected as was that of a citizen of old Rome. I am clearly of opinion that rather than have the common class of vagrants, paupers, and other outcasts of Europe, that we had better be as we are and trust to the natural increase of our population for inhabitants.

If the motion made by the gentleman from South Carolina should obtain, such people will find an easy admission indeed to the rights of citizenship; much too easy for the interests of the people of America. Nay, sir, the terms required by the bill on the table are, in my mind, too easy.

I think, before a man is admitted to enjoy the high and inestimable privileges of a citizen of America, that something more than a mere residence among us is necessary. I think he ought to pass some time in a state of probation and, at the end of the term, be able to bring testimonials of a proper and decent behavior. No man who would be a credit to the community could think such terms difficult or indelicate. If bad men should be dissatisfied on this account and should decline to emigrate, the regulation will have a beneficial effect; for we had better keep such out of the country than admit them into it. I conceive, sir, that an amendment of this kind would be reasonable and proper. All the difficulty will be to determine how a proper certificate of good behaviour should be obtained. I think it might be done by vesting the power in the grand jury or district courts to determine on the character of the man, as they should find it.

Mr. Page: I observed before, Mr. Chairman, that the European policy did not apply to the United States. I gave my reasons for it; they are such as have not been controverted, and I presume cannot.

With respect to the idea of excluding bad men from the rights of citizenship, I look upon it as impracticable. Hard terms of admission may exclude good men, but will not keep out one of the wretches alluded to; they will come in various forms, and care little about citizenship.

If we make use of the grand jury for this purpose, as proposed by the member from Georgia (Mr. Jackson) we must, to complete the plan, authorize the grand jury to indict such emigrants as are unworthy to become citizens and expel them. We must add an inquisition, and as it will not be suf- *1115* ficient for our views of having immaculate citizens, we should add censors and banish the immoral from amongst us. Indeed, sir, I fear, if we go on as is proposed now, in the infancy of our Republic, we shall in time require a test of faith and politics of every person who shall come into these States.

As to any precautions against admitting strangers to vote at elections, though I think them of less importance than some gentlemen, I object not to them but contend that every man, upon coming into the States and taking the oath of allegiance to the Government and declaring his desire and intention of residing therein, ought to be enabled to purchase and hold lands, or we shall discourage many of the present inhabitants of Europe from becoming inhabitants of the United States.

Mr. Burke thought it of importance to fill the country with useful men such as farmers, mechanics, and manufacturers and, therefore, would hold out every encouragement to them to emigrate to America. This class he would receive on liberal terms; and he was satisfied there would be room enough for them and for their posterity for five hundred years to come. There was another class of men whom he did not think useful, and he did not care what impediments were thrown in their way; such as your European merchants and factors of merchants who come with a view of remaining so long as will enable them to acquire a fortune, and then they will leave the country and carry off their property with them. These people injure us more than they do us good and, except in this last sentiment, I can compare them to nothing but leeches. They stick to us until they get their fill of our best blood, and then they fall off and leave us. I look upon the privilege of an American citizen to be an honorable one, and it ought not to be thrown away upon such people. There is another class also that I would interdict, that is the convicts and criminals which they pour out of British jails. I wish sincerely some mode could be adopted to prevent the importation of such; but that, perhaps, is not in *1118* our power. The introduction of them ought to be considered as a high misdemeanor.

. . .

1.8 Theodore Sedgwick: "America has opened to her view a more rich and glorious prospect than ever was presented to man."*

[Note by the editors. The naturalization law that was enacted in 1791 authorized citizenship to free white persons on these conditions: residence for two years in the United States, including one year under the jurisdiction of the court hearing the petition, proof satisfactory to the court of good character, and a promise on oath or affirmation to support the Constitution of the United States.

Text of the bill for revision of the Naturalization Act of 1791, under consideration in the following debate in 1794, appears not to be available. The remarks of Representative Sedgwick that are printed here were directed to a motion by Representative Samuel Dexter of Massachusetts that required two credible witnesses to

---

* Remarks by the Representative from Massachusetts in the House of Representatives, December 22, 1794. *Annals*, 3d Congress, 2nd session, pp. 1005-1008.

testify on oath that they believed the petitioner to be of good moral character and attached to the welfare of the United States. The statute subsequently enacted required five years residence in the United States, an oath to support the Constitution of the United States, and a finding of good moral character by the judges, but did not specify that witnesses should testify in behalf of the petitioner.]

America, he said, if her political institutions should on experience be found to be wisely adjusted, and she shall improve her natural advantages, 1006 had opened to her view a more rich and glorious prospect than ever was presented to man. She had chosen for herself a Government which left to the citizen as great a portion of freedom as was consistent with a social compact. All believed the preservation of this Government, in its purity, indispensable to the continuance of our happiness.

The foundation on which it rested was general intelligence and public virtue; in other words, wisdom to discern and patriotism to pursue the general good. He had pride, and he gloried in it, in believing his countrymen more wise and virtuous than any other people on earth; hence he believed them better qualified to administer and support a Republican Government. This character of Americans was the result of early education, aided indeed by the discipline of the Revolution.

In that part of the country with which he was best acquainted, the education, manners, habits, and institutions, religious and civil, were Republican. The community was divided into corporations, in many respects resembling independent republics, of which almost every man, the qualifications were so small, was a member. They had many important and interesting concerns to transact. They appointed their executive officers, enacted bye laws, raised money for many purposes of use and ornament. Here, then, the citizens acquired the habits of temperate discussion, patient reasoning, and a capacity of enduring contradiction. Here the means of education and instruction are instituted and maintained. Public libraries are purchased and read. These are (said he) the proper schools for the education of Republican citizens. Thus are to be planted the seeds of Republicanism. If you will cultivate the plants which are to be reared from these seeds, you will gather an abundant harvest of long continued prosperity.

Much information (he said) might be obtained by the experience of others, if, in despite of it, we were not determined to be guided only by a visionary theory. The ancient Republics of Greece and Rome (said he) see with what jealousy they guarded the rights of citizenship against adulteration by foreign mixture. The Swiss nation (he said) in modern times, had not been less jealous on the same subject. Indeed, no example could be found in the history of man to authorize the experiment which had been made by the United States. It seemed to have been adopted by universal practice as a maxim, that the Republican character was no way to be formed but by early education. In some instances, to form this character, those propensities which are generally considered as almost irresistible, were opposed and subdued. And shall we (he asked) alone adopt the rash theory that the subjects of all Governments, Despotic, Monarchical, and Aristocratical, are, as soon as they set foot on American ground, qualified to participate in administering the sovereignty of our country? Shall we hold the benefits of American citizenship so cheap as to invite, nay, almost bribe, the discontented, the ambitious, and the avaricious of every country to accept them? *1007*

We had (he said) on this subject not only example, but warning. Will gentlemen (said Mr. S.) recollect the rage of ages which existed in the country from which we came, between the Saxon, Danish, and Norman emigrants and the natives of the country? The cruelties, the oppressions, the assassinations, in a word, the miseries to which this gave birth? Perhaps it might be said that in this instance the emigrants were hostile invaders. But the same events took place in the decline of the Roman empire between the emigrants who were invited to occupy the vacant frontiers and the ancient inhabitants, although the former ought to have been united to the latter by every principle of affection and gratitude.

By these and almost an infinity of other instances it would not be rash to conclude that the undeviating principles of human nature, whenever the inhabitants of one country should be permitted to settle in another, by national affections an union would be formed, unfriendly not only to the ancient inhabitants but also to social order. Our own experience was not, he believed, in opposition to the general observation. Although this reasoning was to his mind conclusive against a general and indiscriminate admission of aliens to the rights of citizenship, yet he did not wish it should go to a complete exclusion.

It was said, in support of what was termed our liberal policy, that our country wanted commercial capital; that we had an immense tract of vacant territory; and that we ought not, with the avarice of a miser, to engross to ourselves the exclusive enjoyment of our political treasures.

Mr. Sedgwick said he had never been convinced, that we ought to make so great a sacrifice of principle for the rapid accumulation of commercial capital. He had never been convinced that by an improvement of our own resources, it would not accumulate as fast as might be for the public benefit. We heard much of equality. Property was in some sense power; and the possession of immense property generated daring passions which scorned equality, and with impatience endured the restraints of equal laws. Property was undoubtedly to be protected as the only sure encouragement of industry, without which we should degenerate into savages. But he had never been convinced that the anxiety with which we wished an accumulation of capital in the hands of individuals, was founded on correct Republican reflection. The ardent ambition inspired by the possession of great wealth and the power of gratifying it, which it conferred, had in many instances disturbed the public peace, and in not a few destroyed liberty.

The vacant lands, which some with so much avidity wished to see in the occupation of foreigners, he considered as the best capital stock of the future enjoyment of Americans, as an antidote against the poison of luxury, as the nursery of robust and manly virtue, and as a preventive of a numerous class of citizens becoming indigent and therefore dependent. Whenever the time should arrive (and may that period be very distant) when there should no longer be presented to 1008 the poor a decent competence and independence, as the effect of industry and economy (which would generally be the case when lands were no longer to be obtained on their present easy and reasonable terms) then that description of men, now perhaps the most happy and virtuous, would become miserable to themselves and a burden to the community. Now the man who entered on the stage of life without property had a reasonable assurance that a few years of industry and economy would give him independence, competence, and respectability. The prospect gave relish and effect to his labors. He planted himself on the frontiers, and cultivated in his posterity every useful and manly virtue. This was his treasure, and it was a glorious one.

Mr. S. said he considered America as in possession of a greater stock of enjoyment than any other people on earth. That it was our duty to husband it with care. Yet he could not altogether exclude such virtuous individuals, as might fly here, as to an asylum against oppression. On the one hand, he would not dissipate our treasures with the thoughtless profusion of a prodigal; nor would he, on the other, hoard them, as in the unfeeling grasp of a miser. Our glorious fabric (said he) has been cemented by the richest blood of our country, and may it long continue to shelter us against the blasts of poverty, of anarchy, and of tyranny.

. . .

chapter **2**

The Constitution

CHARACTER AND PURPOSE

2.1 Roger Nelson: "How honorably different is the American
Constitution!"*

. . .

Previous to an inquiry into the constitutionality of the proposed
project, he would just observe that constitutions themselves were
things of recent date. Before the American Revolution the word
itself was never fully understood. Lexicographers who attempted to
define it never could agree. There was no practice whereupon to try
its meaning. No power on earth had a Constitution before the
American States. True, England has long boasted of possessing a
Constitution, and so satisfied were her statesmen and politicians of
the reality of this imaginary being that they have extolled it to the
skies. The glorious Constitution of England, her pride, and the envy
of the world! Fine words truly; but where is the thing itself to be
found? Is it reduced to writing? No. Who has seen it? No man. Is it

* From a speech by the Representative from Maryland in the House of
Representatives, January 8, 1805, arguing that the Constitution did not permit
Congress to recede to Maryland and Virginia the territory those states had
given for a national capital. *Annals*, 8th Congress, 2nd session, p. 906.

35

known to any man? If it be, no two agree as to what the boasted Constitution of Britain is.

How different, how honorably different, is the American Constitution! With us it is reduced to writing. It is in every man's hand; it is known to the whole world, and every citizen agrees in its true and legitimate meaning. He would take this opportunity of expressing his voice, and of holding up his hand in resisting the doctrine of construction and inference formerly set up, whereby the tenor and effect of that invaluable instrument was likely to be changed. He knew that artful and ingenious men might twist and turn, and make it, like the word republican, to mean anything or nothing, as best suited their nefarious designs. But this declaration and these attacks upon the body of that sacred work, were introduced by insinuating and artful lawyers, aided by the villany of judges, and accepted by men employed in the administration of our public and most important national affairs.

. . .

2.2 John Pope: "This Republican system depends more upon the virtue and intelligence of the people and the responsibility of their public servants, than paper restrictions."*

. . .

Much alarm and delusion have been artfully spread through the country about a violation of the Constitution and a consequent destruction of our republican institutions. I fear the people are unfortunately led to believe that the security of their liberty depends too much upon paper barriers, and too little upon their own virtue and intelligence. It appears to me that the Constitution is occasionally made a mere stalking horse to serve the purposes of unprincipled demagogues and pretended lovers of the people to get into power to the exclusion of honest men. They, with great address, distract and inflame the public mind about some nice Constitutional question or abstract proposition and thereby bring the people to decide, not which candidate is the most entitled to their confidence, but who rides the finest electioneering hobby.

We are misled very much, I believe, by theories and terms more

---

* From a speech by the Senator from Kentucky in the Senate, February 15, 1811, supporting a bill to continue the life of the Bank of the United States. *Annals*, 11th Congress, 3d session, pp. 233-234.

applicable to other Governments than our own. In Great Britain they speak with great propriety of the Government and people, because there is in that country an immense power independent of the people. But here, where every public functionary is responsible to, and the Government in the hands of a majority of the people, those terms do not appear to me applicable in the sense in which they are used in other countries.

My reflections and practical observations on the Government incline me to the opinion that, with regard to measures of general policy not assailing individual liberty or right or the independence of any State, there is not that danger to be apprehended from a liberal construction of the Constitution which gentlemen seem to imagine. So long as the Government is in the hands of the people, measures affecting the whole nation, if 234 oppressive or inconvenient, will be resisted and corrected by the public feeling and opinion. This is not mere theory. Look at the State of Connecticut, one of the best regulated democracies in ancient or modern times, whose Legislature is as omnipotent as the British Parliament. What people enjoy more real liberty and independence? In what country is to be found more practical, intelligent republicanism? Those principles which secure the rights of the citizen and the responsibility of their public servants are held sacred, but the Legislature is, I believe, unrestricted with regard to measures of general policy.

It is a truth which ought to be deeply impressed on the American mind, that the preservation of this republican system depends more upon the virtue and intelligence of the people and the responsibility of their public servants, than paper restrictions.

. . .

2.3   John Page: "The Constitution was formed on a supposition of human frailties."*

. . .

. . . It is not sufficient . . . to say, as some gentlemen have said, that Congress is incapable of partiality or absurdities, and that they are as far from committing them as my colleagues or myself. I tell them the Constitution was formed on a supposition of human

* From a speech by the Representative from Virginia in the House of Representatives, February 7, 1792, opposing a bill to encourage and regulate cod fisheries. *Annals*, 2nd Congress, 1st session, p. 394.

frailty and to restrain abuses of mistaken powers. The Constitution has been said by some one to be, like answers of the oracles of old, capable of various and opposite constructions; that it has been ingeniously contrived, like some of them, to suit two events—a Republican or a Monarchical issue. I will not pretend to say that this is not, in some instances, too just an observation. Nor will I undertake to deny that it was not the intention of some of the Convention that such ambiguities might be in their Constitution, to correspond with the critical and ambiguous state of the American mind respecting Government. But I will boldly affirm that, whatever the theories of that day might lead some to think respecting the application of Monarchical principles to the Government of the United States, no one can at this day pretend that they are applicable to their circumstances, their dispositions, or interests, or even are agreeable to the wishes of the people.

Even before the adoption of the Constitution, when the rights of men had not been so thoroughly investigated as they since have been, it must be remembered that whole States, and large and respectable minorities in other States, complained of and objected to the Aristocratical and Monarchical features of the new Government. In vain did the friends of the new Government—friends of order, of union, or of liberty—contend that the powers granted by the Constitution which appeared so alarming were such as would never be exerted but when all good men would acknowledge the necessity of exercising them, and that, indeed, they would be explained or restrained by some future amendments. The sagacious and eloquent [Patrick] Henry shook his head at such promises, sighed, and submitted to the will of the majority—a small one, indeed—but foretold, from his knowledge of the human heart, what would be done and said in justification of every measure which might extend the power of Congress.

. . .

COMPACT OF STATES OR ACT OF THE PEOPLE?

[Note by the editors. The Constitution, as originally adopted, provided that presidential electors should vote for two men for the offices of President and Vice President, without designating which of the two was preferred for President; that the Presidency should go to the man receiving the most votes, and the Vice Presidency should go to the man receiving the next highest number of votes (provided in each case that the man had received the votes of a majority of all electors). In 1800, the presidential electors gave the same number of votes to Thomas Jefferson and Aaron Burr, and the House of Representatives was required to determine which of the two should be President, the other becoming Vice President. In making the choice, Representatives were required to vote as state delegations, each state delegation having one vote; if the Representatives from any state were equally divided on the question, no vote would be counted for that state. There were sixteen states in the Union in 1800; nine of the state delegations would have to go for the same man to make him President. The first vote, on February 11, was eight for Jefferson, six for Burr, and two delegations not voting because equally divided. Five days later, on the thirty-sixth ballot, the deadlock was broken, and Thomas Jefferson was elected on a vote of ten against four, with two states not voting.

The bitterness excited by this struggle led to insistent demands for a change in method of choosing the President and Vice President, and these demands produced the twelfth amendment to the Constitution. There was great difference of judgment, however, as to whether any change was required and, if required, what the change ought to be. This was one of the most important debates in the early years of Congress, and parts of it will appear at several places in this volume. In the two items immediately following (selections 2.4 and 2.5), we are presented with opposing views as to how the Constitution obtained its authority.]

2.4 Benjamin Huger: "Is it not in its essence a compact, a perfect compromise of the interests, powers, influence and rights of a number of independent societies who have united for their common advantage?"*

Let me ask, what is the Constitution of the United States? From what sources did it originate? In what manner, by whom, from what causes, upon what principles, in what spirit, was it originally

* From a speech by the Representative from South Carolina in the House of Representatives, October 28, 1803, opposing a proposed constitutional amendment. *Annals,* 8th Congress, 1st session, pp. 521-526.

adopted? Is it not a federative Government, agreed upon between thirteen distinct and separate sovereignties, for their mutual defence and protection? 522

Is it not, in its essence, a compact, a bargain, a perfect compromise of the interests, powers, influence, and rights of a number of independent societies, who have united for their common advantage, and who are no further bound or pledged to each other than by the articles and conditions in the written contract—the Constitution—which has been acceded to by them all? And is it not upon the spirit in which . . . that compact was originally formed, that every amendment to, or alteration in it, should be predicated? These questions must all be necessarily answered in the affirmative. The inhabitants of these United States did not then, in forming the Federal Constitution, act in mass as one people, nor can the abstract principles borrowed from different authors on the primeval formation of political societies apply to them. The worn-out theory of a number of insulated beings assembled together in an extensive plain and led by their common wants and necessities to form themselves into a body politic, cannot be applied to the Federal Government, nor can inferences drawn from notions of this kind afford correct grounds upon which to build or support alterations and amendments in the national compact.

Thirteen Colonies, at this time composing the United States, spread over an extensive continent, having been threatened with a privation of their rights and liberties, were induced to form a league, offensive and defensive, and to unite for their mutual and common defence. After a bloody though not inglorious contest, they severed themselves forever from the mother country, and they became and were acknowledged as thirteen independent and distinct Republics or Sovereignties. Under what gloomy and critical circumstances they found themselves for some few years after the close of the war, it would be superfluous for me to detail to this House. Let it suffice to say that their situation was such as seriously to alarm all classes of our citizens and to threaten complete anarchy, perhaps political dissolution, unless some bond of union better adapted to their wants and necessities than the original Confederacy could be established.

That band of worthies therefore, as they have been aptly styled, were sent from twelve, I believe, of the States, who, having met together in convention, ultimately formed that compact, which, having been since ratified by all the States, now happily unites us in one great Union. But by whom and by what authority were the members of the Convention delegated? Whom did they represent when assembled together? They were not, it must be acknowledged, even in the degree that the members of this House are, the immediate representatives of the people inhabiting that part of this vast continent in which the United States are comprised. They were not selected by the people at large, nor did they represent them in their original and individual capacities. No, sir, they were sent to represent the interests and views of thirteen distinct sovereignties. They were appointed by the governments of the different States and they held their authority from the States, as 523 States, and not from the people of the United States generally and indiscriminately. When met therefore, in convention, their object was not to form one general consolidated government for the inhabitants scattered over this vast territory, but to modify still further and to draw still closer the bands of alliance by which these States were already connected. And it cannot surely be forgotten that one of the strongest objections, one of those most insisted on against the Constitution, was, that federative principles had not been sufficiently retained, or rather that they had been totally abandoned, and the Constitution approached too nearly to a consolidation of the different members of the Confederacy, and one general national Government.

. . .

The great outlines of the Constitution were, I presume, Mr. Speaker, agreed on without much difficulty and pretty generally acquiesced in. It was understood on all hands that the Government should be formed on republican principles—that the great departments of which it must necessarily consist should be distinct, and, as far as possible, independent of each other. The difficulty was in the detail, and more especially in respect to the quantum of State sovereignty which was to be yielded to the Union, and the degree of influence which was to be respectively given up or retained by the large and small states. . . . 524 The basis of a republican government, however, is no doubt the will of the people; and that will could only be expressed and brought into action in a country so extensive as ours by representation and elections.

How then was that representation to be apportioned and those elections organized? To adopt the most common and simple princi-

ple in the abstract, and allow the representation to depend entirely
on numbers and the elections to be made indiscriminately and without modification by the people at large would have been to put an
end at once and at one blow to all State sovereignty, to amalgamate
the inhabitants of thirteen free and independent Republics into one
common mass, and to place the smaller and more feeble completely
and forever at the mercy of the more powerful and larger States.

But was this done? Was such a result desirable? Would the
States at that day have acquiesced in any similar arrangement?
Most certainly not; and, consequently, a totally different modification and compromise took place. The Legislative department of the
Government was divided into two distinct branches—a Senate and
House of Representatives. In the latter, it is true, the principle of
numbers and population was, to a certain degree, adopted, yet still
under very important modifications and with evident deviation from
the abstract principle. In the first place, a certain class of people who
unfortunately existed in one portion of the Union, though not allowed any immediate interest themselves in the Government and
regarded rather as property than as beings entitled to any civil or
political rights, were included at a certain ratio in the calculation of
the number of Representatives who were to have a seat in this
House. This difficult and knotty point happily settled, it was in the
second place determined that the members of this body, though
understood to be the immediate representatives of the people, should
not be elected by the people of the United States at large, as one
people; but its share of the whole representation according to the
ratio and in conformity to the compromise above specified was
apportioned to each respective State, and is to be exclusively elected
by the people of that State.

Notwithstanding every modification, however, which could be
devised, it was evident and perfectly understood that although the
smaller States would have a voice and proportionate vote, yet the
interest and the will of the larger must virtually prevail in the House
of Representatives, and that they would in fact dispose of this body
at their will. As a partial check, therefore, as some little safeguard
against this overweening power on their part, the federative principle was completely retained in its utmost purity and without the
smallest modification, in the other branch of Legislature, the Senate;
and not only an equal vote and representation is given to all the

States, however large or however small, but the members who compose the Senate are not even to be elected by the people of the several States, but are to be chosen by, and immediately to represent, the government of each individual State. The diffi- 525 culties which presented themselves in organizing the Legislative department of the Government, being thus surmounted and compromised, another question no less embarrassing and difficult to solve, arose, viz.: in what manner the Executive powers ought to be disposed of. . . .

The members of the Convention, however, were too well acquainted with the feelings and sentiments of the American people to hesitate long on this point, and it was consequently determined that the Executive powers should be lodged in the hands of a single individual, under the title of President, who should hold his office during the term of four years, at the end of which period a new election should take place. But the real difficulty in the organization of this department under our Constitution now naturally suggests itself to the mind, viz: how, and by whom, this President was to be elected; for it must be obvious that all these jealousies and conflicting views and interests of the large and small States, which had been happily compromised as relates to the Legislative author- 526 ity, would, of course, apply with increased force in the case of the Executive.

To divide this branch, as had been done in the former instance, would be, as I have already shown, to enfeeble it, to deprive it of all energy, to render it insufficient and entirely unequal to the purposes for which it was intended. If the Executive power, on the other hand, was to be vested in a single person and he elected by the people of the United States, or even on the modified principles upon which the members of the House of Representatives were to be elected, it followed of necessity that the larger States would elect whom they pleased, and consequently the Executive branch of the Government would be entirely under their control and the champion and promoter of their views and interests. But the large States have an entire control over one of the two Houses of which the National Legislature is composed, and an equality of votes (with all the advantages accruing from superior strength and power, and consequently superior influence) in the other. If, then, in addition to all this, the election of the Executive is put in their hands, you add

strength to the strong, grant more power to those already too powerful, and yield up virtually to the large States that branch of the Government which not only was to have a partial veto on the proceedings of the Legislature but would probably give impulse to the
whole, and be always on the watch and ever ready to avail itself of
such favorable occurrences and favorable moments as might best
enable them to carry into execution their projects of aggrandizement
and encroachment on their more feeble associates. On the other
hand, the larger States, to whom fortune and the nature of the case
necessarily gave a prepondering influence in this instance, could
scarcely be expected to make a sacrifice of this advantage to the
jealousies and fears of the small and weaker, and suffer them, as a
thing of course, to take possession of the Executive branch of the
Government. In this dilemma, what was done by the Convention?

As usual a compromise took place, and as nearly as possible
upon the same principles upon which every other provision of the
Constitution is predicated. It was decided that the Executive power
should rest in a single individual. It was agreed that he should be
elected, not by the people at large, not by the people of each State in
the first instance; but by a number of Electors (equal to the combined
representation of the States in the Senate, and that of the people of the
several States in the House of Representatives) elected by the people
of the several States, in the proportion to which they might be respectively entitled according to the complicated ratio which had been
adopted. . . .

2.5   George W. Campbell: "I am of opinion that our Government was formed by the people of the United States, in their capacity
as such, and not by the several States convened in their State capacities."*

. . . I am, sir, of opinion that our Government was formed by
the people of the United States, in their capacity as such, by their
immediate representatives in the General Convention, and not by the
several States convened in their State capacities. The words of the

---

* From a speech in the House of Representatives by the Representative
from Tennessee, supporting the proposed constitutional amendment that Benjamin Huger opposed in the preceding selection, December 8, 1803. *Annals*,
8th Congress, 1st session, pp. 718-719, 722-723.

Constitution are: "We, the people of the United States, in order to form a more perfect Union," &c., and not we, the United States, in our State capacity, which I presume would have been the language used had the framers of the Constitution intended to have formed a Government for the States united in their State capacities. And though the State interests, as such, are regarded in our Government and their sovereignties represented, whereby it may be considered as partaking in some degree of the federative principle, yet this will not prove our Constitution to be a Confederation of States in the extent contended for in their State capacities; but only shows that the framers of the Constitution intended, by thus regarding the State rights and sovereignties as such, to qualify and limit the operations of the General Government with regard to the several State Governments and their respective interests and rights.

The laws that are made by the General Government are binding on the 719 people of the United States at large, and not on the State Governments; for though the State Governments are limited by and bound not to violate the Constitution of the United States, yet they certainly cannot be controlled or in any manner bound by the legislative acts of the General Government. This, I conceive, shows in a very strong manner that the Union is not a mere Confederation of States. And considering the subject in this view will not tend to produce a consolidation of the General Government so as to encroach upon the rights of the State sovereignties; for the operations of the General Government being felt by the people only in their individual capacities, the State Governments will not be affected so as to infringe their powers or endanger their independence; provided the General Government, in exercising its legislative powers, keep within those bounds prescribed by the Constitution, and does not assume the right of legislating on subjects that properly belong to and are cognizible by the respective State Governments.

I will here observe that the object of every free Government is to lay down a rule of conduct for the people who live under it, by the observance of which their general welfare and happiness may be promoted. Whenever, therefore, the intentions of the people in framing their Government can be ascertained, I conceive it the duty of those who administer the Government to pursue those intentions as nearly as possible. I have always considered it to be the intention of the framers of the Constitution and the true spirit of that instrument, that the Chief Magistrate shall be chosen by the people through their Electors and not by the States represented in this House; and that the provision for electing the President by the House of Representatives, in case no election should be made by the Electors, was intended to guard against an event that might happen, which, if unprovided for, would stop the operations of Government, and not as a mode of election that was desired by any portion of the Union, or contemplated to be introduced when it could be avoided. I conceive, therefore, such measures ought to be adopted as would prevent, as much as possible, the necessity of resorting to that mode of election. . . .

It will, I presume, be admitted that in all free Governments the will of the majority must be considered for the purposes of Government as the will of the nation, and that it ought, therefore, to prevail and control the will of the minority when opposed to it. This, I conceive, sir, is a fundamental principle in our Government. I am, therefore, of opinion that whatever part of our Constitution is found in its operations to contravene this principle ought to be altered, and so modified that the will of the majority of the people should be pursued.

. . . 722

It is certainly true that our Constitution, in some of its features, partakes of the nature of a compact bottomed on a compromise of powers and rights between the small and large States; and this compromise will be found to be confined chiefly to the share which the several States have in the National Legislature, and the consequent effect which that modification produces with regard to the number of Electors of President and Vice President to which each State is entitled according to the provisions of the Constitution. But it will not follow as a necessary consequence that the right of voting by States in this House for President (in the event of the choice being left to the House) was considered as an advantage granted to the small States in order to induce them to come into the Union. I cannot be of opinion that this was considered by the Convention who formed the Constitution as an equivalent given to the small States for any rights or powers by them surrendered to the General Government. If the small States considered it so, they must have esteemed those rights and powers thus surrendered of very small importance indeed. For the event in which they could have the opportunity of exercising the right this mode of election secures to them (of voting by States) is extremely uncertain, and might not occur once in a century. And though it has once happened, it is evident the small States did not in that case unite, nor did the interests of the large and small 723 States seem to be taken into view as opposed to each other.

. . .

CONSTITUTIONAL AMENDMENT: TO CHANGE OR PRESERVE?

2.6 James Jackson and James Madison: "It is possible the abuse of the powers of the General Government may be guarded against in a more secure manner than is now done."*

[Note by the editors. On June 8, 1789, approximately two months after the first session of Congress convened, James Madison arose in the House of Representatives and announced that he would now bring forward a number of amendments to the Constitution which he hoped would be adopted by the method prescribed in Article V of that document. These proposed amendments, he subsequently disclosed, were designed to protect the citizenry from possible abuse of power by the new government. Most of his proposals were finally adopted and became the first ten amendments to the Constitution. Some of the debate on the purpose and merits of these proposals is reported in chapter 10 of this book. At this point we encounter some opinions about the propriety of altering the Constitution so early in its life, and in selection 2.9, different views about how the new language ought to be connected with the language originally adopted.]

Mr. Jackson: I am of opinion we ought not to be in a hurry with respect to altering the Constitution. For my part, I have no idea of speculating in this serious manner on theory. If I agree to alterations in the mode of administering this Government, I shall like to stand

* Remarks made in the House of Representatives by Representatives Jackson of Georgia and Madison of Virginia, in debate on a proposed Bill of Rights, June 8, 1789. *Annals,* 1st Congress, 1st session, pp. 425-426 (Jackson) and pp. 431-433 (Madison).

on the sure ground of experience and not be treading air. What experience have we had of the good or bad qualities of this Constitution? . . .

When the propriety of making amendments shall be obvious from experience, I trust there will be virtue enough in my country to make them. *426*

. . .

Let the Constitution have a fair trial; let it be examined by experience, discover by that test what its errors are, and then talk of amending; but to attempt it now is doing it at a risk, which is certainly imprudent. I have the honor of coming from a State that ratified the Constitution by the unanimous vote of a numerous convention; the people of Georgia have manifested their attachment to it by adopting a State Constitution framed upon the same plan as this. But although they are thus satisfied, I shall not be against such amendments as will gratify the inhabitants of other States, provided they are judged of by experience and not merely on theory. . . .

Mr. Madison: . . . It appears to me that this House is bound by every motive of prudence not to let the first session pass over without proposing to the State Legislatures some things to be incorporated into the Constitution that will render it as acceptable to the whole people of the United States as it has been found acceptable to a majority of them.

. . . *432*

. . . It is possible the abuse of the powers of the General Government may be guarded against in a more secure manner than is now done, while no one advantage arising from the exercise of that power shall be damaged or endangered by it. We have in this way something to gain, and if we proceed with caution, nothing to lose. And in this case it is necessary to proceed with caution; for while we *433* feel all these inducements to go into a revisal of the Constitution, we must feel for the Constitution itself, and make that revisal a moderate one. I should be unwilling to see a door opened for a reconsideration of the whole structure of the Government—for a reconsideration of the principles and the substance of the powers given; because I doubt, if such a door were opened, we should be very likely to stop at that point which would be safe to the Government itself.

But I do wish to see a door opened to consider, so far as to incorporate those provisions for the security of rights, against which I believe no serious objection has been made by any class of our constituents: such as would be likely to meet with the concurrence of two-thirds of both Houses and the approbation of three-fourths of the State Legislatures.

. . .

2.7 Henry St. George Tucker: "We must decide according to our conscience on the Constitutional question; there is no part of this Constitution which requires that doubtful questions shall be referred to the states."*

[Note by the editors. Mr. Tucker supported a resolution that required the creation of a fund to be drawn upon from time to time to pay the costs of constructing internal improvements, including post roads and military roads. It was strongly contended by some members of Congress that the Constitution did not permit the national government to spend money for such purposes; and some members who believed that the national government did have power to do so thought that it might be a good idea, nevertheless, to propose a constitutional amendment which would make that power certain. Mr. Tucker here denies the wisdom of proposing a constitutional amendment under such circumstances.]

. . .

But why, it is asked, not amend the Constitution? The answer is easy. Those who do not believe we possess the power are right in wishing an amendment. Those who believe we have it would be wrong in referring it to the States; and as the Committee were of this opinion, they could not recommend an amendment. For, if 1120 an amendment be recommended and should not be obtained, we should have surrendered a power which we are bound to maintain if we think we possess it. In swearing to support this Constitution, we are not less solemnly bound to maintain all the just powers of the Federal Government than to preserve the States from its encroachments.

° From a speech by the Representative from Virginia in the House of Representatives, March 6, 1818. *Annals*, 15th Congress, 1st session, pp. 1119-1120.

We have no right, therefore, to put in jeopardy a power we believe to have been given us. We must decide according to our conscience, on the Constitutional question, and not refer the matter to State decision. There is no part of this Constitution which declares that doubtful questions shall be referred to the States. If there had been such a provision, it would doubtless not have rendered it necessary in such cases to obtain the acquiescence of three-fourths of the members of the Confederacy.

Suppose we think we possess the power, but refer it to the States for their decision. Six small States may deny it to us, against the general sentiment of the rest of the Union. But suppose we exercise the power, and the States deny its existence. They have, by the Constitution, the power of controlling us. They may provide that we shall not exercise it. It is true they must have a concurrence of fifteen out of twenty States to effect this negative amendment.

It seems indeed as if the struggle was to get the vantage ground which we occupy, if we believe ourselves invested with this power. Such indeed is the peculiar situation of things at the present moment, that it is pretty certain that three-fourths of the States would concur in neither opinion. A majority, it is believed, are in favor of the exercise of this power by the General Government. But, whilst it is evident that no negative amendment can be passed, it is equally certain, that a proposition to amend the Constitution by giving this power to Congress would also fail because those States which believe we have the power would oppose an amendment. They would be right in doing so. For every unnecessary amendment only serves to narrow and circumscribe the construction of the instrument, and, whilst it gives one power, furnishes a weapon by which ten more may be wrested from us. Thus, while it would seem to increase, it in fact diminishes the authority of the General Government, and we should soon find ourselves entangled in inextricable difficulties of construction arising from injudicious and unnecessary amendments. . . .

2.8   George McDuffie: "It is one of the most important rights of the people to make those gradual changes in their political institutions which may be indicated by the changes in the social system."*

. . .

It has often been urged in conversation that, by making amendments of the Constitution, we should impair the popular veneration for that instrument. . . . Nothing can be more dangerous than the inculcation of this sort of superstitious idolatry in this country. Its inevitable tendency is to confound the vices of our system with the system itself; and, in that way to convert the best feelings of the community into the means of preventing the correction of imperfections which time must disclose in all human institutions, and of perpetuating abuses from which no government, administered by men has ever been exempted.

We should never forget (what is our proud distinction) that this Government is founded upon the intelligence of the people; and that, in proportion as their veneration and attachment for the Constitution, proceeds from a discriminating attention to its practical operation, in the same proportion will their liberties be secure and the Government preserved in its purity.

It is, indeed, one of the most important rights of a free people to make those gradual changes in their political institutions, which may be indicated by the changes in the social system, the progress of intelligence, and, above all, by the lights of experience. It is in this way, and in this way only, that the Constitution of a country can be adapted to the condition and circumstances of the people whose liberty it is intended to secure. No constitutional provision can be wise which has not this peculiar adaptation; and no part of the Constitution evinces the wisdom of the Convention more clearly than the provision made for its amendment.

. . .

* From a speech in the House of Representatives by the Representative from South Carolina, supporting a proposed constitutional amendment that would fix for all states a common method of choosing presidential electors, January 16, 1824. *Annals,* 18th Congress, 1st session, p. 1069.

CONSTITUTIONAL AMENDMENT:
TO INTERWEAVE OR APPEND?

2.9   Debate on the First Amendments:*   "On this occasion form
is of some consequence."

The House then resolved itself into a Committee of the Whole,
Mr. Boudinot in the Chair, and took the amendments under consideration. The first article ran thus: "In the introductory paragraph of
the Constitution, before the words 'We the people,' add 'Government
being intended for the benefit of the people, and the rightful establishment thereof being derived from their authority alone.'"

Mr. Sherman: I believe, Mr. Chairman, this is not the proper mode
of amending the Constitution. We ought not to interweave our propositions into the work itself, because it will be destructive of the
whole fabric. . . .

Besides this, sir, it is questionable whether we 708 have the
right to propose amendments in this way. The Constitution is the act
of the people, and ought to remain entire. But the amendments will
be the act of the State Governments. Again, all the authority we possess is derived from that instrument; if we mean to destroy the whole
and establish a new Constitution, we remove the basis on which we
mean to build. For these reasons I will move to strike out that paragraph and substitute another.

The paragraph [which Mr. Sherman then] proposed was to the
following effect:

*Resolved, by the Senate and House of Representatives of the
United States in Congress assembled,* That the following articles be
proposed as amendments to the Constitution, and when ratified by
three-fourths of the State Legislatures, shall become valid to all intents and purposes, as part of the same.

* Representatives Roger Sherman of Connecticut, James Madison of Virginia, and Michael Jenifer Stone of Maryland. Remarks made in the House of
Representatives, August 13, 1789, in the debate on a proposed Bill of Rights.
See the note by the editors under 2.6 above. *Annals,* 1st Congress, 1st session,
pp. 707-708 (Sherman); p. 708 (Madison); p. 710 (Stone).

Under this title, the amendments might come in nearly as stated in the report, only varying the phraseology so as to accommodate them to a supplementary form.

Mr. Madison: Form, sir, is always of less importance than the substance; but on this occasion I admit that form is of some consequence, and it will be well for the House to pursue that which, upon reflection, shall appear to be the most eligible. Now it appears to me that there is a neatness and propriety in incorporating the amendments into the Constitution itself. In that case the system will remain uniform and entire. It will certainly be more simple when the amendments are interwoven into those parts to which they naturally belong than it will if they consist of separate and distinct parts. We shall then be able to determine its meaning without references or comparison; whereas, if they are supplementary, its meaning can only be ascertained by a comparison of the two instruments, which will be a very considerable embarrassment. It will be difficult to ascertain to what parts of the instrument the amendments particularly refer; they will create unfavorable comparisons; whereas, if they are placed upon the footing here proposed, they will stand upon as good foundation as the original work. . . . I am not, however, very solicitous about the form, provided the business is but well completed.

Mr. Stone: It is not a matter of much consequence, with respect to the preservation of the original instrument, whether the amendments are incorporated or made distinct, because the records will always show the original form in which it stood. But, in my opinion, we ought to mark its progress with truth in every step we take. If the amendments are incorporated in the body of the work, it will appear, unless we refer to the archives of Congress, that George Washington and the other worthy characters who composed the convention signed an instrument which they never had in contemplation. The one to which he affixed his signature purports to be adopted by the unanimous consent of the delegates from every State there assembled. Now if we incorporate these amendments, we must undoubtedly go further and say that the Constitution so formed was defective and had need of alteration; we therefore propose to repeal the old and substitute a new one in its place. From this consideration alone, I think we ought not to pursue the line of conduct drawn for us by the committee. This perhaps is not the last amendment the Constitution may receive; we ought therefore to be careful how we set a precedent which, in dangerous and turbulent times, may unhinge the whole.

. . .

part **II**

CONSTITUTIONAL
INTERPRETATION
AND ENFORCEMENT

Introduction

The Constitution is a highly complicated document principally because it calls for a division of functions and powers between three branches of government (a "horizontal" distribution) and a division of powers between the national government and the states (a "vertical" distribution). Those entrusted with activating our constitutional machinery soon found themselves in heated disagreement concerning the nature and purpose of these basic constitutional principles. The reasons for this are not difficult to find. Congress, for instance, by accepting and operating on a liberal or "loose" construction or interpretation of the "necessary and proper" clause did, in many instances, expand national powers to a degree that many felt represented an encroachment on the reserved powers of the states. Debates over this issue, quite naturally, centered around the intended purpose of the vertical division of powers. Likewise, controversies surrounding the proper constitutional interpretation of those provisions relating to the horizontal division of powers (as we will see in greater detail in part III) soon resolved themselves to the very same consideration. Now, in this context, two critical questions, the answers to which were highly instrumental in shaping our constitutional growth, were these: How should Congress, vested with most of the substantive powers of the national government, interpret its powers in light of the Constitution's rather obvious provision for both horizontal and vertical distribution of authority and function? To what extent is Congress constitutionally authorized to make authoritative decisions in these matters?

The answers provided to these questions were varied and conflictive not only because there were few precedents regarding the issues at hand, the usual state of affairs in those early deliberations, but also because those sources that might have provided some guidelines for their resolution were either silent, vague, or even somewhat contradictory. This was especially the case with respect to relevant questions concerning proper vertical distribution of powers. The Philadelphia proceedings, for example, provide us with virtually no information about how the "necessary and proper" clause should be interpreted. We do know that, with each state voting as a unit, this clause was adopted unanimously by the convention. Madison in *Federalist* number forty-four sets forth a probable reason for this unanimity.

Had the convention attempted a positive enumeration of the powers necessary and proper for carrying their other powers into effect, the attempt would have involved a complete digest of laws on every subject to which the Constitution relates; accommodated too, not only to the existing state of things, but to all possible changes which futurity may produce . . .

The opponents of the Constitution, to be sure, did see threats to the residual powers of the states in this and other clauses, but neither Hamilton nor Madison in *The Federalist* came to grips with the essential problems these critics raised. Both maintained that even in the absence of such an express provision these powers would result to the national government by necessary implication and that the means adopted for the exercise of a delegated power must be pursuant to or consistent with the Constitution. Otherwise, Hamilton argued, such laws "will be merely acts of usurpation, and will deserve to be treated as such."

But what would constitute such an unconstitutional encroachment by the national government? Hamilton in *Federalist* number thirty-three offers two concrete examples that he believed would represent flagrant usurpations (national legislation designed "to vary the law of descent in any state" or "to abrogate a land-tax imposed by the authority of a State"), but Madison sets forth a more general and useful formulation in *Federalist* number forty-five:

The former [powers of the national government] will be exercised principally on external objects, as war, peace, negotiation, and foreign commerce; with which last the power of taxation will, for the most part, be connected. The powers reserved to the several States will extend to all the objects which, in the ordinary course of affairs, concern the lives, liberties, and properties of the people, and the internal order, improvement, and prosperity of the State.

And who is to decide, using this standard, when the national government has overstepped its constitutional authority? We find the answers vary. Madison at one point states:

. . . in controversies relating to the boundary between the two juris-dictions, the tribunal [the Supreme Court?] which is ultimately to decide, is to be established under the general government.

A few essays later (number forty-six) he writes:

. . . the ultimate authority, wherever the derivative may be found, resides in the people alone, and that it will not depend merely on the comparative ambition or address of the different governments, whether either, or which of them, will be able to enlarge its sphere of jurisdiction at the expense of the other. Truth, no less than decency, requires that the event in every case should be supposed to depend on the sentiments and sanction of their common constituents.

And Hamilton, addressing himself to much the same question an-swers (in number thirty-three):

. . . the national government, like every other, must judge, in the first instance, of the proper exercise of its powers, and its constituents in the last. If the federal government should overpass the just bounds of its authority and make a tyrannical use of its powers, the people, whose crea-ture it is, must appeal to the standard they have formed, and take such measures to redress the injury done to the Constitution as the exigency may suggest and prudence justify.

Now, the issue of who should have the "last say" in interpreting the Constitution on these and related questions is greatly compli-cated by the fundamental assumption that underlies our entire Con-stitution: The Constitution represents fundamental law embodying the deliberate and real will of its creators. Those agencies, then, created by and operating under its authority are bound by its provi-sions, which can only be changed by the specified amendment proc-ess. We see this belief reflected in Jefferson's *Notes on Virginia,* where he points out that one of the prime defects in the Virginia Constitution of 1776 is that "the ordinary legislature may alter the constitution itself . . ." He notes the "absurdity" of "the ordinary legislature" establishing "*an act above the power of the ordinary legislature.*" Hamilton also held to this view of the Constitution. In *Federalist* number seventy-eight he writes:

No legislative act, therefore, contrary to the Constitution, can be valid. To deny this, would be to affirm, that the deputy is greater than his principal; that the servant is above his master . . .

In what ways does this assumption introduce further complexities with respect to interpretation and enforcement of the Constitution? Here, we can identify at least three that are interrelated. First, because Congress was engaged in the process of giving meaning to fundamental but ill-defined constitutional principles, the "gate" was wide open for some to contend, and not without at least theoretical justification, that Congress, as an agent under the Constitution, had in some instances acted unconstitutionally by contravening or exceeding the authority given to it by the Constitution.

Second, as we have noted, the very nature of the questions with which Congress was dealing seemed to preclude recourse to specific constitutional amendment for their resolution. As Madison intimated in the quotation cited above, to draw such fine lines was not only next to impossible but also potentially dangerous because circumstances that could not be handled within a rigid framework, even some that might conceivably threaten the very existence of the republic, would always arise. There are even considerations beyond these, particularly those noted by Henry St. George Tucker (selection 2.7).

Third, just as Congress is an agent bound by the Constitution, so, too, are the President and the Courts. Thus, any argument to the effect that the President or the Courts should be final arbiters on constitutional meaning was subject to the very same objection levelled at Congress operating in this capacity. To complicate matters even more, when there is a conflict between the interpretations of the Congress and of the Supreme Court, as both are agents bound to uphold the Constitution, there is no reason why Congress is obligated to accept the Court's interpretation or *vice versa*. Nor were any of the solutions to this difficulty offered by Madison or Hamilton satisfactory from this point of view, since the people themselves could change the Constitution only when they acted in their "sovereign" capacities, that is, by amending it.

One of the dilemmas, therefore, facing the early Congresses was, Where should the responsibility for authoritative interpretation of the Constitution rest? Do the people have a right to ignore or resist those laws of the national government they consider unconstitutional? Are they, in fact, duty bound to do so? What recourse do the people have, short of open resistance, if they do regard a law to be a flagrant violation of the Constitution? What role can the states justifiably take in resisting national legislation? Do they have the power and authority to nullify those laws they consider unconstitutional? Can they go so far as to withdraw from the Union? (See selections 3.4 through 3.7.)

Debate, quite naturally, arose over the role of the Judiciary as the arbiter of disputes concerning the meaning of the Constitution. At an early point in the House deliberations controversy developed over the removal powers of the President. Some contended that the Supreme Court should settle whether the Constitution vested removal powers with the President alone or whether removal of subordinate executive officers could only be accomplished through the same processes as appointment, which would, for removal of higher ranking officers, require Senate approval. At this point, questions regarding the Court's power to fix the constitutional boundaries between coordinate departments arose. Does the Court have any more authority to settle such questions involving horizontal distribution of powers than do the other departments? Would acknowledging such a power to reside in the Court place it above and superior to the legislative and executive branches? Why should the Court's interpretation be any more authoritative than congressional interpretation? While this debate involving the Judiciary by all evidences was quite placid, the debates in 1802 over the repeal of certain key provisions of the Judiciary Act of 1801 certainly must rank among the longest and bitterest in congressional history. (See selections 3.8, 3.9, and 8.4.) Several issues were raised during these debates, among them the contention that the Judiciary had the power to authoritatively interpret the Constitution to the extent of nullifying an act of Congress. The proponents of this position asked, Of what good is it to have specific limitations on congressional authority if no check exists to enforce these limitations? Would not the absence of an effective check on Congress lead to a breakdown of the constitutionally prescribed vertical separation and eventually result in a consolidated government? If such authority were not vested with the Judiciary, where could it reside without seriously endangering the ability of the national government to operate effectively? Opponents of this interpretation were not without some questions of their own: Why doesn't the Constitution expressly grant this highly important power to the Supreme Court? If the Court possessed this power, wouldn't it actually be sovereign? And who is to check the Court?

These controversies should not obscure the fact that the function of interpreting the Constitution necessarily devolved upon Congress. In chapters 4 and 5 we see some of the important problems surrounding congressional interpretation with respect to vertical distribution of powers. Perhaps the most important consideration in these interpretations is the general view that prevailed concerning the proper roles of the state and national governments. Among the finest statements on the nature and purpose of the vertical distribution are those found in selections 4.1 through 4.4. Here we see the difficulties encountered in determining, at an early stage of our development, whether a specific program or policy is local or national in character. Moreover, in selections 4.3 through 4.8 questions concerning the general nature of the system are explored: Which institutions were designed to embody the "federative" principle and which the "national"? To what extent is the federative principle designed to protect the small states from the large? To what degree did the original mode of selection of the President incorporate federative or national principles? Do the small states have more to fear from large states than they do from the national government?

In chapter 5. the debates center on interpretations of the specific language of the Constitution and give rise to still other questions. To what extent should the fact that the national government was intended to be a government of delegated and specific powers dictate the meaning of and the powers to be derived from the "general welfare" and "necessary and proper" clauses? How should these clauses be interpreted in order to maintain effective and meaningful vertical distribution of authority? What are reasonable canons of interpretation of specific constitutional provisions? What role should precedent play. either legislative or judicial, in settling questions of constitutionality relative to these and other clauses of the Constitution? (See also selections 3.2 and 3.4.)

These early debates, occurring in the first years of experience under a new Constitution, could not settle all the questions relating to constitutional interpretation and enforcement. But it must be said that, in one way or another, they do point to all those great questions that have stood at the center of controversy throughout our history.

chapter **3**

The Constitution:
interpretation and enforcement

LEGISLATIVE INTERPRETATION

3.1 Debate on the Removal Power: * "There is not one Government on the face of the earth, so far as I recollect, in which provision is made for a particular authority to determine the limits of the Constitutional division of power between the branches of Government."

[Note by the editors. One of the most important accomplishments of Congress in its first session was the creation of the principal executive or administrative departments of the new national government. The Constitution expressly provides for the President, with or without the advice and consent of the Senate, to appoint principal officers, but it contains no instructions for the removal of officers except in instances where impeachment is appropriate. Debate in the Senate was not reported, but members of the House considered at length what provisions for removal were permitted by the Con-

---

° Representatives James Madison and Alexander White of Virginia. Remarks in the House of Representatives, June 18, 1789. *Annals,* 1st Congress, 1st session, pp. 500-501 (Madison's first speech); p. 516 (White); pp. 546-547 (Madison's second speech).

stitution and how the question of what was permitted could be authoritatively determined. The remarks presented here are directed toward the question: May Congress decide the question of constitutionality and specify a removal process in the statute creating a department?]

Mr. Madison: . . . Another species of argument has been urged against this clause. It is said that it is improper, or at least unnecessary, to come to any decision on this subject. It has been said by one gentleman that it would be officious in this branch of the Legislature to expound the Constitution so far as it relates to the division of power between the President and Senate.

It is incontrovertibly of as much importance to this branch of the Government as to any other, that the Constitution should be preserved entire. It is our duty, so far as it depends upon us, to take care that the powers of the Constitution be preserved entire to every department of Government; the breach of the Constitution in one point will facilitate the breach in another; a breach in this point may destroy that equilibrium by which the House retains its consequence and share of power; therefore we are not chargeable with an officious interference. Besides, the bill, before it can have effect, must be submitted to both those branches who are particularly interested in it; the Senate may negative, or the President may object if he thinks it unconstitutional.

But the great objection drawn from the source to which the last arguments would lead us is, that the Legislature itself has no right to expound the Constitution; that wherever its meaning is doubtful, you must leave it to take its course until the Judiciary is called upon to declare its meaning. I acknowledge, in the ordinary course of Government, that the exposition of the laws and Constitution devolves upon the Judiciary. But I beg to know upon what principle it can be contended that any one department draws from the Constitution greater powers than another, in marking out the limits of the powers of the several departments? The Constitution is the charter of the People to the Government; it specifies certain great powers as absolutely granted, and marks out the departments to exercise them. If the Constitutional boundary of either be brought into question, I do not see that any one of these independent departments has more right than another to declare their sentiments on that point.

Perhaps this is an omitted case. There is not one Government on the face of the earth, so far as I recollect, there is not one in the United States, in which provision is made for a particular authority to determine the limits of the Constitu- 501 tional division of power between the branches of the Government. In all systems there are points which must be adjusted by the departments themselves, to which no one of them is competent. If it cannot be determined in this way, there is no recourse left but the will of the community, to be collected in some mode to be provided by the Constitution or one dictated by the necessity of the case. It is therefore a fair question whether this great point may not as well be decided, at least by the whole Legislature as by a part, by us as well as by the Executive or Judiciary? As I think it will be equally Constitutional, I cannot imagine it will be less safe that the exposition should issue from the Legislative authority than any other; and the more so, because it involves in the decision the opinions of both those departments whose powers are supposed to be affected by it. Besides, I do not see in what way this question could come before the judges, to obtain a fair and solemn decision. But even if it were the case that it could, I should suppose, at least while the Government is not led by passion, disturbed by faction, or deceived by any discolored medium of sight, but while there is a desire in all to see and be guided by the benignant ray of truth, that the decision may be made with the most advantage by the Legislature itself.

. . .

Mr. White: . . . Without entering into the evils which may arise, as gentlemen on both sides of the House have done, let us consider whether greater evils will not arise from our explaining the Constitution at this time. If such events as I have apprehended should arise from our attempt to exercise an unconstitutional authority, it would more than counterbalance any possible good that can result from our decision within a moderate period of time. But is there any necessity for the measure? If the Constitution has given this power to the President, which some gentlemen suppose, cannot he exercise it without our passing an act on the subject? If the Constitution has not given it to him, shall we go beyond the limits that are set us in order to extend it to him? I hope not. But it seems a difficult point to determine whether he has or has not this power by the Constitution, because some gentlemen contend he has, others that he has not. Why need we be concerned to determine this point? It will be better to leave the construction to himself; if it should become necessary to exercise this authority, let him consider its powers. I will venture to say, the occasion for the exercise of it will be a better comment on the Constitution than any we can give; it will better explain it to the people, and more perfectly reconcile it to them than any law from the Legislature.

. . .

Mr. Madison: The question now seems to be brought to this, whether it is proper or improper to retain these words in the clause, provided they are explanatory of the Constitution. I think this branch of the Legislature is as much interested in the establishment of the true meaning of the Constitution as either the President or Senate. And when the Constitution submits it to us to establish offices by law, we ought to know by what tenure the office should be held; and whether it should depend upon the concurrence of the Senate with the President, or upon the will of the President alone; because gentlemen may hesitate in either case, whether they will make it for an indefinite or precise time. If the officer can be removed at discretion by the President, there may be safety in letting it be for an indefinite period. If he cannot exert his prerogative, there is no security even by the mode of impeachment; because the officer may intrench himself behind the authority of the Senate and bid defiance to every other department of Government. In this case, the question of duration would take a different turn. Hence it is highly proper that we and our constituents should know the tenure of the office. And have we not as good a right as any branch of the Government to declare our sense of the meaning of the Constitution?

Nothing has yet been offered to invalidate the 547 doctrine, that the meaning of the Constitution may as well be ascertained by the legislative as by the judicial authority. When the question emerges as it does in this bill, and much seems to depend upon it, I should conceive it highly proper to make a legislative construction. In another point of view it is proper that this interpretation should now take place, rather than at a time when the exigency of the case may require the exercise of the power of removal. At present, the disposition of every gentleman is to seek the truth, and abide by its guidance when it is discovered. I have reason to believe the same disposition prevails in the Senate. But will this be the case when some individual officer of high rank draws into question the capacity of the President, with the Senate, to effect his removal? If we leave the Constitution to take this course, it can never be expounded until the President shall think it expedient to exercise the right of removal, if he supposes he has it; then the Senate may be induced to set up their pretensions. And will they decide so calmly as at this time, when no important officer in any of the great departments is appointed to influence their judgments? The imagination of no member here, or of the Senate, or of the President himself, is heated or disturbed by faction. If ever a proper moment for decision should offer, it must be one like the present.

. . .

3.2 Henry Clay: "This doctrine of precedents, applied to the Legislature, appears to me to be fraught with the most mischievous consequences."*

[Note by the editors. This item and selection 3.3 are from debate on a bill to continue in force the Bank of the United States, an institution established by act of Congress in 1791. The power of Congress to establish a bank was disputed from the time its creation was proposed. Alexander Hamilton and Thomas Jefferson, members of President Washington's Cabinet, submitted memoranda examining the Constitution's grant of authority to the national government, Hamilton contending that Congress could and Jefferson contending that Congress could not establish a bank. Their memoranda, both submitted in 1791, are reprinted in several collections of documents; e.g. Henry S. Commager, ed., *Documents of American History*, 7th ed., Nos. 93 and 94 (New York: Appleton-Century-Crofts, 1963), pp. 156-160. Discussions in Congress of the issue of authority under the Constitution appear below in selections 5.4 and 5.5. The remarks reported at this point reveal conflicting

* From a speech by the Senator from Kentucky in the Senate, February 15, 1811. *Annals*, 11th Congress, 3d session, pp. 216-218.

views as to whether previous legislation had settled the issue of
constitutionality before 1811.]

. . .

Gentlemen contend that the construction which they give to the
Constitution has been acquiesced in by all parties, and under all
Administrations; and they rely particularly on an act which passed
in 1804 for extending a branch to New Orleans, and another act, of
1807, for punishing those who should forge or utter forged paper of
the bank. . . . *217*

When gentlemen attempt to carry this measure upon the ground
of acquiescence or precedent, do they forget that we are not in West-
minster Hall? In courts of justice the utility of uniformity of decision
exacts of the judge a conformity to the adjudication of his prede-
cessor. In the interpretation and administration of the law this
practice is wise and proper; and without it, everything depending
upon the caprice of the judge, we should have no security for our
dearest rights. It is far otherwise when applied to the source of
legislation. Here no rule exists but the Constitution; and to legislate
upon the ground merely that our predecessors thought themselves
authorized, under similar circumstances, to legislate, is to sanctify
error and perpetuate usurpation. But if we are to be subjected to
the trammels of precedents, I claim, on the other hand, the benefit
of the restrictions under which the intelligent judge cautiously receives them. It is an established rule that to give to a previous adjudication any effect, the mind of the judge who pronounced it must
have been awakened to the subject, and it must have been a deliberate opinion formed after full argument. In technical language, it
must not have been *sub silentio*. Now, the acts of 1804 and 1807,
relied upon as pledges for the rechartering this company, passed not
only without any discussions whatever of the Constitutional power
of Congress to establish a bank, but I venture to say, without a
single member having had his attention drawn to this question. I
had the honor of a seat in the Senate when the latter law passed;
probably voted for it; and I declare, with the utmost sincerity, that
I never once thought of that point; and I appeal confidently to
every honorable member who was then present to say if that was not
his situation.

This doctrine of precedents, applied to the Legislature, appears to me to be fraught with the most mischievous consequences. The great advantage of our system of government over all others is, that we have a written Constitution defining its limits and prescribing its authorities; and that, however for a time faction may convulse the nation and passion and party prejudice sway its functionaries, the season of reflection will recur, when calmly retracing their deeds, all aberrations from fundamental principle will be corrected. But once substitute practice for principle, the expositions of the Constitution for the text of the Constitution, and in vain shall we look for the instrument in the instrument itself. It will be as diffused and intangible as the pretended Constitution of England; and it must be sought for in the statute book, in the fugitive journals of Congress, and in reports of the Secretary of the Treasury. What would be *218* our condition if we were to take the interpretations given to that sacred book, which is or ought to be the criterion of our faith, for the book itself? We should find the Holy Bible buried beneath the interpretations, glosses, and comments of councils, synods, and learned divines, which have produced swarms of intolerant and furious sects, partaking less of the mildness and meekness of their origin than of a vindictive spirit of hostility towards each other. They ought to afford us a solemn warning to make that Constitution, which we have sworn to support, our invariable guide.

. . .

3.3 Peter B. Porter: "The commentaries of courts are not to furnish the principles upon which I am afterwards to legislate."*

. . .

But, Mr. Chairman, . . . a new argument [has been advanced] in support of the constitutionality of this bank—an argument not deduced from the provisions of the Constitution itself but founded on prescription. He tells us that this bank was originally incorporated by a Congress fully competent and qualified to decide on its

* From a speech by the Representative from New York in the House of Representatives, January 18, 1811. *Annals*, 11th Congress, 3d session, pp. 642-644.

constitutionality; that its existence is almost coeval with the Government; that it has been countenanced by all succeeding Administrations; that laws have been passed to enforce the provisions of the original charter; and therefore the Constitutional question must be considered as settled, adjudicated, and at rest.

Whatever may be the opinion of the gentlemen of the *long robe,* I cannot for myself yield to this *643* doctrine of *prescriptive* Constitutional rights. It may answer in England where they have no constitution; or where, rather, as they choose to explain it, immemorial usage or prescription are evidence of what their Constitution is. It may do in Connecticut—(it is not my design to derogate from the respectability of that State, nor of its institutions)—it may be good doctrine in Connecticut, where ancient customs and *steady habits* are their constitution. But, sir, doctrine should never be tolerated in this House, where every member has a *printed Constitution* on his table before him—a Constitution drawn up with the greatest care and deliberation; with the utmost attention to perspicuity and precision. A Constitution, the injunctions of which, as we in our best judgments shall understand them and not as they shall be interpreted to us by others, we are solemnly bound, by our oaths, to obey.

It is true that this bank was originally established by a Congress competent to judge of its constitutionality. It is equally true that a respectable minority of that Congress opposed the passage of the law on the ground of its unconstitutionality; and if I have been rightly informed, it is also true that the then President, General Washington, in giving his sanction to that law did it with more doubt and hesitation than almost any other act of his Administration.

It is true that subsequent Congresses of different political complexions have passed laws enforcing the provisions of the original charter; and that no attempts have been made to repeal it. But it is equally true that all this might be done away with the most perfect propriety and consistency, although they totally disbelieved in its constitutionality. I need not state to this House, that this is not a law in the ordinary course of legislation—a law prescribing a common rule of conduct for the government of the citizens of the United States at large—liable to be repealed at any time; and the obligations of which would cease with its repeal. This, sir, is not the nature of the law, but it is a law in the nature of a contract between the Government and certain individuals, and the existence of it was extended to twenty years. The moment this contract was made, and its operations commenced, private rights were vested; and it would have been a breach of national faith to have repealed it. The original Congress had the same right that we have to judge of the constitutionality of a law; and having, under that right, passed this law or made this contract, we are bound to carry it, as a contract, into execution. As a contract, every successive Congress, of whatever materials composed, is one party to it; and it is well known that a party cannot violate the obligations of his own contract; but, on the contrary, is bound to carry them into effect. It was competent in the State governments to have opposed the execution on the ground of its unconstitutionality; but, perhaps under all circumstances, they acted a wise and discreet part in not attempting it. The national faith was pledged in the passage of this law. The national credit, which it was at that 644 time and which indeed it is at all times of the first importance to support, was at stake on the faithful execution of this contract; and it was better to suffer for twenty years, under an unconstitutional law, rather than to attempt so violent a remedy—a remedy which would have crippled the credit of the nation in its infancy.

But, sir, because these were proper considerations with our predecessors and the States to suffer the continuance of this law, does it follow that now, when that law has expired by its own limitation, when the obligations of that contract are complied with and discharged, when the national faith is emancipated, that they are motives for us to make a new unconstitutional contract? No, sir. The question now is a question *de novo*. It is a question of conscience in the interpretation of the letter and spirit of the Constitution; unembarrassed by any collateral considerations; and as such I shall feel bound to vote upon it. It is the province of the Executive and judicial departments to explain and direct the practical operation of each particular law; and I must submit to the decisions. But the commentaries of courts are not to furnish the principles upon which I am afterwards to legislate. It is to this book (the Constitution) so justly dear to us all, and not to the books of reports, that we must look as a guide to direct us in the path of our oath and our duty.

. . .

POPULAR RESISTANCE

3.4 Debate on the Alien and Sedition Acts: *   "If we are ready
to violate the Constitution we have sworn to defend, will the people
submit to our unauthorized acts?"

[Note by the editors. Three measures were enacted in 1798 to
protect the national government and its officials from acts of violence
and from verbal attacks. Two of the measures authorized the President to send out of the country aliens who might endanger the safety
of this country, and one measure (applying to both aliens and American citizens) forbad and penalized a number of acts, including ut-
terances that were false, malicious, and scandalous and intended to
bring the government of the United States into disrepute, involve it
in war, or in any other manner weaken or obstruct it. Chapter 12
draws more heavily on debates relating to this legislation; and the
last mentioned of these measures, the Sedition Act of 1798, is printed
at that point. The remarks we now examine are directed to the question of what people might and ought to do in case they believed, as
some Congressmen believed, that these measures were in conflict
with the Constitution.]

Mr. Livingston: . . . The first section provides that it shall be lawful
for the President "to order all such aliens as he shall judge dangerous
to the peace and safety of the United States, or shall have reasonable
grounds to suspect are concerned in any treasonable or secret machinations against the Government thereof, to depart out of the United
States, in such time as shall be expressed in such order."

Our Government, sir, is founded on the establishment of those
principles which constitute the difference between a free Constitution and a despotic power; a distribution of the Legislative, Executive, and Judiciary powers into several hands; a distribution strongly

---

* Representatives Edward Livingston of New York, John Allen of Connecticut, and Albert Gallatin of Pennsylvania. Remarks in the House of Representatives. Livingston, June 21, 1798; Allen and Gallatin, July 5, 1798. *Annals*,
5th Congress, 2nd session, pp. 2007-2008, 2013-2014 (Livingston); pp. 2094-
2096 (Allen); pp. 2110-2111 (Gallatin).

marked in the three first and great divisions of the Constitution. By the first, all Legislative power is given to Congress, the second vests all Legislative [Executive?] functions in the President, and the third declares that the Judiciary powers shall be exercised by the Supreme and Inferior Courts. Here then is a division of the Governmental powers strongly marked, decisively pronounced, and every act of one or all of the branches that tends to confound these powers, or alter this arrangement, must be destructive of the Constitution. Examine then, sir, the bill on your table, and declare whether the few lines I have repeated from the first section do not confound these fundamental powers of Government, *2008* vest them all in the more unqualified terms in one hand, and thus subvert the basis on which our liberties rest.

. . . *2013*

. . . if, regardless of our duty as citizens and our solemn obligation as representatives; regardless of the rights of our constituents; regardless of every sanction, human and divine; if we are ready to violate the Constitution we have sworn to defend—will the people submit to our unauthorized acts? Will the States sanction our usurped power? Sir, they ought not to submit; they would deserve the chains which these measures are forging for them if they did not resist. For let no man vainly imagine that the evil is to stop here, that a few unprotected aliens only are to be affected by this inquisitorial power. The same arguments which enforce those provisions against aliens apply with equal strength to enacting them in the case of citizens. . . . Either the offences described in the act are crimes, or they are not. If they are, then all the humane provisions of the Constitution forbid the mode of punishment, or preventing them, equally as relates to aliens and citizens. If they are not crimes, then the citizen has no more safety by the Constitution than the alien has; for all those provisions apply only to *crimes*. So that, in either event, the citizen has the same reason to expect a similar law to the one now before you; which subjects his person to the uncontrolled despotism of a single man. You have already been told of plots and conspiracies; and all the frightful images that were necessary to keep up the present system of terror and alarm were presented to you. But who were implicated *2014* by these dark hints—these mysterious allusions? They were our own citizens, sir, not aliens. If there is then any necessity for the system now proposed, it is more necessary to

be enforced against our own citizens than against strangers; and I
have no doubt that either in this, or some other shape, this will be
attempted. I now ask, sir, whether the people of America are prepared for this? Whether they are willing to part with all the means
which the wisdom of their ancestors discovered, and their own caution so lately adopted, to secure their own persons? Whether they
are ready to submit to imprisonment or exile whenever suspicion,
calumny, or vengeance shall mark them for ruin? Are they base
enough to be prepared for this? No, sir; they will, I repeat it, they
will resist this tyrannic system; the people will oppose it—the States
will not submit to its operation. They ought not to acquiesce, and I
pray to God they never may.

My opinions, sir, on this subject are explicit, and I wish they may
be known; they are, that whenever our laws manifestly infringe the
Constitution under which they were made, the people ought not to
hesitate which they should obey. If we exceed our powers, we become tyrants and our acts have no effect. Thus, sir, one of the first
effects of measures such as this, if they be not acquiesced in, will be
disaffection among the States and opposition among the people to
your Government—tumults, violations, and a recurrence to first revolutionary principles. If they are submitted to, the consequences will
be worse. After such manifest violation of the principles of our Constitution, the form will not long be sacred; presently, every vestige
of it will be lost and swallowed up in the gulf of despotism.
. . .

[Note by the editors. Mr. Livingston's remarks were directed
to one of the bills authorizing deportation of aliens. The remarks
which follow, by Representatives Allen and Gallatin, are directed to
the bill which, when enacted, became the Sedition Act of 1798.]

Mr. Allen: . . . I will take the liberty of reading to the House another paragraph from the same paper; and it comes from high authority. It is published as the *2095* speech of Mr. Livingston when
we were discussing the Alien bill a few days since, and I presume
is correct. It is a precious disclosure of the principles of certain gentlemen.
. . . *2096*
But, sir, in the same speech the people are instructed that op-

position to the laws, that insurrection, is a duty whenever they think
we exceed our Constitutional powers; but, I ask the gentleman, who
shall determine that point? I thought the Constitution had assigned
the cognizance of that question to the Courts, and so it has. But the
attempt here is to evince, and the doctrine we know is openly
avowed by members of this House, that each man has the right of
deciding for himself, and that as many as are of opinion that the law
is unconstitutional, have a right to combine and oppose it by force.
The people I venerate; they are truly sovereign; but a section, a part
of the citizens, a town, a city, or a mob, I know not; if they oppose
the laws, they are insurgents and rebels; they are not the people.
The people act in their elections by displacing obnoxious Representatives, and by the irresistible force of their opinions; when the people wills, the Government is convinced and obeys. It is too manifest
to admit of doubt or denial that the intention and tendency of such
principles, are to produce divisions, tumults, violence, insurrection,
and blood; all which are intended by the fashionable doctrine of
modern times, which the gentleman terms "a recurrence to first revolutionary principles," from which may God preserve us.

. . .

Mr. Gallatin: . . . [As respects the speech of Mr. Livingston] so far
as he had heard the expressions alluded to, it was not 2111 an invitation to the people, or an opinion that the people should oppose the
alien bill itself as unconstitutional; but merely a general position that
they had a right to resist and would resist unconstitutional and oppressive laws. He [Mr. Gallatin] believed that doctrine to be strictly
correct, and neither seditious or treasonable. The opposite doctrines
of passive obedience and non-resistance had long been exploded.
America had never received them. America had asserted the right of
resisting unconstitutional laws, and the day we were celebrating yesterday (4th of July) is a monument of that right. When and how such
a right should be exercised, was a different and delicate question. It is
a question to be decided by motives of prudence and by principles
of morality. It is a question which America had once decided in the
affirmative. It is a right to which they may, perhaps, in the course of
events be again obliged to resort. God forbid that we should ever
see that day! But it is above all in the power of Government to avert
such an evil by refraining from unconstitutional and arbitrary laws.

Mr. G. added that he was one of those who had the most sincere and strong conviction impressed on his mind that the alien bill was unconstitutional. [The Speaker said, that was not the question.][1] Mr. G. said, that he was not going to make any remarks on that law, or any that could by any one be supposed to be out of order. He meant only to state that, notwithstanding that conviction, his opinion was that an appeal must be made to another tribunal, to the Judiciary in the first instance, on the subject of a supposed unconstitutional law; and that even where no redress could be obtained, he did not think that law [the alien act] alone, and in itself, sufficient to justify resistance and opposition even in those who thought it unconstitutional.

. . .

NULLIFICATION, REBELLION, AND SECESSION

3.5 Josiah Quincy: "Let legislators beware lest by the very nature of their laws they weaken that sentiment of respect for them so important to be inspired, so difficult to be reinstated once it has been driven from the mind."*

[Note by the editors. The American declaration of war against Great Britain in 1812 was preceded by more than a decade of depradations on American commerce by both Great Britain and France. Before resorting to war, Congress adopted a number of measures to remove American shipping from exposure to attack. Legislation in effect at the time of this debate included an embargo on shipping into and from American ports.]

. . .

Mr. Chairman, other gentlemen must take their responsibilities —I shall take mine. This embargo must be repealed. You cannot enforce it for any important period of time longer. When I speak of your inability to enforce this law, let not gentlemen misunderstand me. I mean not to intimate insurrection or open defiance of them [the laws restricting shipping]. Although it is impossible to foresee

---

[1] Brackets those of the *Annals* reporter.
* From a speech by the Representative from Massachusetts in the House of Representatives, November 28, 1808, opposing restrictions on shipping. *Annals*, 10th Congress, 2nd session, pp. 539-541.

in what acts that "oppression" will finally terminate, which, we are told, "makes wise men mad." I speak of an inability resulting from very different causes.

. . .

I ask this House, is there no control to its authority; is there no limit to the power of this National Legislature? I hope I shall offend no man when I intimate that two limits exist: Nature and the Constitution. Should this House undertake to declare that this atmosphere should no longer surround us; that water should cease to flow; that gravity should not hereafter operate; that the needle should not vibrate to the pole: I do suppose, Mr. Chairman—sir, I mean no disrespect to the authority of this House, I know the high notions some gentlemen entertain on this subject—I do suppose—sir, I hope I shall not offend—I think I may venture to affirm, that such a law to the contrary notwithstanding, the air would continue to circulate, the Mississippi, the Hudson, the Potomac, would hurl their floods to the ocean, heavy bodies continue to descend, and the mysterious magnet hold on its course to its celestial cynosure.

Just as utterly absurd and contrary to nature 540 is it, to attempt to prohibit the people of New England, for any considerable length of time, from the ocean. Commerce is not only associated with all the feelings, the habits, the interests, and relations of that people, but the nature of our soil and of our coasts, the state of our population and its mode of distribution over our territory, renders it indispensable. We have five hundred miles of seacoast, all furnished with harbors, bays, creeks, rivers, inlets, basins, with every variety of invitation to the sea, with every species of facility to violate such laws as these. Our people are not scattered over an immense surface, at a solemn distance from each other, in lordly retirement, in the midst of extended plantations and intervening wastes. They are collected on the margin of the ocean, by the sides of rivers, at the heads of bays, looking into the water or on the surface of it for the incitement and the reward of their industry. Among a people thus situated, thus educated, thus numerous, laws prohibiting them from the exercise of their natural rights will have a binding effect not one moment longer than the public sentiment supports them.

Gentlemen talk of twelve revenue cutters additional to enforce the embargo laws. Multiply the number by twelve, multiply it by an hundred, join all your ships of war, all your gunboats, and all your militia, in despite of them all, such laws as these are of no avail when they become odious to public sentiment. Continue these laws any considerable time longer and it is very doubtful if you will have officers to execute, juries to convict, or purchasers to bid for your confiscations. Cases have begun to occur. Ask your revenue officers and they will tell you that already at public sales in your cities, under these laws, the owner has bought his property at less than four per cent upon its real value. Public opinion begins to look with such a jealous and hateful eye upon these laws that even self-interest will not co-operate to enforce their penalties.

But where is our love of order? Where our respect for the laws? Let legislators beware lest by the very nature of their laws, they weaken that sentiment of respect for them, so important to be inspired, and so difficult to be reinstated when it has once been driven from the mind. Regulate not the multitude to their ruin. Disgust not men of virtue by the tendency of your laws, lest, when they cannot yield them the sanction of their approbation, the enterprising and the necessitous find a principal check upon their fear of violating them removed. It is not enough for men in place to exclaim, "the worthless part of society!" Words cannot alter the nature of things. You cannot identify the violator of such laws as these, in our part of the country, for any great length of time, with the common smuggler, nor bring the former down to the level of the latter. The reason is obvious. You bring the duties the citizen owes to society into competition not only with the strongest interests, but, which is more, with the most sacred private obligations. When you present to the choice of a citizen bankruptcy, a total loss of the accumulated wealth of *541* his whole life, or a violation of a positive law restrictive of the exercise of the most common rights, it presents to him a most critical alternative. I will not say how sublime casuists may decide, but it is easy to foretell that nature will plead too strong in the bosom to make obedience long possible. I state no imaginary case. . . .

3.6   Debate on Compulsory Military Service: *   "You who create are not the men that can control the tide of rebellion; you, first of all, shall be overwhelmed by its resistless fury."

Mr. Miller: . . . Your conscription system, in any view of it, ought

* Representatives Morris S. Miller of New York and William P. Duvall of

not to be adopted. The Secretary of War admits that the abuse of power in raising armies is to be dreaded; and he says, too, that "our Constitution has provided ample security against that evil." It has, sir; and if so, it forbids conscription. If the General Government has the "absolute power" which is contended for, I can see no security against the exercise of it. If to-day you can raise men by conscription, to-morrow some military despot may embody anticipated conscripts as the ministers of his vengeance. The guard which our Constitution has placed against the abuse of power in raising armies is this: you must raise them by voluntary enlistment. If you have a right to force the people of this country into your armies, then they have no right left worth preserving. Life and all its comforts are robbed of half their value.

. . . 785

This conscription is not only utterly incorrect and inadmissible in principle, but it will prove arbitrary, hard, and oppressive in practice. It will impose an intolerable burden on the poorer classes of society. Each class is to furnish a man; and the man may be designated by lot: in this way the poorest citizen runs an equal hazard with the most wealthy man in the community. If the rich man is drawn, he has the means and may perhaps hire a substitute, while the poor man must perform the service himself—he must quit his business and family, and leave them dependent for a precarious subsistence on the bounty of their neighbors and friends.

. . . 798

There is another view of this subject which honorable gentlemen ought well to consider. The tendency of your whole system is to destroy the bond of union which connects us together. Let me not be charged with any wish to separate the States; I disclaim it. I have cherished the union of these States with an ardor, with an enthusiasm, not inferior to any other gentleman in or out of this House. But all your measures seem to point to separation. The defence of the States has not been a leading object of this war. The States, however, must be defended; if you will not protect them, if you refuse to pay the expense necessarily incurred for the object, they will take care of themselves. The natural consequence is, the States will preserve their

Kentucky. From debate in the House of Representatives on a bill to make military service compulsory. Miller, December 8, 1814; Duvall, December 9, 1814. *Annals*, 13th Congress, 3d session, pp. 781, 785, 798-799 (Miller) and pp. 807-808 (Duvall).

own resources for their own defence; and the practical result will be a dissolution of the Union.

If you resort to conscription you will have a commentary upon it written in the blood of this country. I beg gentlemen to remember the days when York and Lancaster drew forth their battles. They appear to me to be fast returning. Serious discontents already exist in many parts of the United States. Causes already exist which are claimed to justify a dissolution of the Union; and, rather than submit to a military conscription, there are States who may consider themselves bound by duty and interest to withdraw from this Confederacy. You will say they have not justifiable cause. I entreat you not to afford them a plausible pretext. I am no alarmist; nor is this view of the subject taken for any purpose of threat or intimidation. I give it as my opinion, and you will, I dare say, receive it for as much as it is worth. I have carefully examined this conscription question, with all that seriousness and attention required by the solemnity of the occasion; I have exercised that small measure of talent which it has pleased the Almighty to bestow upon me, and I have arrived at this conclusion: the plan of conscription violates the Constitution; it trenches on the rights of the States, and takes from them their "necessary security," it destroys all claim to personal freedom; it will poison all the comforts of this people. In this 799 belief I can have no hesitation to say, that I think it will be resisted, and that it ought to be resisted.

Sir, I speak not particularly of this bill immediately before your committee—I allude to the conscription system as proposed by the Secretary of War. To use the language of a former member of this House (Mr. Edward Livingston, of New York, on the alien bill in 1798) who was a distinguished leader of the present majority, I ask, whether the people of this country are "base 'enough to be prepared for this? No, sir, they 'will, I repeat it, they will resist this tyrannic' system. The people will oppose—the States 'will not submit to its operation—they ought not to' acquiesce, and I pray to God they never may."

. . .

Mr. Duvall: . . . The attention of the Committee [of the Whole] shall not be claimed much longer by me, for I throw by many remarks which have been made in the course of debate in order to call your reflections to a subject that has been too often agitated to escape reply. I mean the doctrine of rebellion, which has been trumpeted in our ears by more than one member of this body. It is time that gentlemen in the Opposition should allay the fury of passion by the exercise of reason and calm inquiry. Can one individual in this body be found who will advocate principles destructive of the happiness and Constitution of his country? Yes, this House has heard discord and rebellion encouraged and avowed from more than one quarter. The member from New York (Mr. Miller) has declared that this militia system, or, as he terms it, *conscription,* will not be submitted to by the people; that they ought to resist such oppression, such infringements of their rights, and he hoped they would resist.

[Here Mr. Miller rose to explain, and said that the language he had used, were the words of Mr. Livingston, a Democrat, and were delivered in a speech when he was opposed to Mr. Adams's Administration, and he (Mr. M.) now adopted them as his own.][2]

Mr. Duvall said, he had so understood the gentleman, and although he claimed the benefit of the example introduced, it was not on that account the less mischievous and pernicious; that demagogues belonged to all parties, and were equally to be detested and condemned. Let gentlemen who are giving tone and encouragement to rebellion beware of the consequences; for, I tell them, they are treading over a burning volcano that may burst upon them in dreadful ruin. Do they propose to better their conditions, or the condition of their country, by such dangerous and mad contention? If so, let me drive from them far the fatal delusion. Look to the French Revolution, and learn, in time, to avoid the bloody scenes which may and will be reacted in America. How many of all the numerous and daring revolutionists of France are now in existence? Few, indeed, compared to the many who have fallen before the power of that rebellion which owed to them its spring and creation. All France did not produce, with her millions of men, a single individual who could snatch the helm and wield the sword of the nation. Such men are rare creations of nature—five centuries will not produce such another man as the Corsican, who braved the tempest of Revolution, and rode on surges of blood to the imperial throne of France.

Beware, in time, beware, of the fate that will attend your temer-

[2] Brackets those of the *Annals* reporter.

ity; for, believe me when I tell you, you who create are not the men
that can control the tide of rebellion; you, first of all, shall be overwhelmed by its resistless fury. Deceive not yourselves and friends
with the vain and foolish hope that you can "mount the whirl-wind
and direct the storm," for you will be scattered *808* before it "like
chaff before the wind of heaven."

3.7 Henry Clay: "I am a true friend to State rights, but not in
all cases as they are asserted."*

. . .

. . . in the period of 1798-9, what was the doctrine promulgated by
Massachusetts? It was that the States, in their sovereign capacities, had no right to examine into the Constitutionality or expedience
of the measures of the General Government. [Mr. C. here quoted
several passages from the answer of the State of Massachusetts to the
Virginia and Kentucky resolutions concerning the alien and sedition
laws, to prove his position.] We see here an express disclaimer, on
the part of Massachusetts, of any right to decide on the Constitutionality or expediency of the acts of the General Government. But what
was the doctrine which the same State, in 1813, thought proper to
proclaim to the world, and that too when the Union was menaced
on all sides? She not only claimed, but exercised, the right which, in
1799, she had so solemnly disavowed. She claimed the right to judge
of the propriety of the call made, by the General Government, for
her militia, and she refused the militia called for.

There was so much plausibility in the reasoning employed by
that State in support of her modern doctrine of "State rights," that,
were it not for the unpopularity of the stand she took in the late war,
or had it been in other times and under other circumstances, she
would very probably have escaped a great portion of that odium
which has most justly fallen to her lot. The Constitution gives to
Congress power to provide for calling out the militia to execute the
laws of the Union, to suppress insurrections and to repel invasions,
and in no other cases. The militia is called out by the General Government, during the late war, to repel invasion. Massachusetts said,

* From a speech by the Representative from Kentucky in the House of
Representatives, March 13, 1818, upholding the authority of the national government to provide for and pay for internal improvements, including post roads
and military roads. *Annals*, 15th Congress, 1st session, pp. 1363-1364.

as you have no right to the militia but in certain contingencies, she was competent to decide whether those contingencies had or had not occurred. And, having examined the fact, what then? She said all was peace and quietness in Massachusetts, no non-execution of the laws, no insurrection at home, no invasion from abroad, nor any immediate danger of invasion. And, in truth, Mr. C. said, he believed there was no actual invasion for nearly two years after the requisition. Under these circumstances, had it not been for the supposed motive of her conduct, he asked if the case which Massachusetts made out would not be extremely plausible?

Mr. C. said he hoped it was not necessary for him to say that it was very far from his intention to convey anything like approbation of the conduct of Massachusetts. No! his doctrine was that the States, as States, have no right to oppose the execution of the powers which the General Government asserts. Any State has undoubtedly the right to express its opinion, in the form of resolution or otherwise, and to proceed, by Constitutional means to redress any real or even imaginary grievance; but it has no right to withhold its military aid, when called upon by the high authorities of the General Government, much less to obstruct the execution of a law regularly passed. To suppose the existence of such an alarming right, is to suppose, if not dis- *1364* union itself, such a state of disorder and confusion as must inevitably lead to it.

Mr. C. said, that, greatly as he venerated the State which gave him birth and much as he respected the judges of its supreme court, several of whom were his personal friends, he was obliged to think that some of the doctrines which that State [Virginia] had recently held concerning State rights were fraught with much danger. Had those doctrines been asserted during the late war, and related to the means of carrying on that war, a large share of the public disapprobation which has been given to Massachusetts, might have fallen on Virginia. What were these doctrines? The Courts of Virginia have asserted that they have a right to determine on the Constitutionality of any law or treaty of the United States and to expound them according to their own views, even if they should vary from the decision of the Supreme Court of the United States. They have asserted more—that from their decision there could be no appeal to the Supreme Court of the United States, and that there exists in Congress no power to frame a law obliging the court of the State, in the last resort, to submit its decision to the supervision of the Supreme Court of the United States; or, if he did not misunderstand the doctrine, to withdraw from the State tribunals controversies involving the laws of the United States and to place them before the Federal Judiciary.

I am a friend, said Mr. C., a true friend to State rights; but not in all cases as they are asserted. The States have their appointed orbit; so has the Union; and each should be confined within its fair, legitimate, and Constitutional sphere. We should equally avoid that subtle process of argument which dissipates into air the powers of this Government, and that spirit of encroachment which would snatch from the States powers not delegated to the General Government. We shall thus escape both the dangers I have noticed—that of relapsing into the alarming weakness of the Confederation, which was described as a mere rope of sand, and also that other, perhaps not the greatest danger, consolidation. No man deprecates more than I do the idea of consolidation; yet, between separation and consolidation, painful as would be the alternative, he should greatly prefer the latter.

. . .

JUDICIAL REVIEW

[Note by the editors. The remarks printed here as selections 3.8, 3.9, and 3.10 were made in debate on a bill proposing the repeal of the Judiciary Act of 1801. The act of 1801 reorganized the federal court system in the last weeks of John Adams' Administration. For a fuller statement concerning the struggle over the Judiciary, see the editors' note preceding selection 8.3.]

3.8   John Breckinridge: "It is said that the different departments of Government are to be checks on each other, and that the
courts are to check the Legislature. If this be true, I would ask where
they got that power, and who checks the courts when they violate
the Constitution."*

Mr. President. . . . I beg leave to say a few words in answer

---

* From a speech by the Senator from Kentucky in the Senate, February 3, 1802, on a bill to repeal the Judiciary Act of 1801. *Annals,* 7th Congress, 1st session, pp. 178-180.

to an argument which has been much pressed to-day. I did not intend to rise again on this subject, especially at so late an hour (about five o'clock) and I promise to detain the House but a few minutes.

I did not expect, sir, to find the doctrine of the power of the courts to annul the laws of Congress as unconstitutional, so seriously insisted on. I presume I shall not be out of order in replying to it. It is said that the different departments of Government are to be checks on each other, and that the courts are to check the Legislature. If 179 this be true, I would ask where they got that power, and who checks the courts when they violate the Constitution? Would they not, by this doctrine, have the absolute direction of the Government? To whom are they responsible? But I deny the power which is so pretended. If it is derived from the Constitution, I ask gentlemen to point out the clause which grants it. I can find no such grant. Is it not extraordinary that if this high power was intended, it should nowhere appear? Is it not truly astonishing that the Constitution, in its abundant care to define the powers of each department, should have omitted so important a power as that of the courts to nullify all the acts of Congress which, in their opinion, were contrary to the Constitution?

Never were such high and transcendent powers in any Government (much less in one like ours, composed of powers specially given and defined) claimed or exercised by construction only. The doctrine of constructions, not warranted by the letter of an instrument, is dangerous in the extreme. Let men once loose upon constructions, and where will you stop them. Is the *astutia* of English judges, in discovering the latent meanings of law-makers, meanings not expressed in the letter of the laws, to be adopted here in the construction of the Constitution? Once admit the doctrine that judges are to be indulged in these astute and wire-drawn constructions, to enlarge their own power and control that of others, and I will join gentlemen of the opposition in declaring that the Constitution is in danger.

To make the Constitution a practical system, this pretended power of the courts to annul the laws of Congress cannot possibly exist. My idea of the subject, in a few words, is, that the Constitution intended a separation of the powers vested in the three great departments, giving to each exclusive authority on the subjects committed to it. That these departments are co-ordinate, to revolve each within the sphere of their own orbits without being responsible for their own motion, and are not to direct or control the course of others. That those who made the laws are presumed to have an equal attachment to and interest in the Constitution; are equally bound by oath to support it, and have an equal right to give a construction to it. That the construction of one department of the powers vested in it is of higher authority than the construction of any other department; and that, in fact, it is competent to that department to which powers are confided exclusively to decide upon the proper exercise of those powers: that therefore the Legislature have the exclusive right to interpret the Constitution in what regards the law-making power, and the judges are bound to execute the laws they make. For the Legislature would have at least an equal right to annul the decisions of the courts, founded on their construction of the Constitution, as the courts would have to annul the acts of the Legislature, founded on their construction.

Although, therefore, the courts may take upon them to give decisions which impeach the constitutionality of a law and thereby, for a time, *180* obstruct its operations, yet I contend that such a law is not the less obligatory because the organ through which it is to be executed has refused its aid. A pertinacious adherence of both departments to their opinions would soon bring the question to issue, in whom the sovereign power of legislation resided, and whose construction of the law-making power should prevail.

If the courts have a right to examine into and decide upon the constitutionality of laws, their decision ought to be final and effectual. I ask then, if gentlemen are prepared to admit that in case the courts were to declare your revenue, impost and appropriation laws unconstitutional, that they would thereby be blotted out of your statute book and the operations of Government be arrested? It is making, in my opinion, a mockery of the high powers of legislation. I feel humbled by the doctrine, and enter my protest against it. Let gentleman consider well before they insist on a power in the Judiciary which places the Legislature at their feet. Let not so humiliating a condition be admitted under an authority of resting merely on application [implication?] and construction. It will invite a state of things which we are not justified by the Constitution in presuming will happen, and which (should it happen) all men of all parties must deplore.

3.9   John Bacon: "The Judiciary have no more right to prescribe, direct, or control the acts of the other departments of the Government than the other departments of the Government have to prescribe or direct those of the Judiciary."*

However I may differ in opinion from some with whom I have the honor generally to agree, I may not deny but must frankly acknowledge the right of judicial officers of every grade to judge for themselves of the constitutionality of every statute on which they are called to act in their respective spheres. This is not only their right, but it is their indispensable duty thus to do. Nor is this the exclusive right and indispensable duty of the Judiciary department. It is equally the inherent and the indispensable duty of every officer, and I believe I may add, of every citizen of the United States.

The Constitution is emphatically the law of the 983 land. It certainly cannot be less so than the statute made present pursuant thereto. It is indeed paramount with us to all other human laws that can be made. In whatever capacity I may be called to act, where the law is to be the rule of my conduct, if two laws are found to clash with each other, in such case I cannot be governed by them both. Of necessity, therefore, I must either not act at all, or reject both, or else determine which shall give way. Should the Constitution and statute be found to contradict each other, the former, with me, must be preferred. But although this is a right of which every officer of the United States, as such, is constitutionally possessed; yet for the due exercise of this, as also of all other such rights, he is responsible. He is not vested with a right to do wrong.

We have heard much of late about the peculiar and absolute independence of the Judiciary. Although this is a term unknown in the Constitution as applying particularly to the Judiciary department of the Government, yet it may and ought to be admitted to be in a certain sense and in some respects true. The Judiciary are so far independent of the Legislative and Executive departments of Gov-

* Remarks by the Representative from Massachusetts in the House of Representatives, February 17, 1802, relating to a bill to repeal the Judiciary Act of 1801. *Annals,* 7th Congress, 1st session, pp. 982-983. Mr. Bacon's remarks are identified in the *Annals* as "supplemental to his speech" delivered on February 17; it is not clear whether these remarks were delivered orally.

ernment, that these, neither jointly or separately, have a right to prescribe, direct, or control its decisions. It must judge for itself, otherwise the decisions made in that department would not be the decisions of that but of some other department or body of men. The Constitution and the laws made pursuant thereto, are the only rule by which the Judiciary, in their official capacity, are to regulate their conduct. The same is the case with other departments. The Judiciary have no more right to prescribe, direct, or control the acts of the other departments of the Government than the other departments of the Government have to prescribe or direct those of the Judiciary. . . .

3.10   James A. Bayard: "Of what importance is it to say, Congress are prohibited from doing certain acts, if no legitimate authority exists in the country to decide whether an act done is a prohibited act?"*

Upon the main question, said Mr. B., whether the judges hold their offices at the will of the Legislature, an argument of great weight and 645 according to my humble judgment of irresistible force, still remains. The Legislative power of the Government is not absolute, but limited. If it be doubtful whether the Legislature can do what the Constitution does not explicitly authorize; yet there can be no question that they cannot do what the Constitution expressly prohibits. To maintain, therefore, the Constitution, the judges are a check upon the Legislature. The doctrine I know is denied, and it is therefore incumbent upon me to show that it is sound.

It was once thought by gentlemen who now deny the principle, that the safety of the citizen and of the States rested upon the power of the judges to declare an unconstitutional law void. How vain is a paper restriction if it confers neither power nor right! Of what importance is it to say Congress are prohibited from doing certain acts, if no legitimate authority exists in the country to decide whether an act done is a prohibited act? Do gentlemen perceive the consequences which would follow from establishing the principle that Con-

---

* From a speech by the Representative from Delaware in the House of Representatives, February 20, 1802, opposing a bill to repeal the Judiciary Act of 1801. *Annals,* 7th Congress, 1st session, pp. 644-648.

gress have the exclusive right to decide upon their own powers? This principle admitted, does any Constitution remain? Does not the power of the Legislature become absolute and omnipotent? Can you talk to them of transgressing their powers when no one has a right to judge of those powers but themselves? They do what is not authorized, they do what is inhibited, nay, at every step they trample the Constitution under foot; yet their acts are lawful and binding, and it is treason to resist them. How ill, sir, do the doctrines and professions of these gentlemen agree! They tell us they are friendly to the existence of the States; that they are the friends of a federative, but the enemies of a consolidated, General Government, and yet, sir, to accomplish a paltry subject, they are willing to settle a principle which, beyond all doubt would eventually plant a consolidated Government with unlimited power upon the ruins of the State governments. Nothing can be more absurd than to contend that there is a practical restraint upon a political body who are answerable to none but themselves for the violation of the restraint, and who can derive from the very act of violation undeniable justification of their conduct.

If, said Mr. B., you mean to have a Constitution, you must discover a power to which the acknowledged right is attached of pronouncing the invalidity of the acts of the Legislature which contravene the instrument. Does the power reside in the States? Has the Legislature of a State a right to declare an act of Congress void? This would be erring upon the opposite extreme. It would be placing the General Government at the feet of the State governments. It would be allowing one member of the Union to control all the rest. It would inevitably lead to civil dissension and a dissolution of the General Government. Will it be pretended that the State courts have the exclusive right of deciding upon the validity of our laws? I admit that they have the right to declare an act of Congress void. But this right they enjoy in practice, and it ever essentially must 646 exist, subject to the revision and control of the courts of the United States. If the State courts definitively possessed the right of declaring the invalidity of the laws of this Government, it would bring us in subjection to the States. The judges of those courts being bound by the laws of the State, if a State declared an act of Congress unconstitutional, the law of the State would oblige its courts to determine the law invalid. This principle would also destroy the uniformity of obligation upon all the States, which should attend every law of this Government. If a law were declared void in one State, it would exempt the citizens of that State from its operation whilst obedience was yielded to it in the other States. I go further and say, if the States or State courts had a final power of annulling the acts of this Government, its miserable and precarious existence would not be worth the trouble of a moment to preserve. It would endure but a short time as a subject of derision, and, wasting into an empty shadow, would quickly vanish from our sight.

Let me now ask if the power to decide upon the validity of our laws resides with the people? Gentlemen cannot deny this right to the people. I admit that they possess it. But if, at the same time, it does not belong to the courts of the United States, where does it lead the people? It leads them to the gallows. Let us suppose that Congress, forgetful of the limits of their authority, pass an unconstitutional law. They lay a direct tax upon one State and impose none upon the others. The people of the State taxed contest the validity of the law. They forcibly resist its execution. They are brought by the Executive authority before the courts upon charges of treason. The law is unconstitutional, the people have done right, but the courts are bound by the law and obliged to pronounce upon them the sentence which it inflicts. Deny to the courts of the United States the power of judging upon the constitutionality of our laws, and it is vain to talk of its existing elsewhere. The infractors of the laws are brought before these courts, and if the courts are implicitly bound, the invalidity of the laws can be no defence.

There is, however, Mr. Chairman, still a stronger ground of argument upon this subject. I shall select one or two cases to illustrate it. Congress are prohibited from passing a bill of attainder; it is also declared in the Constitution that "no attainder of treason shall work corruption of blood or forfeiture, except during the life of the party attainted." Let us suppose that Congress pass a bill of attainder, or they enact that any one attained of treason shall forfeit to the use of the United States all the estate which he held in any lands or tenements. The party attainted is seized and brought before a federal court and an award of execution passed against him. He opens the Constitution and points to this line, "no bill of attainder or *ex post facto* law shall be passed." The attorney for the United States reads the bill of attainder.

The courts are bound to decide, but they have only the alternative of pronouncing the law or the Constitution invalid. It is left to them only to 647 say that the law vacates the Constitution, or the Constitution avoids the law. So in the other case stated, the heir, after the death of his ancestor, brings his ejectment in one of the courts of the United States to recover his inheritance. The law by which it is confiscated is shown. The Constitution gave no power to pass such a law. On the contrary, it expressly denied it to the Government. The title of the heir is rested on the Constitution, the title of the Government on the law. The effect of one destroys the effect of the other; the court must determine which is effectual.

There are many other cases, Mr. Chairman, of a similar nature to which I might allude. There is the case of the privilege of habeas corpus, which cannot be suspended but in times of rebellion or of invasion. Suppose a law prohibiting the issuing of the writ at a moment of profound peace. If in such case the writ were demanded of a court, could they say, it is true the Legislature were restrained from passing the law, suspending the privilege of this writ at such a time as that which now exists, but their mighty power has broken the bonds of the Constitution and fettered the authority of the court. I am not, sir, disposed to vaunt, but standing on this ground I throw the gauntlet to any champion upon the other side. I call upon them to maintain that in a collision between a law and the Constitution, the judges are bound to support the law, and annul the Constitution. Can the gentlemen relieve themselves from this dilemma? Will they say, though a judge has no power to pronounce a law void, he has a power to declare the Constitution invalid.

The doctrine for which I am contending is not only clearly inferable from the plain language of the Constitution, but by law has been expressly declared and established in practice since the existence of the Government.

The second section of the third article of the Constitution expressly extends the judicial power to all cases arising under the Constitution, the laws, & c. The provision in the second clause of the sixth article leaves nothing to doubt. "This Constitution, and the laws of the United States which shall be made in pursuance thereof, & c. shall be the supreme law of the land." The Constitution is absolutely the supreme law. Not so the acts of the Legislature. Such only are the law of the land as are made in pursuance of the Constitution.

I beg the indulgence of the Committee one moment, while I read the following provision from the twenty-fifth section of the judicial act of the year seventeen hundred and eighty-nine:

"A final judgment or decree in any suit in the highest court of law or equity of a State in which a decision in the suit could be had, where is drawn in question the validity of a treaty or statute of, or an authority exercised under, the United States, and the decision is against their validity, & c. may be re-examined and reversed or affirmed in the Supreme Court of the United States, upon a writ of error."

Thus, as early as the years 1789, among the first 648 acts of the Government, the Legislature explicitly recognised the right of a State court to declare a treaty, a statute, and authority exercised under the United States, void, subject to the revision of the Supreme Court of the United States; and it has expressly given the final power to the Supreme Court to affirm a judgment which is against the validity either of a treaty, statute, or an authority of the Government.

I humbly trust, Mr. Chairman, that I have given abundant proofs from the nature of our Government, from the language of the Constitution, and from Legislative acknowledgment, that the judges of our courts have the power to judge and determine upon the constitutionality of our laws.

. . .

chapter 4

The federal structure

THE DISTRIBUTION OF GOVERNMENTAL AUTHORITY

4.1 Roger Griswold: "The Government of the United States is not a consolidated Government; it is strictly federal."*

. . .

The Government of the United States is not a consolidated Government; it is strictly federal, and its friends are of course federalists. It is true that this branch of the Legislature (the House of Representatives) bears many marks of a consolidation. We are the Representatives of the people of the respective States, and in this respect the principle of consolidation may be considered as existing in this House. But in the Senate, nothing but the federative principle is seen. In that body each State is not only represented as a sovereign State, but the representation is equal; nor can the size, population, or wealth of a State increase or diminish its rights or its vote on that floor. In the election of a President, the federative principle is likewise discernable [sic]. That officer is elected by Electors, chosen

* From a speech by the Representative from Connecticut in the House of Representatives, December 8, 1803, opposing a proposed constitutional amendment intended to alter the method of electing the President and Vice President. See editors' note, selection 2.4. *Annals,* 8th Congress, 1st session, pp. 745-746.

in such manner as the State Legislatures shall direct, and to consist of a number of Electors equal to the Senators and Representatives of each State. By this arrangement, the choice of President is controlled by the States; and although the large States have a greater influence in the election than the small States, yet this influence is not entirely regulated by population. The votes to which each State is entitled for its Senators increases the influence of the small States; and it is in consequence of this that the State of Rhode Island now gives four votes for President when, upon the principle of consolidation, she would be entitled to no more than two. The votes of Delaware, on the same principle, would be reduced from three to one.

There is not a feature of our Government more strongly marked than this of its Confederation, nor any to which the people are more strongly attached. And it would be impossible to submit any proposition which could create more alarm than a direct project of consolidating the States into one Government. The States always have [preserved] and probably will continue to preserve with jealousy their sovereignty and independence. The present Government, it is well known, grew out of the old Confederation; in which form the States were in every respect equal—each State having one vote in the National Congress. The innovation which was made on the pure federative principle by the 746 present Constitution was the result of necessity and compromise. But still, as has been already observed, the federative principle is distinctly preserved and remains the great and leading feature of the Constitution.

It has been often repeated that the Constitution of the United States was the result of compromise between the large and the small States. This is undoubtedly true, and the basis of this compromise ought to be considered as sacred—never to be shaken whilst the Constitution endures. After mutual concessions by the large and small States (for both may be considered as conceding something) the principles by which the influence of each State is balanced in the Legislative and Executive departments may be fairly considered as constituting the basis of this compromise. It results from this, that every attempt to diminish the influence of large States on the one hand or to weaken that of the small States on the other, is sapping the foundation of our Confederacy. The power to amend the Constitution was not given to authorize the change of any radical principle in which particular States might be interested. This power, it is well known, was given for very different purposes.

I have made these general observations, because it has appeared to me that every proposal to amend the Constitution ought to be first tested by the nature and scope of the Constitution itself; and if it shall be found to interfere with the rights of States, or with any fundamental principle of the compact, it ought to be rejected, although it may promise some temporary advantages in the eyes of speculative men. It cannot be too often repeated, that in considering projects for changing the Constitution, we ought to consider what the Constitution is and not what it ought to be in the opinion of individuals. Our Government is in fact a Confederacy, and as such we are bound to respect the rights of each party to the compact.

. . .

4.2 Philip P. Barbour: "The fundamental principle on which the whole Constitution was based: by a wise distribution of power, to assign to the General and to the several State Governments, each its own proper orbit in which to move for the general good."*

. . .

When the Constitution was about to be formed, the great problem which occupied the minds of its framers was the determination what powers should be conceded by the States to the Federal Government, and what powers should be retained by the States. If too much should be granted, the General Government, like Aaron's serpent, would soon swallow up the State governments; if, on the other hand, too little were conceded, the Federal Government would be inefficient for the purposes of its institution. The *1006* one error threatened liberty, the other threatened internal peace and order.

In these delicate and difficult circumstances, the authors of the Constitution determined on a compromise between these opposite interests, and the compromise rested on one general principle, subject however to a few modifications. That general principle was this: that whenever the object to be obtained was one which required the concentrated strength of the whole Confederacy, the power to effect it was reposed in the Federal Government; thus the

* From a speech by the Representative from Virginia in the House of Representatives, January 13, 1824, opposing a bill to provide for surveys, plans, and estimates relating to construction of roads and canals. *Annals*, 18th Congress, 1st session, pp. 1005-1007, 1013.

raising of armies and constructing of fleets for the national defence were objects which no individual State could effect, and they, with other powers of the like character, were therefore confided to the General Government; and because they could not be effected without the requisite pecuniary means, the Constitution, on the same principle, gave Congress power to raise a revenue. There were other objects, also, which from their nature could not be managed with the requisite concert by thirteen distinct independent sovereignties such as the regulation of foreign commerce and the making of treaties, which, therefore, were intrusted to the General Government. He cited these instances as illustrations and exemplifications to show what kind and order of powers the reason and spirit of the Constitution deposited in the hands of the Federal Government.

But while, from necessity, powers of this character were ceded, all powers which had relation to matters of internal regulation, all that might be denominated municipal powers, were reserved to the States. These States had each a government of its own, and the authors of the Constitution wisely judged that these governments were fully competent to take the superintendence of their own internal concerns, and were, from their situation, likely to be more intimately acquainted with these concerns and therefore best adapted to their proper management. This distinction of power, Mr. B. insisted, was the general, fundamental principle on which the whole Constitution was based; and it would prove the best guide in investigating any part of that instrument; the object of which had been, by a wise distribution of power, to assign to the General and to the several State Governments, each its own proper orbit, in which to move for the general good.

Yet this general principle was susceptible of and had received some modifications. Some few of the municipal powers, of a special and particular character had, for wise reasons, been transferred to the General Government. An instance of which was found in the exclusive jurisdiction given to that government over the spot where its seat should be fixed; the reason of this was, obviously, that the free exercise of its functions might be preserved, unawed by any influence that might otherwise be exerted over them in consequence of the territorial jurisdiction of any particular State. So the General Government had the power to regulate commerce between the States, and to fix a standard of weights and measures; for which, as in the former instance, there was a special reason, viz: the necessity for uniformity, an object which *1007* could not have been attained, had these powers been left where on the general principle they belonged, that is with the several States. There were but few powers of this description placed in the General Government; and on investigation it would be found that, in every individual case, there was a special individual reason for the grant which rendered it a proper exception. [Mr. Barbour here read extracts, in confirmation of his position, from "The Federalist," No. 45.][1]

Now, said Mr. B., if the principle I have stated furnishes a sound rule for the interpretation of the Constitution, might I not stop here and ask whether the subject of internal improvements is not characterized by every thing which can bring it within the class of municipal powers? Whether, in the language of the book I have just quoted, the able commentary of the authors of the Constitution themselves, it is not a system of "measures to promote internal order, improvement, and prosperity?"
. . . *1013*

In conclusion, Mr. B. said that he had endeavored to present to the House a fair, and at the same time, brief statement of his views on this subject; he had long been settled in the opinion that, however desirable or advantageous internal improvements might be, Congress, by the Constitution, had no power to make them. . . .

THE LOCATION OF POWER
OVER GOVERNMENT

4.3   Michael Jenifer Stone and Roger Sherman: "The people of the United States are like masters prescribing to their servants the several branches of business they would have each perform."*

[Note by the editors. In the first session of Congress under the new Constitution, the House of Representatives "directed" the Secre-

---

[1] Brackets those of the *Annals* reporter.
* Remarks made in the House of Representatives by Representatives Stone of Maryland and Sherman of Connecticut, in debate on Hamilton's plan for support of the public credit, February 23, 1790. *Annals,* 1st Congress, 2nd session, pp. 1312-1313 (Stone) and p. 1317 (Sherman).

tary of Treasury to report to it a plan for the support of the public credit. In response to this instruction, Secretary Alexander Hamilton on January 9, 1790, submitted comprehensive proposals which, among other things, recommended that the national government assume the outstanding debts of the several states and that the combined debt of the national and state governments be funded and paid off on a fixed schedule. These recommendations precipitated one of the greatest debates which took place in the national government during the formative years of our constitutional system.]

Mr. Stone: A strong binding force, exterior, or interior, is supposed essentially necessary to keep together a Government like ours; and of all the bands of political connexion, perhaps there is none stronger than that which is formed by a uniform, compact, and efficacious chain or system of revenue. A greater thought could not have been conceived by man; and its effect, I venture to predict, if adopted by us, and carried into execution, will prove to the Federal Government walls of adamant, impregnable to any attempt upon its fabric or operations. I have viewed it with some degree of attention, and I see the subject rise into gigantic height.

. . .

I think, sir, wherever the property is, there will be the power. And if the General Government has the payment of all the debts, it must, of course, have all the revenue; if it possesses the whole revenue, it is equal, in other words, to the whole power; the different States will then have little to do; important talents will *1313* not be necessary to be employed in the administration of the State Governments; if they are not found to be necessary, the fair presumption is, they will not be employed. Men of consequence and great abilities will hardly go into a Legislature where their usefulness is circumscribed to trifling or uninteresting points. What is likely to be the effect of this? I presume, that hereafter the Legislatures of particular States will be composed of men who hold their talents at a cheaper rate. The same principle will operate throughout the whole routine of State business—the Legislative, Executive, and Judicial; and the operations of the Government will partake of the weakness and imbecility of its administration. In proportion as the State Governments decline in consequence, men will look up to the General Government; and in proportion as they decline in their importance, so will the Federal Government rise in consequence.

It has been very doubtful whether there can be a confederated Government where the laws are to operate on individuals, and not on States. Indeed it has been a doubt whether a Confederated Government remains, when the General Government possesses the power of the purse; and whether that circumstance does not swallow up the idea of an absolute existence of a State Government. I believe the truth of this will be demonstrated by recourse to historic facts. Every confederated Republic which has given the superintending body the power of the purse, has found every effort of the individual States insufficient to keep the compression of that band from holding them tightly together; neither exterior nor interior force has yet been able to separate the parts of a Government formed on this principle. Hence, sir, I am led to believe, that if the whole revenue of the several States is taken into the power of Congress, it will prove a band to draw us so close together, as not to leave the smallest interstice of separation. . . .

. . .

Mr. Sherman: It appears to me, that the objections of the gentleman from Maryland are not sufficient to prevent our adoption of this proposition. His objection is, that it will give a greater degree of importance to the General Government, while it will lessen the consequence of the State Governments. Now, I do not believe it will have that effect. I consider both Governments as standing on the broad basis of the people; they were both instituted by them, for their general and particular good. The Representatives in Congress draw their authority from the same source as the State Legislatures; they are both of them elected by the people at large, the one to manage their national concerns, and the other their domestic, which they find can be better done by being divided into lesser communities, than the whole Union; but to effect the greater concerns, they have confederated; therefore, every thing which strengthens the Federal Government, and enables it to answer the end for which it was instituted, will be a desirable object with the people.

It is well known, we can extend our authority no further than to the bounds the people have assigned. If we abuse this power, doubtless, the people will send others to correct our faults, or, if necessary, alter the system; but we have every reason to believe the people will be pleased with it, and none suppose that the State

Governments will object. They are the supreme power, within their own jurisdiction, and they will have authority over the States, in all cases, not given to the General Government, notwithstanding the assumption of the State debts.

If it was a question between two different countries, and we were going to give the British Parliament power, by assuming our debts, of levying what taxes they thought proper, and the people of America were to have no voice in the appointment of the officers who were to administer the affairs of Government, the experiment would be dangerous to this country; but, as the business is to be conducted by ourselves, there can be no ground for apprehension. The people of the United States are like masters prescribing to their servants the several branches of business they would have each to perform. It would not comport with their interest if the Federal Government was to interfere with the Government of particular States; while, on the other hand, it would injure their interests to restrict the General Government from performing what the Federal Constitution allows them. It is the interest of each and of the whole, that they both should be supported within their proper limits.

. . .

4.4 James A. Bayard: "In the Senate the States are completely and exclusively represented. But on this floor there subsists no relation to States; we are solely related to the people."*

[Note by the editors. Immediately after completion of the second national census, Congress proceeded to reapportion the House of Representatives. In the two speeches that are partially printed here, Representative Bayard supported a motion to fix a ratio of 30,000 population for each seat in the House, instead of the ratio of 33,000 which appeared in the bill as introduced. The result, if the smaller number were fixed, would be to increase the number of members in the House.]

* From two speeches in the House of Representatives by the Representative from Delaware on a bill to reapportion the House of Representatives. *Annals*, 7th Congress, 1st session, pp. 365-366 (January 4, 1802) and pp. 378-379 (January 5, 1802).

Mr. Bayard (*on January 4*): . . . He never had believed that the strength of the Government was to be increased by extending the power of the Executive. But he believed its strength would be increased by augmenting the numbers of that House which would invigorate the affections of the people; and he believed that by thus increasing the energies of this body, more power would be conferred on the Government by an addition of ten members than would be conferred by giving it an army of 10,000 men.

The gentleman from Virginia [Mr. Randolph] had denied that this House was the representative of the people, affirming it to be the representative of the States. Mr. B. hoped, if he misinterpreted his ideas, that the gentleman would explain.

Mr. Randolph would explain. He had said that this House was not the representative of the people over the United States, but the representative of the people of the individual States in their sovereign State capacities.

Mr. Bayard considered the opinion of the gentleman incorrect, and thought it extremely important that on this point correct ideas should be entertained. He viewed the representation in that House as national, and he considered himself as much the Representative of Virginia as the gentleman himself. In this House we have no other 366 relation to the States than that which regards our origin. We form a great national body, designed for national purposes and as soon as we come here we lose our State characters. The Government is of a mixed kind. In the Senate the States are completely and exclusively represented. But on this floor there subsists no relation to States. We are solely related to the people, and our representation is in proportion to the numbers of the people.

There was one argument to him conclusive. A majority of Representatives may bind a majority of States; and the Repesentatives of three or four States, forming that majority, may bind the whole Union.

Mr. B. knew that the arguments he had urged had been met by the expression of a fear that this body might gain an influence that would outweigh the several States; and that this Government might become too strong for the governments of the States. But his fear was that the governments of the States might become too strong for this Government. . . .

Mr. Bayard (*on January 5*): . . . Mr. B. said he was not governed
in the opinion he had adopted in relation to the ratio by the consideration solely of State interest. His great object was to augment the
members of the Representative branch of the Government. He believed that the strength of the National Government existed in that
House; and by increasing the members of this House, its weight and
strength were augmented. He confessed it to be his object to make
the General Government so strong as to be able, with equal certainty, to control the largest as the smallest States. It was now able
to govern the small States; but if one of the largest should deny and
resist the authority of the Union, he doubted the ability of the Government to enforce obedience to its laws. He had occasionally advocated an increase of Executive authority. He had then been
charged with views unfriendly to republicanism. He was now contending for an increase of the weight of the popular branch of the
Government.

He was actuated by the same motive which had always induced
him to give his support to the Executive. His uniform object had
been, and would continue to be, to maintain the independence of
the General Government, and to render it efficient enough to curb
the ambitions and to repress the dominating spirit which was inseparable from the large States. His voice had never been to vary
the relative powers of the Executive and Representative branches;
but generally by increasing 379 the strength to confirm the stability
of the Government. An opportunity now presented itself of promoting the same object by augmenting the weight of the popular
branch; he embraced it with more zeal than he had ever felt in the
support of the Executive prerogative. He rejoiced in an occasion
which enabled him to manifest, that the true object of his views
was not inimical to the equal rights and Constitutional liberties of
his country.

He was firmly convinced that the House of Representatives
was, and necessarily would be, the main pillar of the General Government. While this branch retained the attachment and possessed
the confidence of the nation the Government would endure, but if
any State could succeed in weaning the affections of the people from
this House and transferring their confidence exclusively to the States
the Government would perish. He wished to enlarge the field of

action and employment under this Government. So small a number occupy the ground upon the floor of this House that the talents and ambition of the mass of men aspiring to distinction are directed to State objects, and seeking the aggrandizement of the States, eventually become hostile to the General Government. The representation of the country was too sparse, it was not sufficiently united and bound to the bosom of the nation.

. . .

LARGE STATES vs. SMALL STATES

[Note by the editors. The three selections that follow (4.5 to 4.7) are drawn from debate on a proposed constitutional amendment intended to alter the method of electing the President and Vice President. The circumstances leading to the demand for change are set forth immediately preceding selection 2.4. The specific language before the Senate, and to which the next three speeches are addressed, was proposed in a motion by Senator William C. Nicholas of Virginia. The significant variances of the proposed language from the language that was then in the Constitution are underlined by the editors. Senator Nicholas' motion read as follows: "In all future elections of President and Vice President, the Electors *shall name in their ballots the person voted for as President, and, in distinct ballots, the person voted for as Vice President,* of whom one at least shall not be an inhabitant of the same State with themselves. The *person voted for as President,* having a majority of the votes of all the Electors appointed, shall be the President; and *if no person have such majority, then from the three highest on the list of those voted for as President,* the House of Representatives shall choose the President in the manner directed by the Constitution. The *person having the greatest number of votes as Vice President,* shall be the Vice President; and *in case of an equal number of votes for two or more persons for Vice President,* they being the highest on the list, the Senate shall choose the Vice President from those having such equal number, in the manner directed by the Constitution; but no person constitutionally ineligible to the office of President, shall be eligible to that of Vice President of the United States." *Annals,* 8th Congress, 1st session, p. 84 (November 23, 1803).]

4.5 Samuel White: "Let me ask gentlemen if they are prepared to vest in the five larger States, or even in a smaller number of them, whenever they shall be pleased to exercise it, the exclusive power of appointing the President and Vice President of the United States."*

. . .

. . . sir, if this amendment succeeds, if you designate the person voted for as President and the person voted for as Vice President, you hold out an irresistible temptation to contracts and compromise among the larger States for these offices; it will be placing the choice of the two highest officers in the Government so completely in their power that the five largest States, viz: Massachusetts, New York, Pennsylvania, Virginia, and North Carolina, may not only act in every previous arrangement relative to the appointment of these officers without the necessity of consulting the other twelve, but may totally exclude them from any participation in the election. The whole number of Electors, according to the present representation in Congress, will be one hundred and seventy-seven; these five States will have ninety-six of them, a clear majority of eight, and should they agree among themselves they can say absolutely who shall be the President. The other twelve States will not have even the humble privilege of choosing between their candidates; for their whole number of votes being but eighty-one given to the candidate for the Vice Presidency as President, would be but thrown away, since the other would still have his designated majority of eight for that place.

Should it be said that such a coalition is improbable, I answer that my opinion is different and it is enough for me that it is possible. Again, sir, counting only the States of Massachusetts, New York, Pennsylvania, and Virginia, these four will be found to be entitled to eighty-two Electors, wanting seven of a majority of the whole number; so that, leaving North Carolina among the smaller States, if they unite and can by any species of influence, by promises of offices, bribery, or corruption, gain over to their interest but seven

* From a speech by the Senator from Delaware in the Senate, December 2, 1803. *Annals,* 8th Congress, 1st session, pp. 145-146.

of the Electors belonging to the other States, they can in like manner appoint who they please. I might go on to show that lopping even Massachusetts from the list, the other four, viz: New York, Pennsylvania, Virginia, and North Carolina could with very little difficulty effect the same object, since they are entitled to seventy-seven Electors. And now let me ask gentlemen representing the twelve smaller States if they are prepared to yield up not only the high and honorable ground upon which the Constitution has placed them in the House of Representatives in case of an election for a President to be had there, but to vest in the five larger *146* States, or even in a smaller number of them, whenever they shall be pleased to exercise it, the exclusive power of appointing the President and Vice President of the United States?

. . .

4.6 Uriah Tracy: "Any attempts to destroy this balance should be watched with a jealous eye."*

. . .

I shall attempt to prove, sir that the resolution before us contains principles which have a manifest tendency to deprive the small States of an important right secured to them by a solemn and Constitutional compact, and to vest an overwhelming power in the great States. And, further, I shall attempt to show that in many other points the resolution is objectionable and, for a variety of causes, ought not to be adopted.

. . . *160*

It may be proper, in this place, to explain my meaning when I make use of the words "small" and "great," as applicable to States.

Massachusetts has been usually called a great State; but, in respect to all the operations of this resolution she must, I think, be ranked among the small States. The district of Maine is increasing rapidly and must, in the nature of things, soon become a State. To which event its location, being divided from what was the ancient Colony of Massachusetts, by the intervention of New Hampshire, will very much contribute. I believe there is a Legislative provision

---

* From a speech by the Senator from Connecticut in the Senate, December 2, 1803. *Annals*, 8th Congress, 1st session, pp. 159-165.

of some years' standing, authorizing a division at the option of Maine. When this event shall occur Massachusetts, although in comparison with Connecticut and Rhode Island will not be a small State; yet, in comparison with many others must be so considered. I think myself justifiable, then, for my present purposes, in calling Maine, New Hampshire, Massachusetts, Rhode Island, Connecticut, Vermont, New Jersey, Delaware, Maryland, and South Carolina, small States. They are limited in point of territory, and cannot reasonably expect any great increases of population for many years, not, indeed, until the other States shall become so populous as to discourage emigration with agricultural views; which may retain the population of the small States as seamen or manufacturers. This event, if it ever arrives, must be distant. A possible exception only may exist in favor of Maine; but, when we consider its climate and a variety of other circumstances, it is believed to form no solid exception to this statement.

By the same rule of deciding, the residue of the States must be called great; for although Georgia and several others are not sufficiently populous at this time to be considered relatively great States, yet their prospect of increase, with other circumstances, fairly bring them within the description, in respect to the operation of the measure now under consideration.

. . . *161*

If we attend to the Constitution, we shall immediately find evident marks of concession and compromise, and that the parties to these concessions were the great and small States. And the members of the Convention who formed the instrument have, in private information and public communications, united in the declaration that the Constitution was the result of concession and compromise between the great and small States. In this examination of the Constitution it will be impossible to keep out of view our political relations under the first Confederation. We primarily united upon the footing of complete State equality—each State had one, and no State had more than one, vote in the Federal Council or Congress. With such a Confederation we successfully waged war and became an independent nation. When we were relieved from the pressure of war that Confederation, both in structure and power, was found inadequate to the purpose for which it was established. Under these circumstances the States, by their Convention, entered into a new agreement upon principles better adapted to promote their mutual security and happiness.

But this last agreement or Constitution, under which we are now united, was manifestly carved out of the first Confederation. The small States adhered tenaciously to the principles of State equality; and gave up only a part of that federative principle, complete State equality, and that, with evident caution and reluctance. To this federative principle they were attached by habit; and their attachment was sanctioned and corroborated by the example of most if not all the ancient and the modern Confederacies. And when the great States claimed a weight in the Councils of the nation proportionate to their numbers and wealth, the novelty of the claim, as well as its obvious tendency to reduce the sovereignty of the small States, must have produced serious obstacles to its admission. Hence it is, that we find in the Constitution but one entire departure from the Federal principle. The House of Representatives is established upon the popular principle, and given to numbers and wealth, or to the great States, which, in this view of the subject, are synonymous. It was thought by the Convention that a consolidation of the States into one simple Republic would be improper. And the local feelings and jealousies of all, but more especially of the small States, rendered a consolidation impracticable.

The Senate, who have the power of a legislative check upon the House of Representatives and many other extensive and important powers, is preserved as an entire federative feature of Government as it was enjoyed by the small States, under the first Confederacy.

In the article which obliges the Electors of President to vote for one person not an inhabitant of the same State with themselves, is discovered State jealousy. In the majorities required for many purposes by the Constitution, although there were other motives for the regulations, yet the jealousy of the small States is clearly discernible. Indeed, sir, if we peruse the Constitu- 162 tion with attention, we shall find the small States are perpetually guarding the federative principle, that is, State equality. And this, in every part of it, except in the choice of the House of Representatives, and in their ordinary legislative proceedings. They go so far as to prohibit any amendment [of the Constitution] which may affect the equality of States in the Senate.

This is guarding against almost an impossibility, because the Senators of small States must be criminally remiss in their attendance and the Legislatures extremely off their guard, if they permit such alterations which aim at their own existence. But, lest some accident, some unaccountable blindness or perfidy, should put in jeopardy the federative principle in the Senate, they totally and forever prohibit all attempts at such a measure. In the choice of President, the mutual caution and concession of the great and small States, is, if possible, more conspicuous than in any other part of the Constitution.

. . . *163*

The great States naturally wished for a popular choice of First Magistrate. This mode was sanctioned by the example of many of the States in the choice of Governor. The small States claimed a choice on the federative principle, by the Legislatures, and to vote by States; analogies and examples were not wanting to sanction this mode of election. A consideration of the weight and influence of a President of this Union must have multiplied the difficulties of agreeing upon the mode of choice. But as I have before said, by mutual concession they agreed upon the present mode, combining both principles and dividing between the two parties, thus mutually jealous, as they could, this important privilege of electing a Chief Magistrate.

This mode then became established, and the right of the small States to elect upon the federative principle, or by States, in case [the presidential electors fail to choose a President] cannot with reason and fairness be taken from them, without their consent and on a full understanding of its operation; since it was meant to be secured to them by the Constitution and was one of the terms upon which they became members of the present Confederacy; and for which privilege they gave an equivalent to the great States, in sacrificing so much of the federative principle or State equality.

The Constitution is nicely balanced with the federative and popular principles; the Senate are the guardians of the former, and the House of Representatives of the latter; and any attempts to destroy this balance, under whatever specious names or pretences they may be presented, should be watched with a jealous eye. Perhaps a fair definition of the Constitutional powers of amending is, that you may upon experiment so modify the Constitution in its practice and operation, as to give it, upon its own principles, a more complete effect. But this [proposed change which is now before us] is an attack upon a fundamental principle established after a long deliberation and by mutual concession; [an attack upon] a principle of essential importance to the instrument itself and an attempt to wrest from the small States a vested right and . . . to increase the power and influence of the large States.

I shall not pretend, sir, that the parties to this Constitutional compact cannot alter its original essential principles, and that such alterations may not be effected under the name of amendment. But, let a proposal of that kind come forward in its own proper and undisguised shape. Let it be fairly stated to Congress, to the State Legislatures, to the people at large, that the intention is to change an important federative feature in the Constitution, which change in itself and all its consequences will tend to a consolidation of this Union into a simple Republic. Let it be fairly stated, that the small States have too much agency in the important article of electing a Chief Magistrate and that the great States claim the choice; and we shall then have a fair decision. If the Senators of the small States, and if their State Legislatures, will then quietly part with the right they have, no person can reasonably complain. *164*

Nothing can be more obvious, than the intention of the plan adopted by our Constitution for choosing a President. [The Constitution now provides that] the Electors are to nominate two persons, of whom they cannot know which will be President. This circumstance not only induces them to select both from the best men; but gives a direct advantage into the hands of the small States even in the electoral choice. For they [the Electors of small States] can always select from the two candidates set up by the Electors of large States, by throwing their votes upon their favorite, and of course giving him a majority; or, if the Electors of the large States should, to prevent this effect, scatter their votes for one candidate, then the Electors of the small States would have it in their power to elect a Vice President. So that, in any event, the small States will have a considerable agency in the election.

But if the discriminating or designating principle is carried as contained in this resolution, the whole, or nearly the whole right and

agency of the small States, in the electoral choice of Chief Magistrate, is destroyed and their chance of obtaining a federative choice by States if not destroyed, is very much diminished.
. . . *165*

I am not without my fears, Mr. President, that this is but the beginning of evils and that this Constitution, the bulwark of the feeble members of the Confederacy; the protection of the weak against the strong; the security of the small against the great; the last, best hope of man, with a view to stability in a free Government and to the preservation of liberty in a Republic; is destined to undergo changes and suffer innovations till there be no residue worth preserving and nothing left which ambition will condescend to overturn.
. . .

4.7 John Taylor: "The controversy is not between larger and smaller States, but between the people of every State and the House of Representatives."*

The opposition to this discriminating amendment to the Constitution is condensed into a single stratagem, namely: an effort to excite the passion of jealousy in various forms. Endeavors have been made to excite geographical jealousies—a jealousy of the smaller against the larger States—a jealousy in the people against the idea of amending the Constitution; and even a jealousy against individual members of this House. . . .

So far as these efforts have been directed towards a geographical demarcation of the interests of the Union into North and South in order to excite a jealousy of one division against another; and so far as they have been used to create suspicions of individuals, they have been either so feeble, inapplicable, or frivolous as to bear but lightly upon the question and to merit but little attention. But the attempts to array States against States because they differ in size and to prejudice the people against the idea of amending their Constitution, bear a more formidable aspect and ought to be repelled, because they are founded on principles the most mischiev-

* From a speech by the Senator from Virginia in the Senate, December 2, 1803. *Annals,* 8th Congress, 1st session, pp. 180-183.

ous and inimical to the Constitution, and could they be successful, are replete with great mischiefs.

Towards exciting this jealousy of smaller States against larger States, the gentleman from Connecticut (Mr. Tracy) had labored to prove that the federal principle of the Constitution of the United States was founded in the idea of minority invested with operative power. That, in pursuance of this principle, it was contemplated and intended that the election of a President should frequently come into the House of Representatives, and to divert it from thence by this amendment would trench upon the federal principle of our Constitution and diminish the rights of the small States bestowed by this principle upon them. This was the scope of his argument to excite their jealousy, and is the amount also of several other arguments delivered by gentlemen on the same side of the question. . . .

This idea of federalism ought to be well dis- *181* cussed by the small States, before they will suffer it to produce the intended effect —that of exciting their jealousy against the larger. To him it appeared to be evidently incorrect. Two principles sustain our Constitution: one a majority of the people, the other a majority of the States; the first was necessary to preserve the liberty or sovereignty of the people; the last, to preserve the liberty or sovereignty of the States. But both are founded in the principle of majority; and the effort of the Constitution is to preserve this principle in relation both to the people and the States, so that neither species of sovereignty or independence should be able to destroy the other. Many illustrations might be adduced. That of amending the Constitution will suffice. Three-fourths of the States must concur in this object, because a less number or a majority of States might not contain a majority of people; therefore, the Constitution is not amendable by a majority of States lest a species of State sovereignty might, under color of amending the Constitution, infringe the right of the people. On the other hand, a majority of the people residing in the large States cannot amend the Constitution lest they should diminish or destroy the sovereignty of the small States, the federal Union, or federalism itself. Hence a concurrence of the States to amend the Constitution became necessary, not because federalism was founded in the idea of minority, but for a reason the very reverse of that idea—that is, to cover the will both of a majority of the people and a majority of States, so as to preserve the great element of self-government, as it regarded State sovereignty, and also as it regarded the sovereignty of the people.

. . . *182*

Under this view of the subject, the amendment ought to be considered. Then the question will be, whether it is calculated or not to cause the popular principle, applied by the Constitution in the first instance, to operate perfectly, and to prevent the abuse of an election by a minority? If it is, it corresponds with the intention, diminishes nothing of the rights of the smaller States, and, of course affords them no cause of jealousy.

Sir, it could never have been the intention of the Constitution to produce a state of things by which a majority of the popular principle should be under the necessity of voting against its judgment to secure a President, and by which a minor faction should acquire a power capable of defeating the majority in the election of President, or of electing a Vice President contrary to the will of the electing principle. To permit this abuse would be a fraudulent mode of defeating the operation of the popular principle in this election in order to transfer it to the federal principle—to disinherit the people for the sake of endowing the House of Representatives; whereas it was an accidental and not an artificial disappointment in the election of a President, against which the Constitution intended to provide. A fair and not an unfair attempt to elect was previously to be made by the popular principle before the election was to go into the House of Representatives. And if the people of all the States, both large and small, should, by an abuse of the election design of the Constitution, be bubbled out of the election of Executive power, by leaving to them the nominal right of an abortive effort, and transferring to the House of Representatives the substantial right *183* of a real election, nothing will remain but to corrupt the election in that House by some of those abuses of which elections by diets are susceptible, to bestow upon Executive power an aspect both formidable and inconsistent with the principles by which the Constitution intended to mould it.

The great check imposed upon Executive power was a popular mode of election; and the true object of jealousy which ought to attract the attention of the people of every State is any circumstance tending to diminish or destroy that check. It was also a primary intention of the Constitution to keep Executive power independent of Legislative; and although a provision was made for its election by the House of Representatives in a possible case, that possible case never was intended to be converted into the active rule so as to destroy in a degree the line of separation and independency between the Executive and Legislative power.

The controversy is not therefore between larger and smaller States, but between the people of every State and the House of Representatives. Is it better that the people—a fair majority of the popular principle—should elect Executive power; or, that a minor faction should be enabled to embarrass and defeat the judgment and will of this majority, and throw the election into the House of Representatives? This is the question. If this amendment should enable the popular principle to elect Executive power, and thus keep it separate and distinct from legislation, the intention of the Constitution, the interest of the people, and the principles of our policy will be preserved; and if so, it is as I have often endeavored to prove in this debate, the interest of the smaller States themselves that the amendment should prevail. For, sir, is an exposure of their Representatives to bribery and corruption (a thing which may possibly happen at some future day when men lose that public virtue which now governs them) an acquisition more desirable than all those great objects best (if not exclusively) attainable by the election of Executive power by the popular principle of the Federal Government, as the Constitution itself meditates and prefers?

. . .

chapter **5**

Delegated and reserved powers

GENERAL WELFARE AND THE SPENDING POWER

5.1   James Madison: "I have always conceived that this is a limited Government, tied down to the specified powers."*

. . .

It is supposed by some gentlemen that Congress have authority not only to grant bounties in the sense here used, merely as a commutation for drawbacks, but even to grant them under a power by virtue of which they may do anything which they may think conducive to the "general welfare." This, sir, in my mind raises the important and fundamental question, whether the general terms which had been cited are to be considered as a sort of caption or general description of the specified powers and as having no further meaning and giving no further power than what is found in that specification; or as an abstract and indefinite delegation of power extending to all cases whatever; to all such, at least, as will admit the application

* From a speech by the Representative from Virginia in the House of Representatives, February 6, 1792, opposing a bill providing payment of subsidies to owners of vessels engaged in cod-fisheries. *Annals,* 2nd Congress, 1st session, pp. 386-389.

of money, which is giving as much latitude as any Government could well desire.

I, sir, have always conceived—I believe those who proposed the Constitution conceived, and it is still more fully known and more material to observe that those who ratified the Constitution conceived—that this is not an indefinite Government, deriving its powers from the general terms prefixed to the specified powers, but a limited Government tied down to the specified powers which explain and define the general terms. The gentlemen who contend for a contrary doctrine are surely not aware of the consequences which flow from it, and which they must either admit or give up their doctrine.

It will follow, in the first place, that if the terms be taken in the broad sense they maintain, the particular powers afterwards so carefully and distinctly enumerated would be without any meaning and must go for nothing. It would be absurd 387 to say, first, that Congress may do what they please, and then that they may do this or that particular thing; after giving Congress power to raise money and apply it to all purposes which they may pronounce necessary to the general welfare, it would be absurd, to say the least, to superadd a power to raise armies, to provide fleets, &c. In fact, the meaning of the general terms in question must either be sought in the subsequent enumeration which limits and details them, or they convert the Government from one limited, as hitherto supposed, to the enumerated powers, into a Government without any limits at all.

It is to be recollected that the terms "common defence and general welfare," as here used, are not novel terms, first introduced into this Constitution. They are terms familiar in their construction, and well known to the people of America. They are repeatedly found in the old Articles of Confederation where, although they are susceptible of as great latitude as can be given them by the context here, it was never supposed or pretended that they conveyed any such power as it now assigned to them. On the contrary, it was always considered as clear and certain that the old Congress was limited to the enumerated powers, and that the enumeration limited and explained the general terms. . . .

The novel idea now annexed to these terms, and never before entertained by the friends or enemies of the Government, will have a further consequence which cannot have been taken into the view of the gentlemen. Their construction would not only give Congress the complete Legislative power I have stated—it would do more—it would supersede all the restrictions understood at present to lie on their power with respect to the Judiciary. It would put in the power of Congress to establish courts throughout the United States, with cognizance of suits between citizen and citizen, and in all cases whatsoever. This, sir, seems to be demonstrable; for if the clause in question really authorizes Congress to do whatever they think fit, provided it be for the general welfare, of which they are to judge, and money can be applied to it, Congress must have power to create and support a Judiciary Establishment with a jurisdiction extending to all cases favorable, in their opinion, to the general welfare in the same manner as they have power to pass laws and apply money, providing in any other way for the general welfare. I shall be reminded, perhaps, that according to the terms of the Constitution, the Judicial Power is to extend to certain cases only, not to all cases. But this circumstance can have no effect in the argument, it being presupposed by the gentlemen that the specification of certain objects does not limit the import of general terms. Taking these terms 388 as an abstract and indefinite grant of power, they comprise all the objects of Legislative regulation, as well such as fall under the Judiciary article in the Constitution as those falling immediately under the Legislative article; and if the partial enumeration of objects in the Legislative article does not, as these gentlemen contend, limit the general power neither will it be limited by the partial enumeration of objects in the Judiciary article.

There are consequences, sir, still more extensive, which, as they follow clearly from the doctrine combated, must either be admitted or the doctrine must be given up. If Congress can apply money indefinitely to the general welfare, and are the sole and supreme judges of the general welfare, they may take the care of religion into their own hands; they may establish teachers in every State, county, and parish, and pay them out of the public Treasury; they may take into their own hands the education of children, establishing in like manner schools throughout the Union; they may undertake the regulation of all roads, other than post roads. In short, everything from the highest object of State legislation down to the most minute object of police, would be thrown under the power of Congress; for every object I have mentioned would admit the application of money, and might be called, if Congress pleased, provisions for the general welfare.

The language held in various discussions of this House is a proof that the doctrine in question was never entertained by this body. Arguments, wherever the subject would permit, have constantly been drawn from the peculiar nature of this Government, as limited to certain enumerated powers, instead of extending, like other Governments, to all cases not particularly excepted. In a very late instance—I mean the debate on the Representation bill—it must be remembered that an argument much urged, particularly by a gentleman from Massachusetts, against the ratio of one for thirty thousand, was that this Government was unlike the State Governments, which had an indefinite variety of objects within their power; that it had a small number of objections only to attend to, and therefore that a smaller number of Representatives would be sufficient to administer it.

Several arguments have been advanced to show that because, in the regulation of trade, indirect and eventual encouragement is given to manufacturers, therefore Congress have power to give money in direct bounties or to grant it in any other way that would answer the same purpose. But surely, sir, there is a great and obvious difference which it cannot be necessary to enlarge upon. A duty laid on imported implements of husbandry would, in its operation, be an indirect tax on exported produce; but will any one say that by virtue of a mere power to lay duties on imports, Congress might go directly to the produce or implements of agriculture or to the articles exported? It is true, duties on exports are expressly prohibited; but if there were no article forbidding them, a power directly to tax exports could never be deduced from a power to tax imports, although such 389 a power might directly and incidentally affect exports.

In short, sir, without going further into the subject, which I should not have here touched on at all but for the reasons already mentioned, I venture to declare it as my opinion that were the power of Congress to be established in the latitude contended for, it would subvert the very foundation and transmute the very nature of the limited Government established by the people of America; and what inferences might be drawn, or what consequences ensue from such a step, it is incumbent on us all well to consider.

. . .

5.2   John C. Calhoun: "Our laws are full of instances of money appropriated without any reference to the enumerated powers."*

. . .

He understood there were, with some members, Constitutional objections. . . . It was mainly urged that the Congress can only apply the public money in execution of the enumerated powers. He was no advocate for refined arguments on the Constitution. The instrument was not intended as a thesis for the logician to exercise his ingenuity on. It ought to be construed with plain, good sense; and what can be more express than the Constitution on this very point? The first power delegated to Congress is comprised in these words: "To lay and collect taxes, duties, imports, and excises: to pay the debts, and provide for the common defence and general welfare of the United States; but all duties, imports, and excises shall be uniform throughout the United States." First—the power is given to lay taxes; next, the objects are enumerated to which the money accruing from the exercise of this power may be applied; to pay the debts, provide for the common defence, and promote the general welfare; and last, the rule for laying the taxes is prescribed—that all duties, imposts, and excises shall be uniform. If the framers had intended to limit the use of the money to the powers afterwards enumerated and defined, nothing could be more easy than to have expressed it plainly.

He knew it was the opinion of some that the words "to pay the debts, and provide for the common defence and general welfare," which he had just cited, were not intended to be referred to the power of laying taxes contained in the first part of the section, but that they are to be understood as distinct and independent powers, granted in general terms; and are gratified by a more detailed enumeration of powers in the subsequent part of the Constitution. If such were in fact the meaning, surely nothing can be conceived more bungling and awkward than the manner in which the framers

* From a speech by the Representative from South Carolina in the House of Representatives, February 4, 1817, supporting a bill to create a fund to be spent in construction of roads and canals. *Annals,* 14th Congress, 2nd session, pp. 855-857.

have communicated their intention. If it were their intention to make a summary of the powers of Congress in general 856 terms which were afterwards to be particularly defined and enumerated, they should have told us so plainly and distinctly; and if the words "to pay the debts, and provide for the common defence and general welfare," were intended for this summary, they should have headed the list of our powers, and it should have been stated that to effect these general objects, the following specific powers were granted. He asked the members to read the section with attention and it would, he conceived, plainly appear that such could not be the intention. The whole section seemed to him to be about taxes. It plainly commenced and ended with it, and nothing could be more strained than to suppose the intermediate words "to pay the debts, and provide for the common defence and general welfare," were to be taken as independent and distinct powers. Forced, however, as such a construction was, he might admit it and urge that the words do constitute a part of the enumerated powers. The Constitution, said he, gives to Congress the power to establish post offices and post roads. He knew the interpretation which was usually given to these words confined our power to that of designating only the post roads; but it seemed to him that the word "establish" comprehended something more.

But suppose the Constitution to be silent, said Mr. C., why should we be confined in the application of money to the enumerated powers? There is nothing in the reason of the thing that he could perceive why it should be so restricted; and the habitual and uniform practice of the Government coincided with his opinion. Our laws are full of instances of money appropriated without any reference to the enumerated powers. We granted, by an unanimous vote or nearly so, fifty thousand dollars to the distressed inhabitants of Caraccas, and a very large sum at two different times to the Saint Domingo refugees. If we are restricted in the use of our money to the enumerated powers, on what principle, said he, can the purchase of Louisiana be justified? To pass over many other instances, the identical power which is now the subject of discussion has, in several instances, been exercised. To look no further back, at the last session a considerable sum was granted to complete the Cumberland road.

In reply to this uniform course of legislation, Mr. C. expected it would be said that our Constitution was founded on positive and written principles, and not on precedents. He did not deny the position; but he introduced these instances to prove the uniform sense of Congress and the country (for they had not been objected to) as to our powers; and surely, said he, they furnished better evidence of the true interpretation of the Constitution than the most refined and subtle arguments.

Let it not be urged that the construction for which he contended gave a dangerous extent to the powers of Congress. In this point of view, he conceived it to be more safe than the opposite. By giving a reasonable extent to the money power, it exempted us from the necessity of giving a strained and forced construction to the other enu- 857 merated powers. For instance, he said, if the public money could be applied to the purchase of Louisiana, as he contended, then there was no Constitutional difficulty in that purchase; but, if it could not, then were we compelled either to deny that we had the power to purchase or to strain some of the enumerated powers to prove our right. It had, for instance, been said that we had the right to purchase under the power to admit new States—a construction, he would venture to say, far more forced than the one for which he contended. Such are my views, said he, on our right to pass this bill.

. . .

5.3 Alexander Smyth: "It will operate as an offer of money in exchange for power."*

. . .

It is contended by the select committee that, even if Congress have no power to construct roads and canals, they may notwithstanding give money to aid in the constructing of roads and canals by the States; that there is a distinction between a power to appropriate money for a purpose, and a power to do the act for which the money is appropriated. I deny to Congress the right to appropri-

---

* From a speech by the Representative from Virginia in the House of Representatives, March 7, 1818, opposing a bill to create a fund to be spent in construction of roads, canals, and other internal improvements. *Annals,* 15th Congress, 1st session, pp. 1145-1147.

ate one shilling of the money of the people except for the purposes of executing their own powers or the powers of the Government or the powers of some department or officer of the Government; for no money can be drawn from the Treasury except in consequence of appropriations made by law; and no law can be passed except such as is necessary and proper to carry into execution the powers granted to Congress, those vested in the Government of the United States, or in some department or officer thereof.

When, therefore, a question arises whether Congress may appropriate money for a certain purpose or not, the answer must depend on that which shall first be given to another inquiry: whether it is necessary and proper for carrying into execution the powers of Congress, or of the Government of the United States, or of some department or officer thereof; and if it is not thus necessary and proper, Congress cannot pass the law to make the appropriation.

The appropriation of money which the select committee propose to make is not an appropriation of money for the general welfare; it is for the improvement of particular sections of country. In making war, maintaining armies and navies, regulating commerce, maintaining a judiciary, and so on, the whole people are concerned; but it is not so as to particular roads and canals. And as roads and canals are of local concern, they ought to be made by local impositions. Suppose that a law should pass according to the proposition of the select committee, and that in Maryland the fund should be applied to make a road from Annapolis to this city; that in Virginia the *1146* fund should be applied to make a road from Winchester to Richmond; should these roads be said to be of general concern, or to provide for the general welfare?

The power of levying money is expressly granted to Congress; and the object is declared to be, to pay the debts and provide for the common defence and general welfare of the United States. It is properly admitted by the select committee that the clause grants no power but to raise money. The common defence and general welfare are to be provided for by expending the money raised in the execution of the other powers expressly granted.

If Congress have greater latitude in making appropriations than in passing other laws, it is not given to them by the Constitution. It results from the circumstance that there exists no check on this power of the National Legislature except solemn promises of its members to support the Constitution. There is little probability of a question respecting the constitutionality of an appropriation law being brought before the judiciary. And as there is no efficient corrective of the power of the Legislature to pass acts of appropriation, we should be the more scrupulous and careful not to transcend the Constitutional authority granted to us by the people.

It does not remove the objection to this appropriation that all the States may share therein. Should that equal participation be considered as removing the objection, then we may make a like appropriation to defray the civil list of each state.

The "beneficent effects" of the proposed measure are urged as furnishing an argument in favor of a liberal construction, that is, a stretch of the Constitution. But who were they that ever seized upon power not granted to them, and did not offer the same argument in their justification? Caesar, Cromwell, and Napoleon overturned the liberties, and seized upon the whole power of their respective nations, with a view to produce "beneficial effects," according to them. The powers of Congress should not be extended by construction, in any case. Should that be done, all the advantages of a written constitution will be lost. Our Constitution will be no better than that of England where the rule of construction is, that whatever has been done may be done again. Although the select committee say that the power will only be felt in "the blessings it confers"; yet the Constitution does not grant to Congress every power that may confer blessings. Every usurpation is dangerous in its tendency. Every additional power tends to the aggrandizement of the General Government. Every surrender of power that the States can be lured to make, tends to their degradation.

I dislike the aspect of this proposition. It will operate as an offer of money in exchange for power. If this power is to be asked for, let the State Legislatures decide upon the expediency of granting it before you place within their reach a sum of money upon condition that they will agree to give you up this power. A State will 1147 have no alternative but to grant the consent required, or submit to the greatest injustice.

Suppose that a State Legislature should refuse its consent, not choosing that the power of the General Government should be exerted in making roads within its territory; what will become of its share of the fund? It is to be withheld, and to remain suspended as a lure to induce the State Legislature to surrender their Constitutional powers. Meantime the fund will be in the name of the State, and daily augmenting; and sooner or later the largeness of the sum will overcome all scruples; the State Legislatures will accept of the money for the benefit of the State, and surrender their rights. If such measures are adopted, you may purchase one power after another, from one State after another, until this Government, like the rod of Aaron, shall have swallowed up all the rest.

. . .

LOOSE vs. STRICT CONSTRUCTION

5.4   Debate on Establishment of a Bank of the United States:* "The doctrine that powers may be implied which are not expressly vested in Congress has long been a bugbear to a great many worthy persons."

Mr. Madison: . . . Is the power of establishing an incorporated Bank among the powers vested by the Constitution in the Legislature of the United States? This is the question to be examined.

After some general remarks on the limitations of all political power, he took notice of the peculiar manner in which the Federal Government is limited. It is not a general grant out of which particular powers are excepted; it is a grant of particular powers only, leaving the general mass in other hands. So it had been understood by its friends and its foes, and so it was to be interpreted.

As preliminaries to a right interpretation, he laid down the following rules:

An interpretation that destroys the very characteristic of the Government cannot be just.

Where a meaning is clear, the consequences, whatever they may

* Representatives James Madison of Virginia and Fisher Ames of Massachusetts. From debate in the House of Representatives on a bill to incorporate a Bank of the United States. Madison, February 2, 1791; Ames, February 3, 1791. *Annals,* 1st Congress, 2nd session, pp. 1896-1902 (Madison) and pp. 1904-1906 (Ames).

be, are to be admitted—where doubtful, it is fairly triable by its consequences.

In controverted cases, the meaning of the parties to the instrument, if to be collected by reasonable evidence, is a proper guide.

Contemporary and concurrent expositions are a reasonable evidence of the meaning of the parties.

In admitting or rejecting a constructive authority, not only the degree of its incidentality to an express authority is to [be] regarded, but the degree of its importance also; since on this will depend the probability or improbability of its being left to construction.

Reviewing the Constitution with an eye to these positions, it was not possible to discover in it the power to incorporate a Bank. The only clauses under which such a power could be pretended are either:

1. The power to lay and collect taxes to pay the debts, and provide for the common defence and general welfare: or,

2. The power to borrow money on the credit of the United States: or,

3. The power to pass all laws necessary and proper to carry into execution those powers.

The bill did not come within the first power. It laid no tax to pay the debts, or provide for the general welfare. It laid no tax whatever. It was altogether foreign to the subject.

No argument could be drawn from the terms "common defence and general welfare." The power as to these general purposes was limited to acts laying taxes for them; and the general purposes themselves were limited and explained by the particular enumeration subjoined. To understand these terms in any sense that would justify the power in question, would give to Con- 1897 gress an unlimited power; would render nugatory the enumeration of particular powers; would supersede all the powers reserved to the State Governments. These terms are copied from the Articles of Confederation; had it ever been pretended that they were to be understood otherwise than as here explained?

. . .

The second clause to be examined is that which empowers Congress to borrow money.

Is this bill to borrow money? It does not borrow a shilling. Is there any fair construction by which the bill can be deemed an exercise of the power to borrow money? The obvious meaning of the power to borrow money is that of accepting it from and stipulating payment to those who are able and willing to lend.

To say that the power to borrow involves a power of creating the ability, where there may be the will, to lend, is not only establishing a dangerous principle, as will be immediately shown, but is as forced a construction as to say that it in- 1898 volves the power of compelling the will where there may be the ability to lend.

The third clause is that which gives the power to pass all laws necessary and proper to execute the specified powers.

Whatever meaning this clause may have, none can be admitted that would give an unlimited discretion to Congress.

Its meaning must, according to the natural and obvious force of the terms and the context, be limited to means necessary to the end and incident to the nature of the specified powers.

The clause is in fact merely declaratory of what would have resulted by unavoidable implication, as the appropriate and, as it were, technical means of executing those powers. In this sense it has been explained by the friends of the Constitution, and ratified by the State Conventions.

The essential characteristic of the Government as composed of limited and enumerated powers would be destroyed, if instead of direct and incidental means, any means could be used which, in the language of the preamble to the bill, "might be conceived to be conducive to the successful conducting of the finances, or might be conceived to tend to give facility to the obtaining of loans." He urged an attention to the diffuse and ductile terms which had been found requisite to cover the stretch of power contained in the bill. He compared them with the terms necessary and proper, used in the Constitution, and asked whether it was possible to view the two descriptions as synonymous, or the one as a fair and safe commentary on the other.

If, proceeded he, Congress, by virtue of the power to borrow, can create the means of lending and in pursuance of these means can incorporate a Bank, they may do any thing whatever creative of like means.

. . .

If, again, Congress by virtue of the power to borrow money can create the ability to lend, they may by virtue of the power to levy money create the ability to pay it. The ability to pay taxes depends on the general wealth of the society, and this on the general prosperity of agriculture, manufactures, and commerce. Congress then may give bounties and make regulations on all of these objects.

The States have, it is allowed on all hands, a concurrent right to lay and collect taxes. This power is secured to them, not by its being expressly reserved, but by its not being ceded by the Con- 1899 stitution. The reasons for the bill cannot be admitted because they would invalidate that right; why may it not be conceived by Congress that a uniform and exclusive imposition of taxes would not less than the proposed Banks "be conducive to the successful conducting of the national finances, and tend to give facility to the obtaining of revenue, for the use of the Government"?

The doctrine of implication is always a tender one. The danger of it has been felt in other Governments. The delicacy was felt in the adoption of our own; the danger may also be felt, if we do not keep close to our chartered authorities.

Mark the reasoning on which the validity of the bill depends! To borrow money is made the end, and the accumulation of capitals implied as the means. The accumulation of capitals is then the end, and a Bank implied as the means. The Bank is then the end, and a charter of incorporation, a monopoly, capital punishments, &c., implied as the means.

If implications, thus remote and thus multiplied, can be linked together, a chain may be formed that will reach every object of legislation, every object within the whole compass of political economy.

The latitude of interpretation required by the bill is condemned by the rule furnished by the Constitution itself.

Congress have power "to regulate the value of money"; yet it is expressly added, not left to be implied, that counterfeiters may be punished.

They have the power "to declare war," to which armies are more incident that incorporated banks to borrowing; yet the power "to raise and support armies" is expressly added; and to this again, the express power "to make rules and regulations for the government of armies"; a like remark is applicable to the powers as to the navy.

The regulation and calling out of the militia are more appertinent to war than the proposed Bank to borrowing; yet the former is not left to construction.

The very power to borrow money is a less remote implication from the power of war than an incorporated monopoly Bank from the power of borrowing; yet, the power to borrow is not left to implication.

It is not pretended that every insertion or omission in the Constitution is the effect of systematic attention. This is not the character of any human work, particularly the work of a body of men. The examples cited, with others that might be added, sufficiently inculcate, nevertheless, a rule of interpretation very different from that on which the bill rests. They condemn the exercise of any power, particularly a great and important power, which is not evidently and necessarily involved in an express power. *1900*

. . . the power of incorporation exercised in the bill could never be deemed an accessory or subaltern power, to be deduced by implication, as a means of executing another power; it was in its nature a distinct, an independent and substantive prerogative, which not being enumerated in the Constitution, could never have been meant to be included in it, and not being included, could never be rightfully exercised.

He here adverted to a distinction, which he said had not been sufficiently kept in view, between a power necessary and proper for the Government or Union and a power necessary and proper for executing the enumerated powers. In the latter case, the powers included in the enumerated powers were not expressed, but to be drawn from the nature of each. In the former, the powers composing the Government were expressly enumerated. This constituted the peculiar nature of the Government; no power, therefore, not enumerated could be inferred from the general nature of Government. Had the power of making treaties, for example, been omitted, however necessary it might have been, the defect *1901* could only have been lamented, or supplied by an amendment of the Constitution. . . . *1902*

It appeared on the whole, he concluded, that the power exercised by the bill was condemned by the silence of the Constitution; was condemned by the rule of interpretation arising out of the Constitution; was condemned by its tendency to destroy the main characteristic of the Constitution; was condemned by the expositions of the friends of the Constitution, whilst depending before the public; was condemned by the apparent intention of the parties which ratified the Constitution; was condemned by the explanatory amendments proposed by Congress themselves to the Constitution; and he hoped it would receive its final condemnation by the vote of this House.

Mr. Ames: . . . In making this reply I am to perform a task for which my own mind has not admonished me to prepare. I never suspected that the objections I have heard stated had existence; I consider them as discoveries; and had not the acute penetration of that gentleman brought them to light, I am sure that my own understanding would never have suggested them.
. . .

Two questions occur; may Congress exercise any powers which are not expressly given in the Constitution, but may be deduced by a reasonable construction of that instrument? And, secondly, will such a construction warrant the establishment of the bank?

The doctrine that powers may be implied which are not expressly vested in Congress has long been a bugbear to a great many worthy persons. They apprehend that Congress, by putting constructions upon the Constitution, will govern by its own arbitrary discretion; and therefore that it ought to be bound to exercise the powers expressly given, and those only.

If Congress may not make laws conformably to the powers plainly implied, though not expressed in the frame of Government, it is rather late in the day to adopt it as a principle of conduct. A great part of our two years labor is lost, and worse than lost to the public, for we have scarcely made a law in which we have not exercised our discretion with regard to the true intent of the Constitution. Any words but those used in that instrument will be liable to a different interpretation. We may regulate trade; therefore we have taxed ships, erected light-houses, made laws to govern seamen, &c., because we say that they are the incidents to that power. The most familiar and undisputed acts of Legislation will show that we have adopted it as a safe rule of action to legislate beyond the letter of the Constitution.

He proceeded to enforce this idea by several considerations, and illustrated it by various examples. He said that the ingenuity of man was unequal to providing, especially beforehand, for all the contingencies that would happen. The Constitution contains the principles which are to govern in making laws; but every law requires an

application of the rule to the case in question. We may err in applying it; but we are to exercise our judgments, and on every occasion to de- *1905* cide according to an honest conviction of its true
meaning.

The danger of implied power does not arise from its assuming
a new principle; we have not only practised it often, but we can
scarcely proceed without it; nor does the danger proceed so much
from the extent of the power as from its uncertainty. While the opposers of the bank exclaim against the exercise of this power by Congress, do they mark out the limits of the power which they will leave
to us with more certainty than is done by the advocates of the bank?
Their rules of interpretation by contemporaneous testimony, the debates of Conventions and the doctrine of substantive and auxiliary
powers, will be found as obscure, and of course as formidable as that
which they condemn; they only set up one construction against
another.

The powers of Congress are disputed. We are obliged to decide
the question according to truth. The negative, if false, is less safe
than the affirmative, if true. Why, then, shall we be told that the
negative is the safe side? Not exercising the powers we have may be
as pernicious as usurping those we have not. If the power to raise
armies had not been expressed in the enumeration of the powers of
Congress, it would be implied from other parts of the Constitution.
Suppose, however, that it were omitted and our country invaded,
would a decision in Congress against raising armies be safer than
the affirmative? The blood of our citizens would be shed and shed
unavenged. He thought, therefore, that there was too much prepos-
session with some against the Bank and that the debate ought to be
considered more impartially, as the negative was neither more safe,
certain, nor conformable to our duty than the other side of the
question. After all, the proof of the affirmative imposed a sufficient
burden, as it is easier to raise objections than to remove them. Would
any one doubt that Congress may lend money, that they may buy
their debt in the market, or redeem their captives from Algiers? Yet
no such power is expressly given, though it is irresistibly implied.
. . . *1906*

Congress may do what is necessary to the end for which the
Constitution was adopted, provided it is not repugnant to the natural
rights of man or to those which they have expressly reserved to them-

selves or to the powers which are assigned to the States. This rule of
interpretation seems to be safe, and not a very uncertain one, independently of the Constitution itself. By that instrument certain powers are specially delegated, together with all powers necessary or
proper to carry them into execution. That construction may be maintained to be a safe one which promotes the good of the society, and
the ends for which the Government was adopted, without impairing
the rights of any man, or the power of any State.

. . .

5.5   Debate on Renewal of the Bank of the United States:*   "The
defined powers may prove only a text, and the implied or resulting
powers may furnish the sermon to it."

Mr. Porter: . . . The mode of reasoning adopted by General [Alex-
ander] Hamilton and the other advocates of implied powers is this:
They first search for the end or object for which a particular power
is given; and this object will be an immediate or ultimate one, as
may best suit the purpose of the argument. Having ascertained the
end or object, they abandon the power; or, rather, they confound the
power and the *object* of it together and make the attainment of the
object and the execution of the power given to accomplish it, con-
vertible terms. Whatever, they say, attains the object for which any
power is given, is an execution of that power.
. . . *636*
     The Constitution of the United States is not, as such reasoning
supposes it to be, a mere general designation of the ends or objects
for which the Federal Government was established, and leaving to
Congress a discretion as to the means or powers by which those ends
shall be brought about. But the Constitution is a specification of the
powers or means themselves by which certain objects are to be accomplished. The powers of the Constitution, carried into execution
according to the strict terms and import of them, are the appropriate

---

* Representative Peter B. Porter of New York and Senators William H.
Crawford of Georgia, James Lloyd of Massachusetts, and William B. Giles of
Virginia. From debate on a bill to continue in force the act of 1791 creating a
Bank of the United States. Porter, January 18, 1811; Crawford, February 11,
1811; Lloyd, February 12, 1811; Giles, February 14, 1811. *Annals,* 11th Con-
gress, 3d session, pp. 634, 636-637 (Porter); pp. 140-142 (Crawford); p. 158
(Lloyd); p. 186 (Giles).

means and the only means within the reach of this Government for the attainment of its ends.

It is true, as the Constitution declares, and it would be equally true if the Constitution did not declare it, that Congress have a right to pass all laws necessary and proper for executing the delegated powers; but this gives no latitude of discretion in the selection of means or powers. A power given to Congress in its Legislative capacity, without the right to pass laws to execute it, would be nugatory; would be no power at all. It would be a solecism in language to call it a power. A power to lay and collect taxes carries with it a right to make laws for that purpose; but they must be laws to lay and collect taxes and not laws to incorporate banks. If you undertake to justify a law under a particular power, you must show the incidentality and applicability of the law to the power itself, and not merely its relation to any supposed end which is to be accomplished by its exercise. You must show that the plain, direct, ostensible, primary object and tendency of your law is to execute the power, and not that it will tend to facilitate the execution of it. It is not less absurd than it is dangerous, first to assume some great, distinct and independent power unknown to the Constitution and violating the rights of the States; and then, to attempt to justify it by a reference to some remote, indirect, collateral tendency which the exercise of it may have towards facilitating the execution of some known and acknowledged power.

This word *facilitate* has become a very fashionable word in the construction of powers; but, sir, it is a dangerous one; it means more than we are aware of. To do a thing and to facilitate the doing of it, are distinct operations; they are distinct means; they are distinct powers. The Constitution has expressly given to Congress the power to do certain things; and it has, as explicitly, withheld from them the power to do every other thing. The power to lay and collect taxes is one thing; and the power 637 to establish banks, involving in its exercise the regulation of the internal domestic economy of the States, is another and totally distinct thing; and the one is therefore not included in the other.

Again, sir, it is contended that the right to incorporate a bank is implied in the power to regulate trade and intercourse between the several States. It is said to be so inasmuch as it creates a paper currency, which furnishes a convenient and common circulating medium of trade between the several States. Money, sir, has nothing more to do with trade than that it furnishes a medium or representative of the value of the articles employed in trade. The only office of bank bills is to represent money. Now, if it be a regulation of trade to create the representative articles or subjects of trade, *a fortiori*, will it be a regulation of trade to create the articles or subjects themselves. By this reasoning then you may justify the right of Congress to establish manufacturing and agricultural companies within the several States; because the direct object and effect of these would be to increase manufactures and agricultural products, which are the known and common subjects of trade. You might with more propriety say that under the power to regulate trade between the States, we have a right to incorporate canal companies; because canals would tend directly to open, facilitate and encourage trade and intercourse between the several States; and, in my humble opinion, sir, canals would furnish a much more salutary, direct and efficacious means for enabling the great body of the people to pay their taxes than is furnished by banks. But, sir, these various powers have never been claimed by the Federal Government; and, much as I am known to favor that particular species of internal improvement, I would never vote to incorporate a company for the purpose of opening a canal through any State, without first obtaining the consent of that State whose territorial rights would be affected by it. There can be no question but canal companies, and agricultural companies, and manufacturing companies, and banking companies may all tend more or less to facilitate the operations of trade; but they have nothing to do with the political regulations of trade; and such only come within the scope of the powers of Congress.

. . .

Mr. Crawford: . . . The right to erect light-houses is exercised because the commerce of the nation or the collection of duties is greatly facilitated by that means; and, sir, the right to create a bank is exercised because the collection of your revenue and the safe-keeping and easy and speedy transmission of your public money is not simply facilitated, but because these important objects are more perfectly secured by the erection of a bank than they can be by any other means in the *141* power of human imagination to devise. We say, therefore, in the words of the Constitution, that a bank is necessary and proper to enable the Government to carry into complete effect the right to lay and collect taxes, imposts, duties, and excises. We do not say that the existence of the Government absolutely depends upon the operations of a bank, but that a national bank enables the Government to manage its fiscal concerns more advantageously than it could do by any other means. The terms necessary and proper, according to the construction given to every part of the Constitution, imposes no limitation upon the powers previously delegated. If these words had been omitted in the clause giving authority to pass laws to carry into execution the powers vested by the Constitution in the National Government, still Congress would have been bound to pass laws which were necessary and proper, and not such as were unnecessary and improper.

. . . *142*

The original powers granted to the Government by the Constitution can never change with the varying circumstances of the country, but the means by which those powers are to be carried into effect must necessarily vary with the varying state and circumstances of the nation. We are, when acting to-day, not to inquire what means were necessary and proper twenty years ago, not what were necessary and proper at the organization of the Government, but our inquiry must be, what means are necessary and proper this day. The Constitution, in relation to the means by which its powers are to be executed, is one eternal *now*. The state of things now, the precise point of time when we are called upon to act, must determine our choice in the selection of means to execute the delegated powers.

. . .

Mr. Lloyd: . . . It is impossible for the ingenuity of man to devise any written system of Government which, after a lapse of time, extension of empire, or change of circumstances, shall be able to carry its own provisions into operation—hence, sir, the indispensable necessity of implied or resulting powers, and hence the provision in the Constitution that the Government should exercise such additional powers as were necessary to carry those that had been delegated into effect. Sir, if this country goes on increasing and extending in the ratio it has done, it is not impossible that hereafter, to provide for all the new cases that may rise under this new state of things, the defined powers may prove only a text and the implied or resulting powers may furnish the sermon to it.

. . .

Mr. Giles: . . . The power to grant charters of incorporation is not an incidental, subordinate, subservient power; it is a distinct, original, substantive power. It is also susceptible of the clearest definition; and not being among the enumerated powers, it seems to me that Congress can have no fair claim to its exercise in any case. If Congress had been expressly authorized to grant charters of incorporation generally, then granting a charter of incorporation to a bank would have been an instance, or among the means, of carrying into effect that enumerated power, and would have been as much connected and affiliated with it as is the erection of custom-houses with the collection of duties; but the power to grant charters of incorporation generally not being expressly given in the Constitution, no particular instance involving the exercise of that power can be inferred by a fair and candid interpretation of the instrument.

I do not mean to exaggerate the consequences which might result from an assumption of the power to grant charters of incorporation, &c. It is sufficient for me to say that it is a power of primary importance; that it involves as many incidental powers in its exercise as any one of the enumerated powers; that it is equal, if not paramount, to any; and, therefore, in my judgment, cannot be assumed by fair construction as incidental and subservient to any; and, of course, not as among the necessary and proper means for carrying any into effect. In fact, in its nature it does not in the smallest degree partake of the derivative, incidental character. It is original, substantive, distinct in itself, and susceptible of the plainest definition. Hence, whilst I am willing to admit that a power which is in its nature incidental and subservient to any enumerated power, and also among the necessary and proper means for carrying it into effect, may be exercised by Congress without the express words of the Constitution, I should be very unwilling to admit that Congress should also exercise a power neither incidental or subservient to any of the enumerated powers, nor among the necessary and proper means for carrying any into effect; still less should I be inclined to this admission when the power thus proposed to be derived, incidentally or constructively, involves in it the exercise of almost unlimited powers. . . .

. . .

part III

SEPARATION
OF POWERS

Introduction

It would be difficult to overstate the extent to which, during the formative years of our republic, the principle of separation of powers was held as axiomatic. Even those with widely differing political philosophies, such as John Adams and Thomas Jefferson, subscribed to this maxim. To be sure, they differed in important particulars concerning its implementation, but both believed that government powers and functions ought to be divided between three principal departments, legislative, executive, and judicial. Every major plan of government submitted to the Constitutional Convention, specifically those of Randolph, Paterson, and Hamilton, incorporated this principle. What is more, even during the stormy debates in some of the state ratifying conventions no one rose to question, much less to criticize, the proposed system because it did embody this principle, dividing the functions and powers of government between three branches. On the contrary, those who were critical of the Constitution wanted assurances and guarantees above and beyond the checks and balances contained in the Constitution that separation of powers would be maintained. The constitutional ratifying conventions of three states (Virginia, North Carolina, and Rhode Island) recommended that the Constitution be amended to declare "That the legislative, executive, and judiciary powers of Government should be separate and distinct . . ." Madison, it would appear, merely reflects and amplifies upon the nature of this consensus concerning the need for separation of powers when he writes in *Federalist* number forty-seven, "No political truth is certainly of greater intrinsic value, or is stamped with the authority of more enlightened patrons of liberty. . . ."

A significant question for understanding both past and present controversies surrounding separation of powers is, Why was this doctrine so generally accepted as axiomatic? For modern scholars, there is no easy answer to this question. The reason for continuing perplexity could well stem, somewhat paradoxically, from the very fact that this maxim was so widely and unquestioningly accepted. After all, why bother to explain or justify a political principle that seems perfectly obvious to everyone? Yet, so much can be said with certainty. A belief did prevail, as Madison states it in *Federalist* number forty-seven, that an "accumulation of all powers, legislative, executive, and judiciary, in the same hands, whether of one, a few, or many, and whether hereditary, self-appointed, or elective, may justly be pronounced the very definition of tyranny." Jefferson is maintaining essentially the same proposition when he writes in his *Notes on Virginia,* "The concentrating of these [legislative, executive and judicial powers] in the same hands is precisely the definition of despotic government. It will be no alleviation that these powers will be exercised by a plurality of hands, and not by a single one. One hundred and seventy-three despots would surely be as oppressive as one." Thus, the framers believed, the construction of a government designed to promote and preserve liberty required separation of governmental powers. In their concern for separation, we see also a deep-seated fear of government as a potential source of tyranny. Madison in *The Federalist,* principally number fifty-one, acknowledges such when he writes of separation of powers in the context of guarding "society against its rulers," obliging government "to control itself," and controlling the "abuses of government." Moreover, throughout the debates of the Constitutional Convention we find this very same concern expressed; namely, that without provision for separation of powers the rulers will eventually use their positions and the very agencies of government to advance their own interests at the expense of the people.

We can also say with equal surety that the framers regarded Congress as the most likely source of governmental tyranny. In the republican form of government they envisioned, the bulk of governmental powers had to be constitutionally vested in Congress. For this reason, among others, they seemed to feel that special precautions had to be taken to provide adequate checks against encroachments from this branch. Although the plan submitted by Paterson (the New Jersey or small state plan) proposed a unicameral legislature, the view soon prevailed that control of legislative authority required two houses that would serve to check one another. As James Wilson remarked, "If the legislative authority be not restrained, there can be neither liberty nor stability; and it can only be restrained by dividing it within itself, into distinct and independent branches."

While there was fairly substantial agreement on these points, almost every page of the convention debates, as recorded by Madison, reveals sharp differences over what checks and balances should be adopted to preserve the necessary separation between the branches. The debates over the executive department illustrate some of the problems facing the framers. Should there be a plural executive or just one? If a single person, should he possess an absolute or qualified veto over acts passed by Congress? What provisions should be made for his removal? What should be his term of office? By what means should he be elected? In the debates over these and like matters, separation of powers was a major consideration. Would election of the President by Congress or one of its houses tend in the long run to make him completely subservient to the will of Congress, particularly if specific provision were made for his re-eligibility? Would plural executives possess sufficient unity and motive to resist legislative encroachments? Would vesting Congress with impeachment and removal powers really serve to destroy the independence of the executive branch?

The Constitution, in a very important sense, can be viewed as a document that presents us with a definite resolution of conflicting ideas concerning the proper powers and relationships between our three branches. And in providing answers to the questions that arose, it established boundaries or certain "rules of the game" which not only have been, but will continue to be—so long as we live under the system it established—significant in the settlement of disputes arising between our branches. But the Constitution did much more than this. We also find in it an initial resolution of what certainly must have been one of the most perplexing and difficult tasks confronting the framers: How to insure that those holding office under the Constitution, vested as they were with far-reaching and important powers, would use those powers to advance and promote the general objectives of the union as stated in the Preamble, not for the purpose of establishing tyranny over the people. Because the framers had a certain objective in mind, we find that our system of separation of powers and checks and balances differs in important particulars from those models set forth by Montesquieu and other political theorists of an earlier period. True enough, quite in keeping with the traditional theories, the framers felt that it was essential to maintain an adequate separation between the branches; but they also wanted to assure that the system would be consistent with the principles of republican government they espoused, that is, that it would respond to the will of deliberate popular majorities and act within limits acceptable to a majority of the population. The resolution of this particular difficulty, it would seem, comes to this: While all the branches are equipped with the means to resist the encroachments of the others, they are all ultimately, either directly or indirectly, accountable to and controlled by the people as a whole. For this reason, none of the branches can represent an insurmountable obstacle to the enactment and implementation of the deliberate will of the people. Beyond this, separation of powers, particularly the division of the legislative branch, helps to force deliberation in policy-making councils.

The Constitution, however, though setting the crucial boundaries for subsequent controversy, actually gives rise to more questions than answers concerning the proper relationship between branches. This was inevitable. The framers simply could not foresee all the conflicts that would arise once their system was "set in motion." What is more, where the framers apparently saw no inconsistency in or incompatibility between key provisions of the Constitution, those entrusted with the function of implementing the Constitution were soon confronted with the tasks of interpreting and applying these provisions to specific controversies in which the contending parties referred to the constitutional language to bolster their respective contentions and, more importantly, to show that their opponents' interpretations of the Constitution led to logical absurdities. As we can readily imagine, in many of these controversies more than one interpretation served to render the provisions in question consistent and compatible with one another. In still other cases, none of the interpretations was completely satisfactory for this purpose. In either event, the participants, quite naturally, resorted to arguments based on expediency or the intent of the Constitution's makers to reinforce their positions. And we must emphasize, these two lines of argument were, at times, fused to the extent that they were inseparable: Those who had the better case in terms of expediency (e.g., cost or simplicity) seemed to feel that they could derive some advantage by arguing that the framers would have placed a high premium on this value. On the other hand, our constitutional system, as it emerged from the Philadelphia convention, would hardly lead one to believe that the framers had valued economy, efficiency, and simplicity above all else. Far from being decisive, debates centered on expediency only served to emphasize some of the difficulties associated with arguments based on the framers' intent.

The debates in part III (chapters 6, 7, and 8) indicate the nature of the controversies surrounding separation of powers in an ongoing system. They also point, in one way or another, to the central difficulty confronting those with the responsibility of resolving these controversies; namely, what were the framers' intentions? While the framers, as we have indicated, certainly believed that the branches ought to be separate, they also felt that responsible and effective government required a certain blending or union of powers. The crucial questions thus became these: When does such blending of powers promote responsible and effective government? Conversely, when does it lead to a breakdown of the necessary separation? Many of the debates in these chapters illustrate these concerns. To what extent should Congress, or at least the Senate, participate in the removal of executive officers? Would such participation tend to undermine the ability of the President to carry out his constitutional duties? Can the President, through judicious use of his appointment powers, actually control congressional decisions on matters of policy most important to him? How much initiative in the formulation of public policy ought Congress to repose in the executive branches? Would any such grants of authority by Congress eventually result in a dangerous union of executive and legislative powers?

A highly complex question of still another order recurs throughout these debates. Does the constitutional language relating to the powers and structures of the branches limit the discretionary authority of Congress (and, presumably, popular majorities as well), even to the extent of spelling out obligations that Congress must act to fulfill. There are three somewhat distinct but highly interrelated aspects of this problem. First, does the Constitution require Congress to perform certain functions relating to the establishment and organization of the other branches? The debates (selection 8.2) concerning the establishment of lower federal courts illustrate this particular dimension. Second, is Congress obligated to support the other branches when they exercise powers within their constitutionally prescribed domain? Chapter 7 dealing with the questions of appropriations for foreign missions and the treaty-making powers should be read with this question in mind. Third, does adherence to the principle of separation of powers, as envisioned by the framers, actually limit the extent of congressional authority relative to the executive and judicial branches? On this matter the debates concerning presidential removal powers (selection 7.1) and repeal of the Judiciary Act of 1801 (selections 8.3 and 8.4) are most enlightening. While these question are prominent in the debates that follow, the answers eventually provided depended in large measure on the conceptions and general views that prevailed concerning the functions and powers that the branches were designed to perform and execute. For this discernment alone, those statements relating to the nature of the system are highly important. But more than this, they give us some insight into the reasons why our system has developed in the way it has.

chapter 6

Separation of powers and the legislative branch

PRINCIPLES: SEPARATION OF POWERS AND CHECKS AND BALANCES

6.1 Richard B. Lee and James Jackson: "The people ought to know what belongs to each department. Upon what can their sense be exercised, unless they know the particular powers invested in every branch."*

Mr. Lee: . . . It is laid down as a maxim in Government by all judicious writers that the Legislative, Executive, and Judicial powers should be kept as separate and distinct as possible in order to secure the liberties of the people. And this maxim is founded on the experience of ages; for we find that however Governments have been established, however modified in their names or forms, if these pow-

---

* Remarks made in the House of Representatives by Representatives Lee of Virginia and Jackson of Georgia, in debate on a bill to establish a Department of Foreign Affairs, the point at issue being: where the power to remove the heads of departments can and ought to be placed. Lee, June 18, 1789; Jackson, June 19, 1789. *Annals,* 1st Congress, 1st session, pp. 524-525 (Lee) and pp. 553-554 (Jackson).

ers are blended in or exercised by one body, the effects are ever the same; the public liberty is destroyed.

The several States, in forming their constitutions, have attended particularly to this sacred maxim. We find they sedulously separated these powers of Government; and many of their declarations of rights were intended to perpetuate the inviolable truth. The framers of the Constitution of the United States came from among the people, who venerated this general principle; they were the select and honored sons of those people who, like them, were impressed with sovereign respect for a truth which supported the great object of a good and free Government. Characters 525 like these, with such impressions, were not likely to forego principles in which they were nurtured. Did they forego them? Examine the result of their deliberations, and see how carefully they are preserved. They have divided our Government into three principal branches, with express declarations that all Legislative power shall vest in one, all Executive in another, and the whole Judicial in a third.

It is our bounden duty to imitate their great example and to support the separation which they have formed. The Legislature has the power to create and establish offices; but it is their duty so to modify them as to make them conform to the general spirit of the Constitution. The people ought to know what belongs to each department; what belongs to the Executive Magistrate and what is expected from him. Upon what can their sense be exercised, unless they know the particular powers invested in every branch? If a mischievous Legislative act be passed, they look to the Legislature; they remonstrate with you and ask, why was this done? If a wicked Executive act is perpetrated, they look to the Executive Magistrate and ask, why did you do this or suffer it to be done? If an improper decision takes place in a court of law, they ask of the Judiciary to correct the error.

It is by separating and keeping distinct these powers that the public jealousy can be directed to those objects which are most necessary to be watched; they can discover the error, and know who to blame. But if the powers are blended, their attention is divided and the responsibility, if not annihilated, is greatly diminished. On the public jealousy, therefore, the freedom of the Government exists; for if the Government is not watched, it either becomes negligent or tyrannical; and to induce the people to keep an observing eye over the actions of men in power, they must have their object specific and single.

Now, as I contend we have the power to modify the establishment of officers, so ought we, Mr. Chairman, to modify them in such a way as to promote the general welfare, which can only be done by keeping the three branches distinct; by informing the people where to look in order to guard against improper Executive acts. It is our duty, therefore, to vest all Executive power belonging to the Government where the convention intended it should be placed. It adds to the responsibility of the most responsible branch of the Government, and, without responsibility, we should have little security against the depredations and gigantic strides of arbitrary power. . . .

. . .

Mr. Jackson: . . . It has been strenuously contended, as necessary to the security of freedom, that the Executive branch of the Government should not be blended with the Legislative, but ought to be divided and kept separate and distinct. Now, that this doctrine exists in practice as well as theory, I beg to be convinced. I do not pretend that such an excellency in Government is undesirable. I only wish permission to ask gentlemen (and will they candidly answer me?) to bring forward a single instance in any Government, when and wheresoever, in which the Executive and Legislative authorities are not blended. Search the annals of history—for I disclaim Utopian politics; search the archives of Rome, the records of Carthage; inspect the historic page of Grecian Republics; examine the Jewish theocracy—and will gentlemen say they can bring evidence of the fact? No, the whole assemblage of ancient Governments, so far as has come within the knowledge of the present age, bears ample testimony against them.

Turn we then to the middle age and not one solitary ray of this benign principle is to be discovered. In that period of Cimmerian darkness, the powers of Government were blended in the most confused chaos.

Let us turn our eyes then to the enlightened hemisphere that brightens on our Atlantic shores. The Governments of Europe are in an improving state; but none, I apprehend, have yet arrived to that perfection which gentlemen have contemplated. That which we have been taught to consider most pure and favorable to liberty, is the Government of Great Britain. There we shall find that the Executive authority is connected with, and forms a part of, the Legislative, and this upon Constitutional ground; it expands itself further, and within its capacious grasp actually holds the Legislative as well as the Executive powers. If we do not find it there, we will not look for it in the despotisms of the East.

Come we then to this country. . . . 554 Look at your own Constitution. Do gentlemen find that it is modelled upon their principles? Are the Legislative, Executive, and Judicial powers kept separate and distinct? No, Mr. Chairman, they are blended; not, to be sure, in so high or dangerous a degree, but in all the possible forms they are capable of receiving; the Executive has a qualified check upon the Legislature; the Legislature exercises the powers of the Judiciary and Executive. Thus, then, I take it, neither our Government nor that of any nation which now exists or hath heretofore existed was strictly founded upon the principles contended for. I call upon gentlemen, therefore, to convince me (for I am open to conviction) how it can be necessary to vest in the President of the United States the power of removal, upon the principle of keeping the Executive department separate and distinct? Gentlemen will not, they cannot, dispute my facts. How then can they contend for inferences, contradicted by such demonstrable and clear hypotheses? . . .

6.2   James A. Bayard: "In all cases where an act is done without power, a check may be found wherever we please to look for it."*

. . .

The case of checks to be derived from the Constitution, I apprehend, may be classed under three heads:

1. Where an express power is given to one branch to control the operations of another.

2. Where a branch of the Government exceeds its powers, and

---

* From a speech by the Representative from Delaware in the House of Representatives, February 27, 1798, opposing a motion to curtail missions to foreign countries. *Annals*, 5th Congress, 2nd session, pp. 1221-1222.

3. Where a general power is given to one branch and a substantive power, included within the terms of it, given to another.

Thus, in the first case, in the Legislature the Senate is a check upon this House and this House upon the Senate and the President upon both; in the Executive, the Senate on the President, as to treaties and appointments; and, in the Judiciary, one Court upon another.

Upon the second head, a case mentioned by the gentleman from Virginia [Mr. Madison] and much relied on, furnishes a striking example. Even the Judges, the gentleman said, are a check upon the Legislature. This arises from the nature of the Legislature, the powers of which are limited. If the Legislature transgress the bounds of their authority, their acts are void, and neither the people nor the Judges are bound by them. So if the President should commission [an officer], after an appointment non-concurred in by the Senate, the commission would be void. And in all cases where an act is done without power, a check may be found wherever we please to look for it.

The third case which has been mentioned is, where the general power of one branch is controlled by a particular power given to another branch. To this head may be assigned another case much relied on by the gentleman from Virginia. The case I refer to is that of a treaty made by the President having war for its object. Now, as the exclusive power to declare war is vested in Congress, I have no hesitation in saying the President has not the power to make a treaty of offensive and defensive alliance. For though such a power may be embraced in the general terms giving the power to make treaties, yet as the right to declare war is distinctly given to Congress, it must operate as an exception to the general treaty-making power. *1222*

These are the cases of legitimate checks which occur to me. But as to the wild doctrine which has been contended for that, wherever one branch of the Government possesses any degree of power, a discretion necessarily accompanies the exercise of it, nothing, I conceive, can be more dangerous, or have a more direct tendency to disorganization. If the principle were asserted by each branch, the operations of the Government must cease. The President might say he was not bound blindly to execute laws which he conceived to be absurd or impolitic. We create offices, he refuses to fill them; we appropriate money, he refuses to apply it; we declare war, he refuses to carry it on, because, consulting his own judgment, he conceived our measures to be unwise and that it would be better for the country to check us by refusing the aid of his Constitutional power to carry our schemes into effect. I beg leave to put a case which comes up to the strongest point of the argument on the other side.

Suppose Congress declare war? This can be done by a majority of both Houses. The President participates [in] the power of appropriating money. Now, suppose war actually declared by a power competent and expressly allowed to judge of its expediency, and the President, afterwards conceiving the war to be unjust or the declaration premature, refuses to concur in an appropriation to support it? In such case, we should be Constitutionally at war, and Constitutionally restrained from carrying it on.

Such are the absurdities which flow from the imported doctrine of checks. Consequences which tend to paralyze the powers of the Constitution, and effectually to stop the wheels of Government.

. . .

THE PRIMACY OF LEGISLATIVE POWER

6.3   Report on Compensation of Congress: "Of all the powers with which the people have invested the Government, that of legislation is undoubtedly the chief."*

. . .

Of all the powers with which the people have invested the Government, that of legislation is undoubtedly the chief. In addition to its own important, ordinary duties, the Legislature is the only power which can create other powers. Departments, with all their duties and offices—with all their emoluments—can emanate from the Legislature alone. Over the most numerous branch of the Legislature, therefore, the people have retained the power of frequent elections; and with this branch alone they have trusted the original exercise of the right of taxation. The members of the House of Representatives are the special delegates and agents of the people in this

* From the report of a select committee created to inquire into legislation fixing the compensation of Congress, House of Representatives, December 18, 1816. *Annals*, 14th Congress, 2nd session, p. 317.

high trust. They, and they alone, proceed immediately from the suffrage of the people. They, and they alone, can touch the mainspring of the public prosperity. They are elected to be the guardians of the public rights and liberties.

Can the people, then, have any greater or clearer interest than that the seats of these their Representatives should be honorable and independent stations, in order that they may have the power of filling them with able and independent men? Is it according to the principles of our Government, that the legislative office should sink in character and importance below any office, even the highest, in the gift of the Executive? Or, can anything be more unpropitious to the success of a free representative Government than that the Representatives of the people should estimate anything higher than their own seats, or should find inducements to look to any other favor than the favor of their constituents?

It would be a most unnatural state of things, in a Republic, if the people should place greater reliance anywhere else than in their own immediate Representatives; or if, on the other hand, Representatives should revolve round any other centre than the interests of their constituents. Through their Representatives, the direct influence and control of the people can alone be felt. In them the rays of their power are collected; and there can be no better criterion by which to judge of the real influence of the people in the Government, than by the degree of respectability and importance attached to the representative character. Evil indeed to the public will that time be, should it ever arrive, when Representatives in Congress, instead of being agents of the people to exercise an influence in government, should become instruments of government to influence the people.

. . .

6.4   John C. Calhoun: "This, then, is the essence of our liberty; Congress is responsible to the people immediately, and the other branches of Government are responsible to it."*

. . .

. . . The question of adequate or inadequate pay to the members

* From a speech by the Representative from South Carolina in the House of Representatives, January 17, 1817, on a bill to alter the compensation of members of Congress. *Annals,* 14th Congress, 2nd session, pp. 575-576.

of Congress is, if he was not greatly mistaken, intimately connected with the very essence of our liberty. This House is the foundation of the fabric of our liberty. So happy is its constitution that in all instances of a general nature, its duty and its interests are inseparable. If he understood correctly the structure of our Government, the prevailing principle is not so much a balance of power as a well-connected chain of responsibility. That responsibility commenced here, and this House is the centre of its operation. The members are elected for two years only; and at the end of that period are responsible to their constituents for the faithful discharge of their public duties. Besides, the very structure of the House is admirably calculated to unite interest and duty. The members of Congress have in their individual capacity no power or prerogative. These attach to the entire body assembled here, and acting under certain forms. We then as individuals are, said Mr. C., not less amenable to the laws which we enact, than the humblest citizen. Such is the responsibility, such the structure, such the sure foundation of our liberty.

If we turn our attention to what are called the co-ordinate branches of our Government, we find them very differently constructed. The Judiciary is in no degree responsible to the people immediately. To Congress, to this body, is the whole of their responsibility. Such, too, in a great measure, is the theory of our Government as applied to the Executive branch. It is true the President is elected for a term of years, but that term is twice the length of ours; and, besides, his election is in point of fact removed in all of the States three degrees from the people; the Electors in many of the States are chosen by the State Legislatures, and where that is not formally the case yet it is in point of fact effected through the agency of those bodies.

But what mainly distinguishes the Legislative and Executive branches, as it regards their *actual* responsibility to the people, is the nature of their operation. It is the duty of the former to enact laws, of the latter to execute them. Every citizen of ordinary infor- 576 mation is capable, in a greater or less degree, to form an opinion of the propriety of the law, and consequently whether Congress has or has not done its duty; but of the execution of the laws, they are far less competent to judge. How can the community judge whether the President, in appointing officers to execute the laws, has in all cases been governed by fair and honest motives, or by favor or corruption?

How much less competent is it to judge whether the application of the public money has been made with economy and fidelity or with waste and corruption! These are facts that can be fully investigated and brought before the public by Congress, and Congress only. Hence it is that the Constitution has made the President responsible to Congress. This, then, is the essence of our liberty; Congress is responsible to the people immediately, and the other branches of Government are responsible to it. . . .

. . .

FRONTIERS OF LEGISLATIVE POWER: APPROPRIATIONS

[Note by the editors. On January 18, 1798, Representative John Nicholas of Virginia introduced in the House of Representatives a motion to specify in the appropriation bill both the particular foreign capitals to which ministers should be sent and the rank (Minister Plenitentiary or Minister Resident) of each such minister. Under previous acts of Congress, the President had determined the places to which ministers should be sent and had fixed the rank (and so determined the salary) of each minister. Mr. Nicholas said he believed our establishment abroad to be too big and that the purpose of his motion was to reduce it to what it had been in an earlier period. His motion is in *Annals*, 5th Congress, 2nd session, p. 852. The speeches that follow support and oppose Nicholas' motion.]

6.5   Albert Gallatin: "Whenever the powers vested in any one department are sufficient to complete a certain act, that department is independent of all the others."*

. . .

We say that Congress, having the sole power of granting money, are judges of the propriety or impropriety of making a grant, and

* From a speech by the Representative from Pennsylvania in the House of Representatives, March 1, 1798, supporting a motion to curtail foreign missions. *Annals*, 5th Congress, 2nd session, pp. 1120-1122.

that they have a right to exercise their discretion therein; whilst those who oppose the amendment upon Constitutional grounds contend that the power of creating the office of public Ministers, vested in the President, imposes an obligation upon Congress to provide an adequate compensation for as many as he shall think fit to appoint. We say that the power of granting money for any purposes whatever belongs solely to the Legislature, in which it is literally vested by the Constitution. They insist that that power in this instance attaches, by implication, to the President, and that Congress are bound to make provision, without having a right to exercise their own discretion.

In order to establish this doctrine, it is asserted that by our Constitution each department may have checks within itself, but has none upon the other; that each department is self-independent, has its own share of powers, and moves uncontrolled within its sphere; that, therefore, whenever a certain authority is by the Constitution vested in any one department it must possess the means to carry that authority into effect, and that the other departments are bound to lend their assistance for that purpose.

Those positions will not stand the test of investigation. Whenever the powers vested in any one department are sufficient to complete a certain act, that department is independent of all the others, and it would be an unconstitutional attempt in any of the others to try to control it. But whenever the powers have been so distributed between two departments, in relation to another certain act, that neither of the two can complete the act by virtue of its own powers, then each department is controlled by the other, not in relation to the operation of its appropriate powers but in relation to the act itself. Each department, in that case, may go as far as its own authority will permit, but no further. The refusal of the other department to exercise its powers in relation to that act, in the same direction and in concurrence with the first department, is no abridgement of the legitimate powers of the first. It is the Constitution which, in that case, abridges the powers of both, and which has rendered the concurrence of both necessary for the completion of the act. If either of the departments, in that *1121* case, after having exercised its own authority towards the completion of the act, shall pretend to have a right to force the powers of the other in the same direction so as to have the act completed against or without its voluntary consent, it is that department which abridges the legitimate exercise of the powers of the other. Thus, in the instance before us, the President may appoint as many public Ministers as he thinks fit, and if he can [induce them to go, he may] send them to their intended mission without the assistance of any act of the Legislature; if he can, as in the case of Consuls, find men who will serve without a salary, he has a right to do it, and thus to act uncontrolled by the Legislature; because, in this supposed instance, his own authority is sufficient to carry into effect his intentions. But further than that he cannot go; for the Constitution, in no part, gives him any power to force the Legislature to grant the money which may be necessary to pay the Ministers. In the same manner the Legislature have a right to appropriate a sum of money for the purpose of paying twenty public Ministers, if they shall in their judgment think so many necessary. But further than that they cannot go; they cannot force the President to appoint twenty Ministers, if he does not think them necessary. In this instance the act is placed partly under the jurisdiction of the Executive, and partly under that of the Legislature—under the jurisdiction of the Executive so far as relates to the creation of the office and to the appointment—under the jurisdiction of the Legislature so far as relates to granting the money—and the concurrence of both departments is necessary to complete the act.

The contrary doctrine leads to a palpable absurdity. For if it be true that any department, having expressed its will in relation to an act upon which it can operate but partially, binds the other departments to lend their assistance in order that its will may be completely carried into effect, it follows that whenever two departments shall differ in opinion as to a certain act we shall have two different wills acting in contrary directions and each binding the other respectively; that is to say, that there is a necessity that the act should, at the same time, be done in two different ways, or in some instances that it should, at the same time, be done and not be done. But the fact is that the true doctrine of those gentlemen, though not openly avowed on the present occasion, is not that each department may act uncontrolled in the exercise of its own appropriate powers; but that they have two standards, one of which they apply to the Executive and another by which they measure the powers of the Legislature; and that, in their opinion, the powers of the Executive are paramount and must limit and control those of the Legislature whenever they happen to move in the same sphere, whenever the execution of an act depends upon the concurrence of both.

This doctrine is as novel as it is absurd. We have always been taught to believe that, in all mixed Governments and especially in our own, the different departments mutually operated as *1122* checks one upon the other. It is a principle incident to the very nature of those Governments; it is a principle which flows from the distribution and separation of Legislative and Executive powers, by which the same act in many instances, instead of belonging exclusively to either, falls under the discretionary and partial authority of both; it is a principle of all our State constitutions; it is a principle of the Constitution under which we now act; it is a principle recognised by every author who wrote on the subject; it is a principle fully established by the theory and practice of the Government of that country from which we derive our political institutions. In Great Britain the power of declaring war is vested in the King; but the power of granting supplies, in order to support the war, is vested in Parliament. It has never been contended there that Parliament were bound by the act of the King in granting money for that purpose; it is, on the contrary, fully understood that a concurrence of opinion is necessary before a war can be carried into effect; that the two departments, in that respect, control and check each other and that war is never declared by the King, unless he can depend on the support of Parliament.

When it is found that the Constitution has distributed the powers in a manner different from that contended for, although there is no clause which directs that Congress shall be bound to appropriate money in order to carry into effect any of the Executive powers, some gentlemen, recurring to metaphysical subtleties and abandoning the literal and plain sense of the Constitution, say that, although we have a Constitutional power, we have not a moral right to act according to our own discretion but are under a moral obligation in this instance to grant the money. It is evident that where the Constitution has lodged the power, there exists the right of acting and the right of discretion. Congress is, upon all occasions, under a moral obligation to act according to justice and propriety.

. . .

6.6 Robert Goodloe Harper: "These two powers—the power of appointment by the President and the Senate, and the power of appropriation in the House—must be made to act as mutual helps, not as mutual obstructions."*

. . .

I shall, Mr. Chairman, . . . consider this amendment as having for its object, and its sole object, too, the establishment of this principle: "that the House of Representatives, by its power over appropriations, has a right to control and direct the Executive in the appointment of foreign Ministers." I shall treat the question which arises upon this amendment as a question of power between this House and the President and Senate, and I shall endeavor to show that the amendment, if carried, would be a direct breach of the Constitution, an alarming usurpation by this branch on the Constitutional powers of the Executive Department.

The supporters of this amendment, avowing its object to be the establishment of a control over the appointment of foreign Ministers, contend that this House have a right to exercise that control, and rely on that part of the Constitution which provides that "no money shall be issued from the Treasury without an appropriation by law." As this House, say gentlemen, must concur in passing all laws, it follows that it may refuse its assent to appropriations. In judging whether it will *1166* give or refuse this assent, it must be guided solely by its own discretion, by its own opinion about the necessity or utility of the object for which an appropriation is wanted. If it should think this object unnecessary, or hurtful, it is bound in duty to withhold the appropriation. Consequently, it may refuse to appropriate for a Minister to Lisbon, Berlin, or any other place, if it should think such Minister, though appointed by the President and Senate, unnecessary or injurious. This I take to be a fair state of the argument.

But gentlemen, while they lay such stress upon this part of the

* From a speech in the House of Representatives by the Representative from South Carolina, opposing the motion which Representative Gallatin supported in the preceding selection, March 2, 1798. *Annals*, 5th Congress, 2nd session, pp. 1165-1169.

Constitution, seem entirely to forget another part—that part which provides that "The President, by and with the advice and consent of the Senate, shall appoint foreign Ministers and Consuls." It will, however, be admitted that these two parts of the Constitution are equally authoritative, and must both have effect; that the whole instrument, like all other instruments, must be taken together, and so construed that none of its provisions may be defeated or rendered nugatory. These two powers, therefore—the power of appointment by the President and the Senate, and the power of appropriation in the House—must be reconciled with each other; must be made to act as mutual helps, not as mutual obstructions. How is this to be done? Certainly not by admitting the doctrine of this amendment, which would utterly destroy one of the powers—would give the House an absolute control over the appointment of Ministers, and reduce the President and Senate to the mere power of making a nomination, which the House might refuse or agree to, according to its good pleasure. This is the plain and necessary consequence of admitting the principle, contended for in support of this amendment, that the House, when called on to appropriate for an officer, legally appointed, may, in the first place, inquire whether the appointment is necessary.

Some other way of reconciling these powers must, therefore, be found out; and which is it? We contend, Mr. Chairman, that it is thus: An office must first be authorized by law; for nobody pretends that the President and Senate can create offices. When the office is thus authorized, the President and Senate exercise their power of appointment, and fill the office. The House of Representatives then exercises its Constitutional power over appropriations, by providing an adequate compensation for the officer. In the exercise of this power, they cannot inquire whether the office was necessary or not; for that has already been determined by the law which authorized it. Neither can they inquire whether the office was properly filled; for that would be to invade the powers of the President and Senate, to whom, by the Constitution, the right of choosing the officer is exclusively referred.

What, then, is their power, and into what may they inquire? They may inquire what is a proper and adequate compensation for such an officer. They may fix the amount of his salary; and, in fixing it, they must be guided by a proper discretion, by a sense of duty, by the nature of the office, the circumstances of the country, and the public service. *1167* Thus the Constitution would be reconciled, and each department would act within its proper sphere. The President and Senate could make no appointment till the office should be authorized by law, consequently there would be no danger of abuse. When they had made the appointment, they could not fix the amount of salary, or order the money to be paid out of the Treasury —another guard against the danger of abuse. When the appointment should be duly made, the House, on the other hand, would be bound to provide an adequate salary, and could not, by refusing it, defeat the law and the appointment, because they might think the one unnecessary, or the other unwise, and this principle would be a guard against any abuse of the powers of the House, would prevent it from invading the province of the other departments, and subverting the principles of the Constitution.

. . .

But, say gentlemen, is the House always bound to appropriate? If the President should appoint an hundred Ministers Plenipotentiary, must the House, without inquiry, give money to support them all? What guard would there then be, they exclaim, against an enormous and abusive extension of the diplomatic establishment?

To this I answer, Mr. Chairman, in the first place, that we have a security in the responsibility of the President. He is elected by the people, and elected every four years. All these appointments, though sanctioned by the Senate, must originate with him, and therefore he is particularly, and almost solely, responsible. His character is at stake. He is a single actor in a most conspicuous theatre, and all eyes are upon him. He is watched with all the jealousy which, in this country particularly, is entertained of Executive power. He is watched by the gentlemen themselves who support this amendment, and who are sufficiently prone to find fault with him and abuse him, even when he acts properly. This he well knows, and consequently [he] will take care to do nothing which may strengthen their hands by giving them ground for censure. Should he act improperly, make foolish or unnecessary appointments, he must disgust his friends and supporters, forfeit the public esteem, and lose his election. He may be even turned out by impeachment before the time for a new election arrives. These, I apprehend, are sufficient securities against wanton misconduct.

I answer, in the next place, that if the President *1168* should think fit to abuse his powers, it is his own concern, and no business of this House, unless indeed we choose to impeach him. We are sent here by the people to exercise our own powers and not to watch over the President, who equally with us derives his powers from the people and is amenable to them and not to this House for the exercise of those powers. We may, indeed, as individuals, censure his conduct, as we may that of any member on this floor, and endeavor to prevent the people from re-electing him; but, as a body, we have nothing to do with him or his conduct but impeach him. If he proposes measures to us which we do not approve, we may reject them in the same manner as he may reject bills which we send up to him; but we have no more right to prevent him, either directly or indirectly, from making such appointments as he pleases than he has to prevent us from passing such votes or resolutions as we please. The interference in one case is equally unconstitutional with the other. It has, indeed, become fashionable with some gentlemen on this floor, to consider this House as "the people," and to speak and act as if the people had delegated to us their general superintending power over the other departments; but this doctrine is unknown to the Constitution, to the utter subversion of which it directly leads. It directly leads to that concentration of powers in one popular body, which it was the main object of the Constitution to prevent, and which it was and is the main object of those gentlemen to introduce; that concentration whereto this amendment is considered and intended, by its supporters, as an introductory step.

I answer, in the last place, Mr. Chairman, that if the President should appoint an hundred Ministers Plenipotentiary, or commit any other such wanton and foolish abuse of his power, it would be an extreme case which would speak for itself and dictate the line of conduct which this House and the country ought to pursue. But we never can legislate on extreme cases. They must be left to suggest and provide their own remedies when they occur. Suppose two-thirds of both Houses, under the influence of some unaccountable madness, should pass a law, in spite of the President, for building fifty ships of the line, to be given to France in order to augment her Navy, or for any other violent purpose. How ought the President and the country to Act? I do not know; these would be extreme cases, and they would carry their own remedies with them. We may as well suppose extreme cases of one kind as of another, and however our own self-love may induce us to think that there is less danger from us than from the President and Senate, and that power, however dangerous in their hands, is perfectly safe as soon as it comes into ours, the Constitution and the framers of it judged otherwise, and they judged rightly. It is infinitely more dangerous in our hands when uncontrolled, because we have less personal responsibility and are far more liable to the influence of passion. When, therefore, these extreme cases occur, we will act accordingly, and 1169 should they obviously require the breach of a law, the necessity will be universally felt and acknowledged and we must break it. All that I contend for is, that the present is not an extreme case, and that these appointments being authorized by law, a law must be broken before we can defeat the appointments, according to the avowed object of this amendment. . . .

. . .

FRONTIERS OF LEGISLATIVE POWER: TREATIES

6.7 Robert Goodloe Harper: "Treaties may bind the nation, may lay the Legislature under the obligations of good faith; but they cannot encroach on the Legislative power, cannot produce a Legislative effect."*

[Note by the editors. The treaty which John Jay, representing the United States, negotiated with Great Britain in 1794 excited bitter controversy within the United States. On June 25, 1795, the Senate declared its consent and advised the President to ratify the treaty, on the condition that the operation of one of the provisions which had excited greatest opposition be suspended. In the next session of Congress, Representative Edward Livingston of New York, anticipating the introduction of measures to fulfill obligations under the treaty, moved the following resolution in the House of Representatives:

From a speech in the House of Representatives by the Representative from South Carolina on the Jay Treaty, March 24, 1796. *Annals,* 4th Congress, 1st session, pp. 748-750, 758-759.

Resolved, That the President of the United States be requested to lay before this House a copy of the instructions given to the Minister of the United States who negotiated the treaty with Great Britain communicated by his Message on the first instant, together with the correspondence and other documents relative to the said Treaty. (*Annals*, 4th Congress, 1st session, pp. 400-401, March 2, 1796.)

Livingston's motion was opposed on the ground that the House of Representatives, having only "legislative" power, had no right to intervene in the treaty-making process, even to the limited extent of calling for information about the negotiation of a particular treaty. This precipitated one of the greatest debates in the first decades of Congress, a main point of concern being, Where are the boundaries between legislative power and the treaty-making power? Representative Harper's examination of this question is the most searching presented in this debate.]

. . .

In order to discover how far these powers [the Legislative and the Treaty-making] could restrict each other, it was necessary to inquire how far they might interfere; and that inquiry would lead us to consider the nature of Treaties and the nature of laws, the origin from which each is derived, the objects on which they act, the manner of their operation, the purposes for which they are intended, and the effects which they are able to produce. If it should appear that in all these respects they were different, that they could neither produce the same effects, operate in the same manner, nor effect the same objects, it would follow that they moved in different spheres in which each operated uncontrollably and supreme, could neither encroach on, interfere with, or restrict each other.

Treaties, he observed, then, derived their origin and their existence from the consent of equals; laws from the authority of a superior. The former were compacts, the latter commands. Treaties derived their sanction from good faith, from national honor, from the interest of the parties to observe them; laws derive their sanction from the authority of the community, which enforces 749 their observance and punishes disobedience. A Treaty stipulates that a thing shall be done; a law commands it. A Treaty of consequence may stipulate that a law shall be passed, but it cannot pass a law; that belongs to the Legislative power.

A Treaty may agree that a tax shall be laid, or a crime shall be punished; but it cannot lay the tax or inflict the punishment—that must be done by a law, and is the exclusive province of the Legislative power. Suppose a Treaty should stipulate that ten per cent. additional duty should be laid on goods imported in Swedish vessels: will any one say that the revenue officers could go on and collect the duty without a law? Surely not. The faith of the nation is bound, and the Legislature is under all that obligation to pass the law which results from considerations of good faith, from the necessity of observing Treaties; but still the effect cannot be produced, the duty cannot be collected, till a law is passed. So, if a Treaty should stipulate that certain acts should be punished with fine, imprisonment, or death, could indictments be founded on the Treaty, and the punishment be inflicted without a law? Certainly not. Treaties, therefore, can never, in their nature, operate as laws, can never produce the effect of legislation. They are compacts and nothing more, and, in the sphere of compacts, they are supreme and unlimited. They may bind the nation, may lay the Legislature under the obligations of good faith; but they cannot encroach on the Legislative power, cannot produce a Legislative effect.

. . .

Thus, he said, it appeared that the Treaty-making and Legislative powers being each supreme in their respective orbits, could not interfere with or restrict each other. Both compacts and laws are *750* necessary to be made; both are essential to the attainment of those advantages which result from civilized society; and the power of making each must exist in every Government. In ours these powers are placed in different departments, which must sometimes co-operate in order to produce the desired effects, but neither could execute the business of the other. The Legislature could not make a compact, nor could the Treaty-making power make a law. It may stipulate, and very often must stipulate, that a thing requiring a law shall be done, but this does not render the law less necessary, and can be no more considered as an invasion of the Legislative power, than a law directing a compact to be made with a foreign nation as an invasion of the Treaty-making power. The law could not produce the effect of a Treaty, nor render the agency of the Treaty-making power less necessary. . . .

He therefore contended that the Treaty-making power was free and unrestricted in the President and Senate; so that a Treaty, when ratified by them as the Constitution requires, became complete in its own nature, perfect as a Treaty, without the concurrence of the House of Representatives; bound the faith of the nation as completely as a Treaty can bind it, and that the House of Representatives had nothing to do with it, but to consider whether and how far they could carry it into effect. In this, and this alone, their agency was necessary; and here, from the nature of the thing, they had a free agency.
. . . 758

The result, he said, of the ideas which he had submitted to the Committee [of the Whole] if they were just, was that the Treaty-making and Legislative powers were entirely distinct and independent. That they moved in different orbits, where each was supreme and uncontrolled, except by its own nature and the Constitution. That the President and Senate under the Treaty-making power could make all sorts of compacts. That Congress, under the Legislative power, could make all laws. That these compacts, however, could never operate as laws, could never produce a Legislative effect, any more than a law could produce the effect of a Treaty. That the Treaty-making power therefore never could invade the Legislative, never could interfere with or be restricted by it. That Treaties when made and complete, as such, were no more than Executory compacts, depending for their execution upon the aid of the Legislature, in giving which aid it must from the nature of things be a free agent. Herein, he said consisted the real security against the abuse of the Treaty-making power; that it could never act without Legislative aid. While that House hold the purse-strings of the people, while no Treaty could produce its effects without a law and the concurrence of that House was necessary in passing the law, there could be no real danger. Great, indeed, was the responsibility which those must take on themselves who should refuse in that House to execute a Treaty. Weighty, indeed, must be the reasons which could induce the House to risk all the consequences which must be expected to result from such a refusal. Few, he believed, would be found hardy enough 759 to risk them in ordinary cases. In some cases they must be risked, and to decide what those cases are, is an object of the soundest discretion. . . .

chapter 7

The President and the
executive branch

THE EXECUTIVE POWER AND PRESIDENTIAL
RESPONSIBILITY

7.1 Debate on the Removal Power:* "I conceive that if any power whatsoever is in its nature Executive, it is the power of appointing, overseeing, and controlling those who execute the laws."

[Note by the editors. Within a month after a number of its members sufficient to form a quorum appeared in the first session of Congress, the House of Representatives took up the task of establishing the administrative departments thought to be needed. The Constitution made provision for the appointment of heads of departments, but was silent as to method of removal. The two ques-

---

* Representatives James Madison and Alexander White of Virginia, Fisher Ames of Massachusetts, and James Jackson of Georgia. Debate in the House of Representatives on a bill to create a Department of Foreign Affairs. Madison's first speech and Ames, June 16, 1789; Jackson and Madison's second speech June 17, 1789; White, June 18, 1789. *Annals*, 1st Congress, 1st session, pp. 462-463 (Madison's first speech); pp. 474-476 (Ames); pp. 486-488 (Jackson); pp. 497-500 (Madison's second speech); pp. 513-514 (White).

tions—whether Congress had authority to specify a method for removal in the law creating a department, and if it did, what that
method ought to be—excited an unusually interesting debate. Some
of the remarks on the first of these questions appear in this book as
selection 3.1. Argument on the second question, we shall now see,
brought forth conflicting views on still broader questions about the
nature of the executive power and the place of the President in our
political system.]

Mr. Madison: It is evidently the intention of the Constitution that
the first Magistrate should be responsible for the Executive department. So far therefore as we do not make the officers who are to aid
him in the duties of that department responsible to him, he is not
responsible to his country. Again, is there no danger that an officer,
when he is appointed by the concurrence of the Senate and has
friends in that body, may choose rather to risk his establishment on
the favor of that branch than rest it upon the discharge of his duties
to the satisfaction of the Executive branch, which is constitutionally
authorized to inspect and control his conduct? And if it should happen that the officers connect themselves with the Senate, they may
mutually support each other, and for want of efficacy reduce the
power of the President to a mere vapor; in which case his responsibility would be annihilated, and the expectation of it unjust. The high
Executive officers, joined in cabal with the Senate, would lay the
foundation of discord and end in an assumption of the Executive
power, only to be removed by a revolution in the Government. I believe no principle is more clearly laid down in the Constitution than
that of responsibility.
. . . *463*

I conceive that if any power whatsoever is in its nature Executive, it is the power of appointing, overseeing, and controlling those
who execute the laws. If the Constitution had not qualified the
power of the President in appointing to office by associating the
Senate with him in that business, would it not be clear that he would
have the right, by virtue of his Executive power, to make such appointment? Should we be authorized, in defiance of that clause in the
Constitution—"The Executive power shall be vested in a President"
—to unite the Senate with the President in the appointment to office?
I conceive not. If it is admitted that we should not be authorized to
do this, I think it may be disputed whether we have a right to asso-

ciate them in removing persons from office, the one power being as much of an Executive nature as the other; and the first only is authorized by being excepted out of the general rule established by the Constitution in these words: "the Executive power shall be vested in the President."

. . .

Mr. Ames: The executive powers are delegated to the President with a view to have a responsible officer to superintend, control, inspect, and check the officers necessarily employed in administering the laws. The only bond between him and those he employs is the confidence he has in their integrity and talents. When that confidence ceases, the principal ought to have power to remove those whom he can no longer trust with safety. If an officer shall be guilty of neglect or infidelity, there can be no doubt but he ought to be removed. Yet there may be numerous causes for removal which do not amount to a crime. He may propose to do a mischief; but I believe the mere intention would not be cause of impeachment. He may lose the confidence of the people upon suspicion, in which case it would be improper to retain him in service. He ought to be removed at any time when, instead of doing the greatest possible good, he is likely to do an injury to the public interest by being continued in the administration.

I presume gentlemen will generally admit that officers ought to be removed when they become obnoxious; but the question is, how shall this power be exercised? It will not, I apprehend, be contended that all officers hold their offices during good behavior. If this be the case, it is a most singular Government. I believe there is not another 475 in the universe that bears the least semblance to it in this particular; such a principle, I take it, is contrary to the nature of things.

But the manner how to remove is the question. If the officer misbehaves, he can be removed by impeachment; but in this case is impeachment the only mode of removal? It would be found very inconvenient to have a man continued in office after being impeached, and when all confidence in him was suspended or lost. Would not the end of impeachment be defeated by this means? If Mr. Hastings, who was mentioned by the gentleman from Delaware (Mr. Vining) preserved his command in India, could he not defeat

the impeachment now pending in Great Britain? If that doctrine obtains in America, we shall find impeachments come too late; while
we are preparing the process, the mischief will be perpetrated and
the offender will escape.

I apprehend it will be as frequently necessary to prevent crimes
as to punish them; and it may often happen that the only prevention
is by removal. The superintending power possessed by the President
will perhaps enable him to discover a base intention before it is ripe
for execution. It may happen that the Treasurer may be disposed to
betray the public chest to the enemy, and so injure the Government
beyond the possibility of reparation, should the President be restrained from removing so dangerous an officer until the slow formal-
ity of an impeachment was complied with, when the nature of the
case rendered the application of a sudden and decisive remedy indispensable.

. . . 476

If this is to be considered as a question undecided by the constitution and submitted on the footing of expediency, it will be well
to consider where the power can be most usefully deposited for the
security and benefit of the people. . . . It will be found that the nature of the business requires it to be conducted by the head of the
Executive. And I believe it will be found even there that more injury will arise from not removing improper officers than from displacing good ones. I believe experience has convinced us that it is
an irksome business; and officers are more frequently continued in
place after they become unfit to perform their duties than turned out
while their talents and integrity are useful. But advantages may result from keeping the power of removal *in terrorem* over the heads
of the officers. They will be stimulated to do their duty to the satisfaction of the principal who is to be responsible for the whole executive department.

. . .

Mr. Jackson: . . . I am, sir, a friend to the full exercise of all the
powers of Government, and deeply impressed with the necessity
there exists of having an energetic Executive. But, friend as I am to
an efficient Government, I value the liberties of my fellow-citizens
beyond every other consideration; and where I find them endangered, I am willing to forego every other blessing to secure them. I

hold it as good a maxim as it is an old one, of two evils to choose the least.

  . . . *487*

It has been observed, that the President ought to have this power to remove a man when he becomes obnoxious to the people or disagreeable to himself. Are we then, to have all the officers the mere creatures of the President? This thirst of power will introduce a treasury bench into the House, and we shall have ministers obtrude upon us to govern and direct the measures of the Legislature, and to support the influence of their master. And shall we establish a different influence between the people and the President? I suppose these circumstances must take place, because they have taken place in other countries. The executive power falls to the ground in England if it cannot be supported by the Parliament; therefore a high game of corruption is played and a majority secured to the ministry by the introduction of placemen and pensioners.

  . . . *488*

But let me ask gentlemen if it is possible to place their officers in such a situation as to deprive them of their independency and firmness; for I apprehend it is not intended to stop with the Secretary of Foreign Affairs. Let it be remembered that the Constitution gives the President the command of the military. If you give him complete power over the man with the strong box, he will have the liberties of America under his thumb. It is easy to see the evil which may result. If he wants to establish an arbitrary authority and finds the Secretary of Finance not inclined to second his endeavors, he has nothing more to do than to remove him and get one appointed of principles more congenial with his own. Then, says he, I have got the army; let me have but the money and I will establish my throne upon the ruins of your visionary republic. Let no gentleman say I am contemplating imaginary dangers, the mere chimeras of a heated brain. Behold the baleful influence of the royal prerogative when officers hold their commissions during the pleasure of the crown!

. . .

Mr. Madison: . . . Every thing relative to the merits of the question, as distinguished from a constitutional question, seems to turn on the danger of such a power vested in the President alone. But when I consider the checks under which he lies in the exercise of this power, I own to you I feel no apprehensions but what arise from the dangers incidental to the power itself; for dangers will be incidental to it, vest it where you please. I will not reiterate what was said before with respect to the mode of election and the extreme improbability that any citizen will be selected from the mass of citizens who is not highly distinguished by his abilities and worth; in this alone we have no small security for the faithful exercise of this power. But, throwing that out of the question, let us consider the restraints he will feel after he is placed in that elevated station.

It is to be remarked that the power in this case will not consist so much in continuing a bad man in office as in the danger of displacing a good one. Perhaps the great danger, as has been observed, of abuse in the executive power lies in the improper continuance of bad men in office. But the power we 498 contend for will not enable him to do this; for if an unworthy man be continued in office by an unworthy President, the House of Representatives can at any time impeach him and the Senate can remove him, whether the President chooses or not. The danger then consists merely in this: the President can displace from office a man whose merits require that he should be continued in it.

What will be the motives which the President can feel for such abuse of his power, and the restraints that operate to prevent it? In the first place, he will be impeachable by this House, before the Senate for such an act of mal-administration; for I contend that the wanton removal of meritorious officers would subject him to impeachment and removal from his own high trust. But what can be his motives for displacing a worthy man? It must be that he may fill the place with an unworthy creature of his own. Can he accomplish this end? No; he can place no man in the vacancy whom the Senate shall not approve; and if he could fill the vacancy with the man he might choose, I am sure he would have little inducement to make an improper removal. Let us consider the consequences. The injured man will be supported by the popular opinion; the community will take side with him against the President; it will facilitate those combinations and give success to those exertions which will be pursued to prevent his re-election. To displace a man of high merit, and who from his station may be supposed a man of extensive influence, are considerations which will excite serious reflections beforehand in the mind of any man who may fill the Presidential chair. The friends of those individuals and the public sympathy will be against him. If this should not produce his impeachment before the Senate, it will amount to an impeachment before the community, who will have the power of punishment, by refusing to re-elect him.

But suppose this persecuted individual cannot obtain revenge in this mode; there are other modes in which he could make the situation of the President very inconvenient, if you suppose him resolutely bent on executing the dictates of resentment. If he had not influence enough to direct the vengeance of the whole community, he may probably be able to obtain an appointment in one or the other branch of the Legislature; and being a man of weight, talents, and influence, in either case he may prove to the President troublesome indeed. We have seen examples in the history of other nations which justifies the remark I now have made. Though the prerogatives of the British King are great as his rank, and it is unquestionably known that he has a positive influence over both branches of the legislative body, yet there have been examples in which the appointment and removal of ministers have been found to be dictated by one or other of those branches. Now if this be the case with an hereditary Monarch, possessed of those high prerogatives and furnished with so many means of influence, can we suppose a President, elected for four years only, dependent upon the popular voice, impeachable by the Legislature, little if at all distinguished for wealth, personal talents, or influence from 499 the head of the department himself—I say, will he bid defiance to all these considerations, and wantonly dismiss a meritorious and virtuous officer? Such abuse of power exceeds my conception. If anything takes place in the ordinary course of business of this kind, my imagination cannot extend to it on any rational principle.

But let us not consider the question on one side only; there are dangers to be contemplated on the other. Vest this power in the Senate jointly with the President and you abolish at once that great principle of unity and responsibility in the executive department which was intended for the security of liberty and the public good. If the President should possess alone the power of removal from office, those who are employed in the execution of the law will be in their proper situation and the chain of dependence be preserved. The lowest officers, the middle grade, and the highest will depend, as they ought, on the President, and the President on the community.

The chain of dependence therefore terminates in the supreme body, namely, in the people, who will possess besides, in aid of their original power, the decisive engine of impeachment.

Take the other supposition: that the power should be vested in the Senate on the principle that the power to displace is necessarily connected with the power to appoint. It is declared by the Constitution that we may by law vest the appointment of inferior officers in the heads of departments, the power of removal being incidental, as stated by some gentlemen. Where does this terminate? If you begin with the subordinate officers, they are dependent on their superior, he on the next superior, and he on—whom? On the Senate, a permanent body, a body by its particular mode of election in reality existing forever; a body possessing that proportion of aristocratic power which the Constitution no doubt thought wise to be established in the system, but which some have strongly excepted against. And let me ask gentlemen, is there equal security in this case as in the other? Shall we trust the Senate, responsible to individual Legislatures, rather than the person who is responsible to the whole community? It is true, the Senate do not hold their offices for life, like aristocracies recorded in the historic page. Yet the fact is, they will not possess that responsibility for the exercise of Executive powers which would render it safe for us to vest such powers in them.

But what an aspect will this give to the Executive? Instead of keeping the departments of Government distinct, you make an Executive out of one branch of the Legislature; you make the Executive a two-headed monster. To use the expression of the gentleman from New Hampshire (Mr. Livermore) you destroy the great principle of responsibility and perhaps have the creature divided in its will, defeating the very purposes for which a unity in the Executive was instituted.

These objections do not lie against such an arrangement as the bill establishes. I conceive that the President is sufficiently accountable to the community; and if this power is vested in him, it will be vested where its nature requires it should 500 be vested. If anything in its nature is executive, it must be that power which is employed in superintending and seeing that the laws are faithfully executed. The laws cannot be executed but by officers appointed for that purpose; therefore, those who are over such officers naturally possess the executive power. If any other doctrine be admitted, what is the consequence? You may set the Senate at the head of the executive department, or you may require that the officers hold their places during the pleasure of this branch of the Legislature, if you cannot go so far as to say we shall appoint them. And by this means, you link together two branches of the Government which the preservation of liberty requires to be constantly separated.

. . .

Mr. White: . . . It is not contended that the power which this bill proposes to vest is given to the President in express terms by the constitution, or that it can be inferred from any particular clause in that instrument. It is sought for from another source, the general nature of executive power. It is on this principle the clause is advocated, or I mistake the arguments urged by my colleague (Mr. Madison). It was said by that gentleman that the constitution having invested the President with a general executive power, thereby all those powers were vested which were not expressly excepted; and therefore he possessed the power of removal. This is a doctrine not to be learned in American Governments; is no part of the constitution of the Union. Each State has an Executive Magistrate; but look at his powers and I believe it will not be found that he has in any one, of necessity, the right of appointing or removing officers. In Virginia, I know all the great officers are appointed by the General Assembly. Few, if any, of a subordinate nature are appointed by the Governor without some 514 modification. The case is generally the same in the other States. If the doctrine of the gentleman is to be supported by examples, it must be by those brought from beyond the Atlantic. We must also look there for rules to circumscribe the latitude of this principle, if indeed it can be limited.

Upon the principle by which the executive powers are expounded must the legislative be determined. Hence we are to infer that Congress have all legislative powers not expressly excepted in the constitution. If this is the case and the President is invested with all executive powers not excepted, I do not know that there can be a more arbitrary Government. The President will have the powers of the most absolute Monarch and the Legislature all the powers of the most sovereign Legislature, except in those particular instances in which the constitution has defined their limits. This I take to be a clear and necessary deduction from the principle on which the clause in the bill is founded.

I will mention the exceptions, and then let gentlemen form their opinion of the Government, if it is thus constituted. The President is limited in the appointment of ambassadors, consuls, judges, and all other officers, and in making treaties, but no further. Take from him these and give him all other powers exercised by Monarchs, and see what they will be. There are also exceptions to the legislative power, such as: they shall not for a certain period prohibit the importation of slaves; that direct taxes shall be apportioned in a particular manner; that duties, imposts, and excises shall be uniform; that they shall grant no titles of nobility, no bill of attainder; no *ex post facto* law shall be passed; no preference in commerce to be given; no money to be drawn but by law. These are the exceptions to the legislative powers. Now give them all the powers which the Parliament of Great Britain have, and what kind of Government is yours? I cannot describe it. It appears to me as absolute and extensive as any despotism. Then we must adhere to the limits described in the constitution. If we advance one step beyond its boundaries, where are we to draw the line to circumscribe our powers or secure the liberties of our fellow-citizens?

. . .

EXECUTIVE LEADERSHIP, INFLUENCE, AND DOMINATION

7.2 Abraham Baldwin and Fisher Ames: "The reasonings of the Secretary, which accompany his reports, are alleged to excite an influence which cannot be resisted."*

Mr. Fitzsimmons offered a resolution to the following purport:

Resolved, As the opinion of this Committee, that measures for the reduction of so much of the public debt as the United States have a right to redeem, ought to be adopted; and that the Secretary of the Treasury be directed to report a plan for the purpose.

* Representatives Thomas Fitzsimons of Pennsylvania, Abraham Baldwin of Georgia, and Fisher Ames of Massachusetts. From debate in the House of Representatives on the resolution of Fitzsimons which is quoted. Fitzsimons, November 19, 1792; Baldwin and Ames, November 20, 1792. *Annals*, 2nd Congress, 2nd session, p. 696 (Fitzsimons); pp. 703-705 (Baldwin); pp. 715-716, 718, 721 (Ames).

Mr. Baldwin: It has been made the duty of the Executive Departments to give information to the Legislature, but this information should relate merely . . . to statements of fact and details of business; but the laws should be framed by the Legislature after they have acquired this information.

. . . *704*

There is a material distinction between receiving information on which to ground a law, and a plan of the law ready formed. The latter mode he was opposed to. Gentlemen have said that we may reject what is proposed. But in this case we will only be exercising a sort of revisionary power, very different from a Legislative one; a very material difference from what is contemplated in the Constitution—the difference between originating and possessing only the right of a negative.

. . .

The objections which he at first entertained to this method of calling for matured plans from the Heads of Departments were growing every day stronger in his mind. The propriety of keeping the Legislative, Judicial, and Executive powers distinct from each other is founded in good sense. It is dangerous to intrust those who have a prospect of deriving some advantage in the execution of a law, to have any hand in framing it. And it is as improper for the Legislative to attend to the execution of a law, as it is for the Executive to meddle in the business of legislation. The principle, if once admitted, may be carried to such lengths as to admit the Judiciary to sit in the House of Representatives; and we shall have them here in their long robes introducing plans of laws, with the Secretaries of the Treasury and War Departments. The strong sense he had of the necessity of keeping the Departments distinct had such force upon his mind as to occasion his opposition even to the introduction of the two Secretaries, the other day, to answer interrogatories in the House. Such a precedent, he feared, might prove a dangerous one, and lean to an interference *705* in more important points. He confessed, however, that in some instances the different Departments of Government must necessarily in some degree be blended; but he insisted that they should be kept separate as much as possible.

Some gentlemen have gone so far as to intimate that the barrier between them is chiefly theoretical, that it is only a paper barrier. To be sure, said he, the barrier laid down in the Constitution for the

separation of the Departments is not a fence to keep out wild beasts
nor a ditch against a savage enemy nor even like the wall of China,
to keep out the Tartars; yet it is not so theoretical as not to be explicitly understood, and we ought to make it as strong and impregnable as if it were a mound.

. . .

Mr. Ames: The great end we have in view is the paying off the public debt. This object, truly important in itself, unites the best sense
and strongest wishes of the country. It is our duty to provide means
for the accomplishment of this end. All agree that a plan is necessary. It must be framed with wisdom and digested with care, so as to
operate with the greatest effect till the whole debt shall be extin-
guished. The true question is, Which is the best mode of framing
this system? . . . *716*

Neither this House nor a select committee are pretended to be
already possessed of the knowledge which is requisite to the framing
a system for a Sinking Fund. The very materials from which this
knowledge is to be gleaned are not in the possession of this House—
they are in the Treasury Department. Without wasting time to prove
this point, common sense will decide instantly that the knowledge of
our financial affairs and of the means of improving them is to be obtained the most accurately from the officer whose duty it is made, by
our own law, to understand them, who is appointed and commissioned for that very purpose, and to whom every day's practice in
his office must afford some additional information of official details
as well as of the operation of the laws. The arguments on both sides
end in the same point, that the information of the Secretary would
be useful. Our object being to prefer that mode of preparing a plan
which is adapted to present us the best, the argument might end
here if it were not that the Constitution is alleged to forbid our resorting to the Secretary.

. . . *718*

It is said, that the Legislative and Executive branches of Government are to be kept distinct, and this reference will produce an
improper blending of them. It is a truth that these Departments are
to be kept distinct; but the conclusion drawn from it is altogether
vague. . . . The President proposes measures to the Legislature in
conformity to the Constitution, yet no one ever supposed that his
doing so is a departure from a just theory. Nor has it, as far as I

know, been ever insinuated till of late, in this or any other country, that the calling for information from officers, any more than the calling for testimony from witnesses, amounts to a transfer of our Legislative duty.

. . . *721*

There is another ground of objection which is urged against the reference. It is said, it gives undue influence to the Treasury. The reasonings of the Secretary, which accompany his reports, are alleged to excite an influence which cannot be resisted. There are two sorts of influence: one, which arises from weight of reason and the intrinsic merit of a proposition; the other, personal influence. As to the former, it is hard to conceive of the influence of reasoning which cannot be analyzed and made capable of exact estimation by the reasoning faculties of those to whom it is submitted; and that estimation, be it what it may, ought to obtain. No one can wish to see it underrated.

. . .

If it be personal influence, independently of reason and evidence, which is apprehended by gentlemen opposed to the reference, for whom do they apprehend it? For themselves, or for us who advocate the motion? Surely, if they do not feel [the pressure of influence] we do not fear it; for we know how to respect their independence of spirit. They would disdain an imputation of the sort [against us]. Their candor will permit us to say [that] if it be a neighborly concern they feel for us, there is no occasion for it.

. . .

7.3 Report on Compensation of Congress: "What is the value to the people of the right of representation, if they have nothing to give which their Representatives will not relinquish for even the smallest appointments of the Executive power?"*

. . .

It is probably the necessary tendency of Government, that patronage and influence should accumulate wherever the Executive

---

* From the report (quoted partially in selection 6.3 above) of a select committee created to inquire into legislation fixing the compensation of Congress, House of Representatives, December 18, 1816. *Annals*, 14th Congress, 2nd session, pp. 317-318.

power is deposited; and this accumulation may be expected to increase with the progress of the Government and the increasing wealth of the nation. To guard as far as possible against the effect of this on the Legislature, the Constitution has prohibited members of Congress from holding, while members, any office under Executive appointment; but it has not restrained them from resigning their seats to accept such appointments, nor from accepting them after their term of service has expired; nor has it prohibited the grant of such offices to their relations, connexions, or dependents. There are hundreds of offices in the gift of the Executive, which, as far as pecuniary emolument is concerned, are preferable to seats in Congress; indeed there are none, except of the very lowest class, which in that respect are not preferable.

Is it for the interest of the people that their Representatives should be placed in this condition? Is it *318* expedient that better service should be commanded for any other department than for the hall of legislation? Or, admitting that offices of high trust and responsibility in the State—such as will be commonly regarded less from motives of pecuniary emolument than from the love of honorable distinction and devotion to the public service—should possess more attractions than the legislative office, is it still fit or expedient that subordinate places in Government such as have no recommendation but the salaries and perquisites belonging to them should have the same influence?

And yet, not only is it well known that persons at every election decline being candidates for the Legislature, but the Government has not been without instances in which members of either House have relinquished their seats in the Congress of the United States to accept offices of a very low grade. Can the public interest require the establishment of a habit of filling such places by candidates taken from the legislative body? Or what is the value to the people of the right of representation, if they have nothing to give which their Representatives will not relinquish for even the smallest appointments of the Executive power? It cannot but tend more, one would think, to the permanent safety of the Republic, that no such hopes or motives should exist; that there should be no inducements of this nature, either to an unfaithful and compliant discharge of official duty, or to a more indirect but not less pernicious exercise of the influence of a public character and a public station.

. . .

7.4 Josiah Quincy: "The spirit of independence is gone whenever the action of the Legislature is identified with the will of the Executive by the potent influence of the office-hoping and the office-holding charm."*

. . .

If there be a principle universally allowed by men of all parties to be the basis of liberty . . . it is that the three great departments of power, the Legislative, Executive and Judicial, ought to be separate and distinct. The consolidation of these three powers into one has been denominated "the definition of despotism." And in proportion as these powers approximate to consolidation, the spirit of despotism steals over us. At the time of the adoption of this instrument, it was an objection raised against it by some of its most enlightened opposers, that its tendency was to such a consolidation, and on this account they strove to rouse the spirit of liberty. But their anticipations had chiefly reference to the forms of the Constitution, and particularly to that qualified control which the Executive has over the acts of the Legislature. They anticipated not at all, or at least very obscurely, that consolidation which has grown and is strengthened under the influence of the office-distributing power vested in the Executive. . . . This state of things is not the less to be deprecated on account of the fact that the forms of the Constitution are preserved while its spirit is perishing. The members of both branches may meet, deliberate, and act, but the spirit of independence is gone whenever the action of the Legislature is identified with the will of the Executive by the potent influence of the office-hoping and the office-holding charm. . . .

But the corruption of which I speak . . . is of a nature neither very gross nor very barefaced. Yet, on 847 these accounts, it is not the less to be deprecated. On the contrary, from its very insidiousness and its appearing so often almost in the garb of a virtue, ought it to be watched and restricted.

Such is its nature that it corrupts the very foundation of action.

---

* From a speech by the Representative from Massachusetts in the House of Representatives, January 30, 1811, supporting a proposed constitutional amendment that would restrict the appointment of members of Congress to executive offices. *Annals,* 11th Congress, 3d session, pp. 846-848.

It springs up out of the human heart and the condition of things, so that it is almost impossible that it should not exist or that it should be altogether resisted. It has its origin in that love of place, which is so inherent in the human heart that it may be called almost an universal and instinctive passion. It cannot be otherwise. For so long as the love of honor and the love of profit are natural to man, so long the love of place (which includes either the one or the other or both) must be a very general and prevalent impulse. It cannot, therefore, but be true as a general principle, and it casts no reflection to admit, that all members of Congress may love offices at least as well as their neighbors.

Now, with the love of place, there is another principle concurrent in relation to members of Congress which is the result of our political condition. [It] is this: that those most desirous of places in the Executive gift will not expect to be gratified except by their support of the Executive. In referring to this principle, as the result of our political condition, I mean to cast no particular reflection on our present Chief Magistrate. It grows out of the nature of political combinations. For, with some highly honorable exceptions it has been true in all and will be true in all future Administrations, that the general way for members of Congress to gain offices for themselves or their relations is to coincide in opinion and vote with the Executive.

Out of the union of these two principles, the love of office and the general impression that coincidence with the Executive is an essential condition for obtaining office, grows that corruption of the very fountain of action, the purification of which is the aim of . . . the amendment . . . under consideration. It exists without any pre-contract with the Executive. He knows our wants without any formal specification from us. And we know his terms without any previous statement from him. The parties proceed together, mutually gratifying and gratified, as occasions offer, and the harmonies of the happy part of the Legislature and the Executive are complete.

And were it not that there is a third party concerned, called the people of the United States, nothing would seem more pleasant or unexceptionable than this partnership in official felicity. But so it is, in truth, that the interests and liberties of the people which we are sent here to consult, will not only be sometimes neglected but at others absolutely sacrificed, while the constituted guardians are gaping after offices for themselves or hunting them up for their relations. The nature of the corruption is such as not only easily to be concealed from the world, but also in a great measure, from the inindividual himself. And so long as that free access which is at present permitted by the Constitution is unrestrained, it will continue and may increase. On 848 every question which arises and has relation to Executive measures, in addition to all the other considerations of honor, policy, justice, propriety, and the like, this also is prepared to be thrown into the scale: that, if a man means to gain office, he must coincide with the Executive. . . .

. . .

LIMITS OF THE PRESIDENT'S AUTHORITY

7.5 Charles Pinckney: "It will be granted that no powers are more important to a nation than those to regulate commerce and to declare war. Are not these powers so great that they ought never to be exercised but by the representatives of the people?"*

Mr. Pinckney said, I feel much pleasure in being present at this discussion, because I have always wished that some parts of this bill, particularly those that relate to the delegation of the powers to the President in the recess of Congress, should be maturely examined in order that I might hear the reasons upon which, what appears to me, so unusual and unconstitutional a delegation of authority has taken place.

. . . 55

This bill is a branch of that system which has been pursued by the friends and supporters of the 56 present Administration for two or three years, with constant and too effectual perseverance, for in-

* From a speech by the Senator from South Carolina in the Senate, February 26, 1800, opposing a bill which would authorize the President to impose and terminate embargoes on shipping to and from certain foreign ports. *Annals*, 6th Congress, 1st session, pp. 54-58. The reporting of Senator Pinckney's address is perhaps the most unsatisfactory reporting that was encountered in selecting the content of this book. The editors therefore made several word changes as well as alterations of punctuation in preparing his remarks for printing here.

creasing the power of the Executive. In a former session we have seen a large army voted, which has since been partly raised and is now resolved to be reduced. There was also an act authorizing the President to raise, if in his opinion the danger was so great as to require it, 10,000 men, as a provisional army, and of his own and sole authority to commission all the officers. There was also in this act a clause authorizing the President to accept of the service of volunteer corps and to appoint all the commissioned officers, although there is an express clause in the Constitution which says that the appointment of all the officers of the militia who may be employed in the service of the United States shall be reserved to the States respectively.

I must confess I view this delegation of power to the President —the power to raise or not to raise this provisional army as in his opinion the dangers of our situation may require, and the power intended to be given by this bill to remit the prohibition of commerce and renew it again, as he pleases, with the whole or any part of the French dominions—I view these two delegations of power as so intimately connected and as standing so precisely on the same principles that, although it may not be perfectly in order, in considering the one I cannot help glancing at the other, inasmuch as they both serve to bring before you the important question: How far does the Constitution authorize Congress to delegate to the President the exercise of such extensive powers?[1]

I have no doubt in my own mind that the Constitution does not authorize the delegation of these authorities, and it is among the reasons that induce me to vote against this bill. It will be granted that no powers are more important to a nation than those to regulate commerce, and to declare war—these, therefore, are both exclusively given to Congress. It is observable that, although the power to make peace is given to the President with the advice and consent

---

[1] This sentence appears as follows in the *Annals:* "I must confess, I view this delegation to the President, of the power to raise this provisional army or not, as in his opinion the danger of our situation may require, and the power intended to be given by this bill, to remit the prohibition of intercourse, and renew it again, with the whole, or any part of the French dominions, as he pleases, as so intimately connected, and as standing so precisely on the same principles, that although it may not be perfectly in order, yet, in considering the one, I cannot help glancing at the other, as they both serve to bring before you the important question, how far the Constitution authorizes Congress to delegate to the President the exercise of such extensive powers."

of two-thirds of the Senate, yet so guarded is the Constitution upon the subject of war that this is given to Congress—they alone can declare war, they alone can regulate commerce. Nor can they constitutionally delegate this exercise of their authorities by any limitations they can annex to the manner in which their agent is to execute them. They are powers so great and so important to the peace and dearest interests of the people that they are vested in Congress— they, and they alone, are to judge from the circumstances before them whether war, or measures that may in their tendency involve a war, are expedient. With them also rests the power to say what shall be the nature of our commerce, or the regulations necessary to its rights and safety; with whom and under what conditions it shall be carried on; with what nations and for what time it shall be interdicted.

And are not these powers so great that they ought never to be exercised but by the representatives of the people? In giving to them exclusively the powers of war and commerce, does not the grant include all their incidental authorities? Where is the part of the Constitution which authorizes their delegation 57 of them? If it has wisely said that delicate and important powers like these ought only to be exercised by the representatives of the people—that they are the only safe depositories of them; that they are to judge when measures ought to be adopted which may in their consequences lead to war; that they alone ought to judge how far commercial prohibitions extending to a whole nation and its territories ought to be carried, when [they ought to be] removed and when again renewed— can they delegate this authority without interfering with the intentions of the Constitution?

The design of that instrument clearly was that no individual should possess the dangerous power of involving this country in war or regulating its commerce. And yet will any man deny that the powers here delegated are such as may, by an unwise and precipitate use of them, lead inevitably to war.

. . . 58

To balance and in some degree to correct this too great influence in the Executive, it ought to be the care of Congress never to add to it if it can be avoided with any kind of convenience, lest they should destroy their own necessary and Constitutional weight in the Government. That as they alone are authorized to put their hands into the pockets of their constituents, they only ought to judge and decide upon those great legislative questions which may lead to requisitions for money or to cramp or touch the means by which alone our citizens can furnish it. That the power to adopt measures that may in their tendency lead to or touch the subject of war or commerce is so intimately connected with the power to tax, that we may just as well suppose that Congress can delegate the right to the President to lay and levy taxes as that they can delegate the authority to regulate commerce in the way this bill proposes.

. . .

chapter **8**

The Judiciary

THE JUDICIAL DEPARTMENT

8.1 William B. Giles: "In the nature of things there can be but two great departments of government, the Legislative and the Executive; it is obvious that the Judiciary is a branch of the Executive department."*

. . .

The theory of three distinct departments in government is, perhaps, not critically correct; and, although it is obvious that the framers of our Constitution proceeded upon this theory in its formation, yet in the practical adjustment of the departments to each other it was found impossible to carry this theory completely into effect. In the nature of things there can be but two great departments in government: the Legislative, whose duty it is to prescribe rules of conduct, or in other words to make laws for the government of the people; the Executive, to carry those laws into effect. But as from the imperfection of language the meaning of the laws is not

* From a speech in the Senate by the Senator from Virginia, supporting a bill to provide for punishment of treason and related crimes, February 11, 1808. *Annals*, 10th Congress, 1st session, pp. 114-116.

definitively understood, the Judiciary department is introduced to explain the meaning of the laws prescribed by the Legislature—to aid the Executive in carrying those laws into effect. Hence, it is obvious that the Judiciary is a branch of the Executive department, and accordingly, under the Constitution, the President appoints all judicial officers and, except the judges, all other officers of the courts hold their offices during his pleasure. . . .

Superficial observers take it for granted that the three great departments of the Government are co-ordinate and independent of each other. It is to be observed that the words *co-ordinate, independent,* are not to be found in any part of the Constitution. They are borrowed from the technical phraseology of another country and do not apply to the Constitution of the United States, at least not without great limitation. If by the word *co-ordinate* is meant that the Judiciary Department is equal in dignity, *co-ordo,* it is admitted. If it be meant in point of time, *co-ordo,* it is not the fact. The Legislative department pre-existed the Judiciary department; for, according to the Constitution, the establishment of the Judiciary department was entrusted to the Legislative department, and of course that department must necessarily pre-exist the department to be established by it, and the fact is well known to be so.

With respect to the word *independent,* as applicable to the Judiciary, it is not correct, nor justified by the Constitution. This term is borrowed from Great Britain, and by some incorrect apprehension of its meaning 115 there, or from some other cause, is applied here to the department itself instead of the officers of the department. In Great Britain the phrase is "an independent judge," not "an independent judicial department." According to the English Constitution, such a phraseology would be absolute nonsense. In this country the terms have been used as synonymous, whereas there is the most palpable difference both in the form and effect of their meaning. An independent department of a Government is conceived to be a department furnished with powers to organize itself, and to execute the peculiar functions assigned to it without the aid, or in other words, independent of any other department. A moment's attention to the Constitution will serve to show that this is not the Constitutional character of our Judicial department. An independent judge may be defined to be a person who, in the exercise of judicial functions, is placed above temptation in the discharge of his judicial duties; or, in other words, a judge who will neither gain nor lose anything by deciding for or against the Government, or for or against any individual or number of individuals; or, a judge whose salary is fixed and who does not hold his office at the pleasure of another person.

In England the King is the fountain of honor and justice, and formerly decided upon the meaning of the laws in his own person. Afterwards, that branch of executive duties was confided to his commissioners, who were appointed by him, held their appointment during his pleasure, and were dependent upon him for their compensations until by the statute of 13 of William III it was declared that the judges should hold their offices during good behaviour. Still, however, their offices were vacated upon the demise of the Crown until the 1st of Anne, when it was declared that the offices of the Judges should not be vacated until six months after the demise of the Crown. And, finally, by a statute of 1st of George III, the salaries of the judges were fixed and it was declared that their offices should not be vacated upon the demise of the Crown. This statute completely established what in England is called *the independence of the judges*. But to infer from this that the judicial department there is independent of the Parliament, would be an absolute misapplication of terms and incompatible with every principle of the British constitution.

From these observations it is not to be inferred that our Constitution is precisely analogous to the British in all these respects, but to show the meaning of the term "independent" in the country from which it was borrowed, and its misapplication to our Constitution. It was his wish to discard these technical, general terms, which rather embarrass than assist us in the correct interpretation of the Constitution. It was his wish to examine the instrument and to deduce our interpretation of it from its own context. For whatever degree of independence is attached either to the judicial department or to the judges themselves, according to the Constitution, it was his wish [that that degree of independence] should be fully enjoyed by the department or the judges *116* without the smallest abatement. But the Constitution, as it is, should be a standard of interpretation, not what it is described to be by general borrowed misapplied phrases.

. . .

A FEDERAL JUDICIAL SYSTEM

8.2   Debate on the Judiciary Act:*   "This principle of establishing Judges of a Supreme Court will lead to an entire new system of jurisprudence, and fill every State in the Union with two kinds of courts."

Mr. Livermore: I now move you, sir, to strike out the whole of this clause. I fear this principle of establishing Judges of a Supreme Court will lead to an entire new system of jurisprudence, and fill every State in the Union with two kinds of courts for the trial of many causes. A thing so heterogeneous must give great disgust. Sir, it will be establishing a Government within a Government, and one must prevail upon the ruin of the other. Nothing, in my opinion, can irritate the inhabitants so generally as to see their neighbors dragged before two tribunals for the same offence. Mankind in general are unfriendly to courts of justice; they are vexed with law-suits for debts or trespasses; and though I do not doubt but the most impartial administration of justice will take place, yet they will feel the imposition burdensome and disagreeable. People in general do not view the necessity of courts of justice with the eye of a civilian; they look upon laws rather as intended for punishment than protection; they will think we are endeavoring to irritate them, rather than to establish a Government to sit easy upon them.

Will any gentleman say that the Constitution cannot be administered without this establish- 784 ment? I am clearly of a different opinion; I think it can be administered better without than with it. There is already in each State a system of jurisprudence congenial to the wishes of its citizens. I never heard it complained that justice was not distributed with an equal hand in all of them; I believe it is so, and the people think it so. We had better then continue them

---

* Representatives Samuel Livermore of New Hampshire, William L. Smith of South Carolina, and Michael Jenifer Stone of Maryland. From debate in the House of Representatives on a bill to establish the Judicial Courts of the United States; enacted, the statute is known as the Judiciary Act of 1789. Livermore, August 24, 1789; Smith and Stone, August 28, 1789. *Annals,* 1st Congress, 1st session, pp. 783-784 (Livermore); pp. 798-801 (Smith); pp. 809-810 (Stone).

than introduce a system replete with expense, and altogether unnecessary.

. . .

Mr. Smith: . . . it seems generally conceded that there ought to be a district court of some sort. The Constitution, indeed, recognizes such a court, because it speaks of "such inferior courts as the Congress shall establish," and because it gives to the Supreme Court only appellate jurisdiction in most cases of a federal nature. But some gentlemen are of opinion that the district court should be altogether confined to admiralty causes; while others deem it expedient that it should be entrusted with a more enlarged jurisdiction and should, in addition to admiralty causes, take cognizance of all causes of seizure on land, all breaches of impost laws, of offences committed on the high seas, and causes in which foreigners or citizens of other States are parties. The committee are now to decide between these two opinions.

After mature reflection, I am inclined to favor the latter. What are the objections advanced against it? A gentleman from New Hampshire has observed, that such an establishment will be unneccessary, expensive, and disagreeable to our constituents. Justice, he observed, could be as well administered in the State as in the district courts; and should the State courts betray any symptoms of partiality, their adjudications would be subject to revision in the Federal Supreme Court which, in his opinion, afforded sufficient security. If the State courts are to take cognizance of those causes which, by the Constitution are declared to belong to the judicial courts of the United States, an appeal must lie in every case to the latter, otherwise the judicial authority of the Union might be altogether eluded. To deny such an appeal, would be to frustrate the most important objects of the Federal Government, and would obstruct its operations. The necessity of uniformity in the decision of the Federal courts is obvious; to assimilate the principles of national decisions and collect them, as it were, into one focus, appeals from all the State courts to the Supreme Court would be indispensable.

It is, however, much to be apprehended that this constant control of the Supreme Federal Court over the adjudication of the State courts, would dissatisfy the people and weaken the importance and authority of the State judges. Nay, more, it would lessen their re-

spectability in the eyes of the people, even in causes which properly
appertain to the State jurisdictions; because the people, being accustomed to see their decrees overhauled and annulled by a superior
tribunal, would soon learn to form an irreverent opinion of their importance and abilities. It appears, therefore, expedient to separate, as
much as possible, the State from the Federal jurisdiction, to draw a
broad line of distinction, to assign clearly to each its precise limits,
and to prevent a clashing or interference between them.
. . . 799

It is very proper that a court in the United States should try offences committed against the United States. Every nation upon
earth punishes by its own courts offences against its own laws. To
seizures on land for breaches of the revenue laws, this power will
not be censured; it would be *felo de se* to trust the collection of the
revenue of the United States to the State judicatures. The disinclina-
tion of the judges to carry the law into effect, their disapprobation
of a certain duty, the rules of the court, or other obvious *800* causes,
might delay or frustrate the collection of the revenue, and embarrass
the National Government. From this view, it appears that the district
court is not clothed with any authority of which the State courts are
stripped, but is barely provided with that authority which arises out
of the establishment of a National Government, and which is indis-
pensably necessary for its support.

Can the State courts at this moment take cognisance of offences
committed on the high seas? If they do, it is under an act of Congress giving them jurisdiction; and, in such cases, the Judge of the
Admiralty is associated with two common law judges: this tribunal
becomes then a federal court for the particular occasion, because it
is established by Congress. The State courts have no jurisdiction of
causes arising from a national impost law, because no such law heretofore existed. Where, then, is the ground of uneasiness suggested
by gentlemen? The foregoing observations must persuade them that
their alarms have been premature. But it is said that there must be
court-houses, judges, marshals, clerks, constables, jails, and gibbets;
that these establishments will occasion a heavy and unnecessary burden, and have a tendency to create disgust in the people.

I readily agree with the gentleman that there are in every community some individuals who will see, with pain, every new institution in the shape of a constable, jail, or gibbet, and who think that

law and courts are an abridgment of their liberty; but I should be
very sorry to concur with him that this is a prevailing opinion. I
think better of our constituents, and am persuaded they are sensible
that those institutions are necessary for the protection of their lives
and property, and grow out of the very nature of a federal Government. Care, indeed, should be taken to prevent their being grievous
and oppressive; but as long as knaves and rogues exist in the world,
and monsters under the form of men preying upon the innocent, so
long will courts and all their concomitants be wanted to redress the
wrongs of the latter, and repress the depredations of the former. . . .

To suppose that there will be a clashing of jurisdiction between
the State and district courts on all occasions, by having a double set
of officers, is to suppose the States will take a pleasure in thwarting
the Federal Government. It is a supposition not warranted by our
fellow-citizens who, finding that these establishments were created
for their benefit and protection, will rather promote than obstruct
them. It is a supposition equally opposed to the power of direct taxation, and to the establishment of State and *801* county courts which
exist in the several States and are productive of no such inconveni-
ence. These several courts will have their limits defined, and will
move within their respective orbits without any danger of deviation.
Besides, I am not persuaded that there will be a necessity for having
separate court-houses and jails; those already provided in the several
States will be made use of by the district courts. . . .

. . .

Mr. Stone: . . . It appears to me that the present Government originated in *necessity,* and it ought not be carried further than *necessity* will justify.

I believe the scheme of the present Government was considered
by those who framed it as dangerous to the liberties of America. If
they had not considered it in this point of view, they would not have
guarded it in the manner they have done. They supposed that it had
a natural tendency to destroy the State Governments; or, on the
other hand, they supposed that the State Governments had a tendency to abridge the powers of the General Government. Therefore
it was necessary to guard against either taking place, and this was
to be done properly by establishing a Judiciary for the United States.

This Judiciary was likewise absolutely necessary because a great many purposes of the Union could not be accomplished by the States from the principle of their government, and could not be executed from a defect in their power. . . . the State courts could not determine between State and State, be- *810* cause their judgment would be ineffectual; they could never carry it into execution. But I apprehend in all other cases the States could execute that authority which is reposed in the United States. Yet I do not doubt but the caution might be necessary for securing to the General Government, in reserve, those very powers, because such abuses may happen in the State courts as to render it necessary for the due administration of justice that the national jurisdiction be carried over such States. But what I am not satisfied of is, whether it is *now* essential that we proceed to make such establishments. . . .

By the Constitution, Congress has a right to establish such inferior courts as they from time to time shall think necessary. If I understand the force of the words "from time to time," it is that Congress may establish such courts when they think proper. I take it they have used another precaution; and this construction is guarded by another clause in the Constitution, where it is provided that the Constitution itself and all laws made in pursuance thereof as well as treaties, shall be the supreme law of the land and the judges in every State are to be bound thereby, any thing in the State laws or constitutions to the contrary notwithstanding. Now can gentlemen be afraid that the State courts will not decide according to the supreme law? If they are, it is in the discretion of Congress to refuse them the opportunity. But the bill gives them a concurrent jurisdiction, and shows that these dangers are not really apprehended. If they give them concurrent jurisdiction, they have the power of giving them complete; and they may delay from time to time the institution of national courts, until they suppose or have experienced the inadequacy of the State courts to the objects granted by the Constitution to the participation of the Judiciary of the United States.

If, sir, the State judges are bound to take cognizance of the laws of the United States, and are sworn to support the General Government, the system before us must have originated from a source different from that from which the Government itself derived its existence. Yet, I admit, sir, that there is a *necessity* for instituting Admiralty courts, though it is not because I consider the power of the State inadequate to that object; but because those courts are not instituted in all of them, and it is proper that there should be a maritime juris-

diction within the bounds of every State to determine cases arising
within the same. . . .

. . .

THE INDEPENDENCE OF THE JUDICIARY

[Note by the editors. The First Congress, in the Judiciary Act
of 1789, brought into existence a Supreme Court, created several district courts, and provided for justices of the Supreme Court to sit
with district court judges to form circuit courts. During President
Adams' Administration Congress reorganized the federal judicial system. The most important statute enlarged the number of circuit
courts and provided for the appointment of sixteen circuit court
judges. President Adams and the Senate promptly filled these circuit
court positions. This judicial reorganization statute was enacted by
the "lame duck" Congress, elected in 1798, which sat from December 1800, to March 3, 1801—the interim between the overwhelming
defeat of President Adams and his party in the elections of November, 1800, and Jefferson's inauguration.

The newly seated Jeffersonians, a substantial majority in both
houses of Congress, promptly repealed the judicial reorganization act
of 1801, and in another act reorganized the federal court system. The
repeal act, by abolishing the sixteen circuit courts, terminated the
offices of the circuit judges whom Adams had appointed in the last
weeks of his Administration.

Pinckney's remarks (selection 8.3) were addressed to one of the
bills considered by the last Congress under President Adams, though
not the one that was finally adopted. The four speeches printed as
selection 8.4 were made during the debate on the bill which, when
enacted, repealed the reorganization act of 1801 and abolished the
offices of the sixteen circuit judges.]

8.3   Charles Pinckney: "It is our duty to guard against every
possibility of influence and corruption."*

It is an established maxim, and I hope will forever remain so,
that the Legislature and Judiciary should be as distinct as the nature

---

* From a speech by the Senator from South Carolina in the Senate, March
5, 1800, supporting a bill to amend the Judiciary Act of 1789. *Annals,* 6th Congress, 1st session, pp. 97, 101.

of our Government will admit; that is, that the same men shall not in a deliberative capacity agree to measures which they shall afterwards have a right to explain and decide upon in a judicial one. The reason is obvious; that the Judges should in a calm and unprejudiced manner explain what the law literally is, and not what it ought to be; that they should not be allowed to carry upon the bench those passions and prejudices which too frequently prevail in the adoption and formation of legislative acts and treaties, and which never fail to give an irresistible bias to the opinions of a Judge who has been concerned in making them. The truth of this reasoning is now so generally conceded, that there is not a man who knows anything of government that will attempt to controvert it; the constitutions of all the States have sanctioned it, and if the opinions of the Federal Convention ought to have weight, they so strongly insisted upon it as even to refuse, after repeated trials, associating the Judges with the President in the exercise of his revisionary power.

. . . *101*

If we recollect the manner in which our Judges are appointed, that circumstance alone should induce us to adopt every mode in our power to render them independent of the Executive. They are appointed by the President, and if the moment after they receive their commissions they were really so independent as to be completely out of his reach— [so independent] that no hope of additional favor, no attempt to caress could be reasonably expected to influence their opinions—yet it is impossible for them ever to forget from whom they have received their present elevation. Hence I have always been of opinion that it was wrong to give the nomination of Judges to the President. It is, however, determined by the Constitution, and while the right continues in him it must in some degree have its effects on the good wishes and influence of a Judge in his favor. He cannot hear anything respecting [the President] in quite so unbiased and impartial a manner as he would was the President unknown to him or had he not received any favor from him.

It is our duty to guard against any addition to this bias which a Judge, from the nature of his appointment, must inevitably feel in favor of the President. It is more particularly incumbent on us when we recollect that our Judges claim the dangerous right to question the constitutionality of the laws and either to execute them or not, as they think proper; a right in my judgment as unfounded and as dan-

gerous as any that was ever attempted in a free government. They however do exercise it, and while they are suffered to do so it is impossible to say to what extent it might be carried. What might be the consequences if the President could at any time get rid of obnoxious laws by persuading or influencing the Judges to decide that they were unconstitutional and ought not to be executed? It will be said this is arguing as if all our officers were corrupt—that we should place no confidence in them—and was truly taking the dark side of the picture. To this I answer that it is our duty to guard against every possibility of influence or corruption—hence springs the necessity of laws. If all our officers were perfect and all our citizens honest and virtuous, there would be no occasion for them; but as it is the nature of men to err and sometimes to be vicious, our laws are incompetent unless they are calculated to meet every contingency.
. . .

8.4 Debate on the Judiciary Repeal Bill:*   "It is admitted that no power derived from the Constitution can deprive the judge of his office, and yet it is contended that by repeal of the law that office can be destroyed."

Mr. Mason: . . . I shall now, sir, trouble you with a few remarks on the expediency of repealing this law. It has been said that there is nothing peculiarly disgustful in this law; that there has been no public clamor excited against it; that it was enacted with solemnity, on calm and deliberate reflection; and that time has not yet been given to test it by experience.

As no [other] member who has taken part in debate was a member of this body when the law passed, I will say something of its history. I am not disposed to excite the sensibility of gentlemen by any remarks which I shall make, or to call up unpleasant recollections of past scenes. But when I hear it said that this law was passed

* Senators Steven T. Mason of Virginia, Gouverneur Morris of New York, and Nathaniel Chipman of Vermont in the Senate; Representative Joseph H. Nicholson of Maryland in the House of Representatives. From debate on a bill to repeal the act of 1801 which reorganized the federal courts. Mason, January, 13, 1802; Morris, January 8, 1802; Chipman, January 19, 1802; Nicholson, February 27, 1802. *Annals,* 7th Congress, 1st session, pp. 66-68 (Mason); pp. 38-40 (Morris); pp. 131-132 (Chipman); pp. 818-819, 822-823 (Nicholson).

with calmness, after mature reflection, and that we are now, in a fit of passion, going to undo what was thus wisely done, I think it necessary that the public should have a correct statement.

It is true, that under the last Administration when there existed (what I trust will never, in an equal degree, exist again) an immoderate thirst for Executive patronage, a proposition was made to establish a new judiciary system; a system worse than the present, as it proposed, according to my recollection, thirty-eight judges instead of 67 sixteen. This law was very near passing. It was, however, rejected in the House of Representatives by a very small majority. But it was circulated as a project of a law among the people. It was illy received. It was thought too rank a thing, and met with general disapprobation throughout the United States, so far as I have been able to learn. After this reception, it was softened down to the plan introduced at the last session. What temper accompanied the progress of the bill in the other House I know not, or, if I did know, would it be proper for me here to say? But with respect to the acts of this body, I am not of opinion they added any dignity to our common course of procedure. The bill was referred to a committee who, though it was [a] very long [bill], reported it without any amendment. . . .

All amendments proposed by the minority were uniformly rejected by a steady, inflexible, and undeviating majority. I confess that I saw no passion, but I certainly did see great pertinacity; something like what the gentleman from Connecticut had termed a *holding fast*. No amendments were admitted. When offered, we were told: no, you may get them introduced by a rider or supplementary bill or in any way you please; but down this bill must go; it must be crammed down your throats. This was not the precise phrase, but such was the amount of what was said.

I will say that not an argument was urged in favor of the bill, not a word to show the necessity or propriety of the change. Yet we are told that there was great dignity, great solemnity in its progress and passage!

But there is something undignified in thus hastily repealing this law! in thus yielding ourselves to the fluctuations of public opinion! So we are told!

But if there be blame, on whom does it fall? Not on us who respected the public opinion when this law was passed, and who still respect it, but on those who, in defiance of public opinion, passed this law after that public opinion had been decisively expressed [in the election of November, 1800]. The revolution in public opinion had taken place before the introduction of this project. The people of the United States had determined to commit their affairs to new agents. Already had the confidence of the people been transferred from their then rulers into other hands. After this exposition of the national will and this new deposit of the national confidence, the gentlemen [of the "lame duck" Congress, elected in 1798] should have left untouched this important and delicate subject—a subject on which the people could not be reconciled to their views, even in the flood-tide of their power and influence. They should have forborne till agents better acquainted with the national will, because more recently constituted its organs, had come into the Government. This would have been more dignified than to seize the critical moment when 68 power was passing from them, to pass such a law as this. If there is error, it is our duty to correct it; and the truth was, no law was ever more execrated by the public.

. . .

Mr. Morris: . . . What will be the effect of the desired repeal? Will it not be a declaration to the remaining judges that they hold their offices subject to your will and pleasure? And what will be the result of this? It will be, that the check established by the Constitution, wished for by the people, and necessary in every contemplation of common sense, is destroyed. It had been said, and truly too, that Governments are made to provide against the follies and vices of men. For to suppose that Governments rest upon reason is a pitiful solecism. If mankind were reasonable, they would want no Government. Hence, checks are required in the distribution of power among those who are to exercise it for the benefit of the people. Did the people of America vest all powers in the Legislature? No; they had vested in the judges a check intended to be efficient—a check of the first necessity, to prevent an invasion of the Constitution by unconstitutional laws—a check which might prevent any faction from intimidating or annihilating the tribunals themselves.

On this ground, said Mr. Morris, I stand to arrest the victory meditated over the Constitution of my country; a victory meditated by those who wish to prostrate that Constitution for the furtherance of their own ambitious views. Not of him who had recommended this measure, nor of those who now urged it—for, on his uprightness and their uprightness, I have the fullest reliance—but of those in the back-ground who have further and higher objects. Those troops that protect the outworks are to be first dismissed. Those posts which present the strongest barriers are first to be taken, and then the Constitution becomes an easy prey.

Let us then, secondly, consider whether we have constitutionally a power to repeal this law. [Here Mr. Morris quoted the third article and first section of the Constitution.][1] I have heard a 39 verbal criticism about the words *shall* and *may,* which appeared the more unnecessary to me as the same word *shall* is applied to both members of the section. For it says "the judicial power, &c., *shall* be vested in one Supreme Court and such inferior courts as the Congress *may,* from time to time ordain and establish." The Legislature, therefore, had without doubt the right of determining, in the first instance, what inferior courts should be established; but when established, the words are imperative, a part of the judicial power shall vest in them. And "the judges shall hold their offices during good behaviour." They shall receive a compensation which shall not be diminished during their continuance in office. Therefore, whether the remarks be applied to the tenure of office or the quantum of compensation, the Constitution is equally imperative. After this exposition, gentlemen are welcome to any advantage to be derived from the criticism on *shall* and *may.*

But another criticism, which but for its serious effects I would call pleasant, has been made, the amount of which is: you shall not take the man from the office, but you may take the office from the man; you shall not drown him, but you may sink his boat under him; you shall not put him to death, but you may take away his life. The Constitution secures to a judge his office; says he shall hold it, that is, it shall not be taken from him during good behaviour; the Legislature shall not diminish, though their bounty may increase, his salary; the Constitution provides perfectly for the inviolability of his tenure. But yet we may destroy the office which we cannot take away, as if the destruction of the office would not as effectually deprive him of it as the grant to another person. It is admitted that no

---

[1] Brackets those of the *Annals* reporter.

power derived from the Constitution can deprive him of the office, and yet it is contended that by repeal of the law that office may be destroyed. Is not this absurd?

It had been said, that whatever one Legislature can do another can undo; because no Legislature can bind its successor, and therefore that whatever we make we can destroy. This I deny on the ground of reason, and on that of the Constitution. What! can a man destroy his own children? Can you annul your own compacts? Can you annihilate the national debt? When you have by law created a political existence, can you, by repealing the law, dissolve the corporation you had made? When by your laws you give to an individual any right whatever, can you by a subsequent law rightfully take it away? No. When you make a compact you are bound by it. When you make a promise you must perform it.

Establish the contrary doctrine and what follows? The whim of the moment becomes the law of the land; your country will be looked upon as a den of robbers; every honest man will fly your shores. Who will trust you, when you are the first to violate your own contracts? The position, therefore, that the Legislature may rightfully repeal every law made by a preceding Legislature, when tested by reason, is untrue. And it is equally untrue when compared with the precepts of the Constitution; for what does the Constitution say? *40* You shall make no *ex post facto* law. Is not this an *ex post facto* law?

. . .

Mr. Chipman: . . . I will here, sir, though it might perhaps have been more properly done before, make a few observations on the independence of the judiciary. It has been said by some gentlemen, in effect, that though the judges ought to be independent of the Executive—though they ought not to hold their offices or salaries dependent on the will of the President, yet in a Government like ours there can be no reason why they should not, like the other departments of the Government, be dependent on public opinion, and on Congress as properly representing that opinion. That if the judges are made thus independent; if Congress cannot remove them by abolishing their offices, or [remove them] in any other way except that of impeachment for misbehaviour, they will become a dangerous body in the State; they may, by their discussions on the constitutionality of a law, obstruct the most important measures of Government for the public good.

Unfortunately for the argument, this doctrine agrees neither with the nature of our Government, which is not vested with the unlimited national sovereignty but from that derives its powers, nor with the positive and solemn declaration of the Constitution. That Constitution is a system of powers, limitations, and checks. The Legislative power is there limited with even more guarded caution than the Executive; because not capable of a check by impeachment, and because it was apprehended that left unlimited and uncontrolled, it might be extended to dangerous encroachments on the remaining State powers.

But to what purpose are the powers of Congress limited by that instrument? To what purpose is it declared to be the supreme law of the land, and as such binding on the courts of the United States and of the several States, if it may not be applied to the derivative laws to test their constitutionality? Shall it be only called in to enforce obedience to the laws of Congress in opposition to the acts of the several States, and even to their rightful powers! Such cannot have been the intention. But, sir, it will be in vain long to expect from the judges the firmness and integrity to oppose a Constitutional decision to a law, either of the national Legislature or to a law of any of the powerful States, unless it should interfere with a law of Congress, if such a decision is to be made at the risk of office and salary, of public character, and the means of subsistence. And such will be the situation of your judges if Congress can, by law or in any other way except by way of impeachment, deprive them of their offices and salaries on any pretence whatever. For it will be remembered that the legislative powers of the several States as well as those of Congress are limited by the Constitution. For instance, they are prohibited, as well as Congress, to pass any bill of attainder or *ex post facto* law. The decisions of the judges upon such laws, and such decisions they have already been called upon to make, may raise against them, even in Congress, the influence of the most powerful States in the Union. In such a situation of the judges, the Constitutional limitation on the Legislative 132 powers, can be but a dead letter. Better would it be they were even expunged.

Thus, sir, it appears that the independence of the judges, even of Congress in their Legislative capacity, is agreeable to the nature

of our Government, to the whole tenor as well as the express letter
of the Constitution. But, sir, at this late stage of the debate I will not
farther enlarge; I will only add that upon these principles and with
these views of the subject I shall give a hearty negative to the resolution on your table.

Mr. Nicholson: . . . We say that we have the same right to repeal
the law establishing inferior courts that we have to repeal the law
establishing post offices and post roads, laying taxes, or raising armies. This right would not be denied but for the construction given
to that part of the Constitution which declares that "the judges both
of the supreme and inferior courts shall hold their offices during
good behaviour."

The arguments of gentlemen, generally, have been directed
against a position that we never meant to contend for: against the
right to remove the judges in any other manner than by impeachment. This right we have never insisted on; we have never in the
most distant manner contended that the Constitution vested us with
the same power that the Parliament of England have, or that is
given to the Legislatures of Pennsylvania, Delaware, New Jersey,
and some others.

Our doctrine is that every Congress has a right to repeal any
law passed by its predecessors, except in cases where the Constitution imposes a prohibition. We have been told that we cannot repeal
a law fixing the President's salary during the period for which he was
elected. This is admitted, because it is so expressly declared in the
Constitution; nor is the necessity so imperious, because at the expiration of every four years, it is in the power of Congress to regulate it
anew, as their judgments may dictate. Neither can we diminish the
salary of a judge so long as he continues in office, because in this
particular the Constitution is express likewise. But we do contend
that we have an absolute, uncontrolled right to abolish all offices
which have been created by Congress, when in our judgment those
offices are unnecessary and are productive of a useless expense.

Let us examine the objections which have been *819* raised to
this upon that part of the Constitution in which it is said that "the
judges both of the supreme and inferior courts shall hold their offices during good behaviour, and shall receive, at stated times, a

compensation for their services, which shall not be diminished during their continuance in office."

It has already been stated by some of my friends, and I shall not therefore dwell upon it, that the prohibition contained in these words was of two kinds: the one applying to the Legislature, and prohibiting a diminution of salary; the other applying to the Executive, and forbidding a removal from office. The first prohibition our adversaries readily admit, but the second, they say, applies as well to the Legislature as to the Executive. I should agree to this, too, were there any necessity for it, but it is not pretended by us that we have the right to remove from office any officer whatsoever—not only a judge, but even a revenue officer; there would, therefore, be no necessity for imposing a restriction upon Congress in relation to a judge any more than in relation to an officer concerned in the collection of the revenue. They are each appointed by the President and Senate, but the Executive officer holds his place at the will of the President, the judge holds his office during good behaviour, and neither [is] subject to removal by the Legislature.

The term good behaviour is said to secure to the judge an estate for life in his office, determinable only upon impeachment for and conviction of bribery, corruption, and other high crimes and misdemeanors, and that inasmuch as his good conduct is the tenure by which he holds his office, he cannot be deprived of it so long as he demeans himself well.

. . . 822

Your supervisors who superintend the collection of your excise duties are appointed by the President and Senate, and hold their offices under the Constitution, not during good behaviour but during the will and pleasure of the President. The tenure by which [one of them] holds his office is completely beyond the power of the Legislature, and they cannot remove him. So long as he can secure the good will of the President, he is to hold his office against the whole world. It is as sacred, in relation to the authority of Congress, as that of a judge. They both hold their offices independent of the Legislature; the one during good behaviour, the other during the pleasure of the President. It is not in our power to remove an excise officer so long as his office continues, any more than to remove a judge, so long as his office continues. The authority vested in us is entirely Legislative, and has nothing to do with the Executive power of removal. Yet is there any man on earth can say that we have not a Constitutional right to repeal the laws laying excise duties, by which the office of supervisor is created? And can any one say that we can remove the supervisor in any other manner than by repealing the law?

We do not contend for the right to remove the judge any more than for the right to remove the supervisor, neither of which we can do, each holding his office independent of us; but we allege that the tenure by which either holds his office cannot prohibit us from re-pealing a law by which the office is created. . . .

I am aware that I may be told that the President, in giving his sanction to the law, at the same time impliedly signifies his consent to the removal of the officer. But permit me to suppose that the President refuses his signature to the law, and tells you that these officers hold their commissions independent of you, and there- 823 fore you have no right to dismiss them; that the Constitution author-izes them to hold their places during his will and pleasure, and that it is his will and pleasure [that] they shall continue in office. Here the tenure is as strong and inviolable by the Legislative power as the tenure of the judge. Yet Congress may, notwithstanding, after-wards pass the law by the concurrence of two-thirds, and destroy this sacred tenure of office.

If, then, the tenure of office in the one case cannot destroy the right to repeal, why shall it destroy it in the other? Both tenures are equally independent of Legislative control—the one securing an es-tate defeasible by misbehaviour, the other securing an estate defea-sible by the will of the President; but neither dependent on Congress for continuance in office, so long as the office itself exists. Gentlemen say we cannot do that by indirect means which we cannot do di-rectly; that is, that we cannot remove a judge by repealing this law, inasmuch as we cannot remove him by direct means. But I have proved beyond the possibility of doubt that we may indirectly re-move an excise officer by repealing the law under which he was ap-pointed, although we have no authority to remove him in any direct manner. If the principle laid down by gentlemen is not true in the one case, it cannot be true in the other.

For my own part, Mr. Chairman, I think no doubt can be enter-tained that the power of repealing, as well as of enacting laws, is inherent in every Legislature. The Legislative authority would be incomplete without it. If you deny the existence of this power, you suppose a perfection in man which he can never attain. You shut the door against a retraction of error by refusing him the benefit of reflection and experience. You deny to the great body of the people all the essential advantages for which they entered into society. This House is composed of members coming from every quarter of the Union, supposed to bring with them the feelings and to be acquainted with the interests of their constituents. If the feelings and the interests of the nation require that new laws should be enacted, that existing laws should be modified, or that useless and unnecessary laws should be repealed, they have reserved this power to themselves by declaring that it should be exercised by persons freely chosen for a limited period to represent them in the National Legislature.

. . .

part **IV**

REPUBLICAN
GOVERNMENT

Introduction

Amid all the controversies surrounding the adoption and interpretation of the Constitution, few questioned that its basic design and its most important particulars were fashioned upon republican principles. Indeed, some were critical of the Constitution because of its republican character. A question, then, of some importance is this: What meaning was attached to the term "republican government" during this early period?

Madison, in *Federalist* number thirty-nine, provides us with one definition that seems to have been widely accepted.

. . . we may define a republic to be, or at least may bestow that name on, a government which derives all its powers directly or indirectly from the great body of the people, and is administered by persons holding their offices during pleasure, for a limited period, or during good behavior.

Beyond any question, republicanism was closely associated with popular control of government; and this meant, as Madison emphasized, control by and responsiveness to "the great body of society," not to an "inconsiderable proportion" or a "favored class of it . . ."

Our Constitution, unique in so many ways, is even more so because it is built upon theoretical foundations and assumptions entirely opposite to those found in most of the traditional theories dealing with the difficulties of establishing stable democratic or republican governments. These theories, widely accepted in Madison's day, hold that an inverse relationship exists between the size of a territory to be governed and the possibility of creating an effective, stable and popularly controlled government. However, if we are to take Madison and others at their word, the Constitution is built upon precisely the opposite assumption; namely, the larger the territory and the more varied the interests within it, the greater the likelihood of establishing such a government. An understanding of this assumption enables us to appreciate more fully why the debates took the form they did. For this understanding, we can most profitably turn to the relevant writings of Madison (principally *Federalist* number ten), since they are generally acknowledged to be the most comprehensive and systematic concerning the theoretical foundations of the Constitution.

Madison, as we have noted, perceived two major sources of tyranny, government and majority factions. In *Federalist* number ten he defines a faction as follows:

> By a faction, I understand a number of citizens, whether amounting to a majority or minority of the whole, who are united and actuated by some common impulse of passion, or of interest, adverse to the rights of other citizens, or to the permanent and aggregate interests of the community.

Though he recognized the threat of minority factions, he rather summarily dismissed the possibilities of their ever gaining control of government to execute their will with the following observation:

> If a faction consists of less than a majority, relief is supplied by the republican principle, which enables the majority to defeat its sinister views by regular vote. It may clog the administration, it may convulse the society; but it will be unable to execute and mask its violence under the forms of the Constitution.

Madison's concern, then, was with preventing majority factions from executing their schemes through the agencies of government or, as he put it, with "controlling" the "effects" of such factions; and he argues that those conditions which are associated with the very extensiveness of the republic will render formation of majority factions extremely difficult. By comparing a republic, that is, a system in which there is representation of the people, with pure or direct democracies, systems in which the people themselves assemble to decide issues of public policy, he attempts to show how majority factions are less likely in the former. Here we can identify some of his major points:

(a) "[T]he delegation of the government . . . to a small number of citizens elected by the rest" in a republican form renders control of government by majority factions less likely than in pure or direct democracies or even small republics. Why? Several reasons are advanced, most of which stem from the belief that representatives will, on the whole, be less susceptible and responsive to the appeals of factions. "Public views" are refined "by passing them through the medium of a chosen body of citizens, whose wisdom may best discern the true interest of their country, and whose patriotism and love of justice will be least likely to sacrifice it to temporary or partial considerations." Beyond this, in a large and extensive republic the probability is greater than it is in small republics that representatives of this character will be elected. First, there are, absolutely speaking, more "fit" characters from which to choose in larger republics. Second, in a larger republic it will be, according to Madison, "more difficult for unworthy candidates to practice with success the vicious arts by which elections are too often carried; and the suffrages of the people being more free, will be more likely to centre in men who possess the most attractive merit and the most diffusive and established characters."

(b) "[T]he greater number of citizens, and greater sphere of country, over which the latter [a republican government] may be extended" serves to prevent the formation of majority factions. On this point Madison writes:

Extend the sphere, and you take in a greater variety of parties and interests; you make it less probable that a majority of the whole will have a common motive to invade the rights of the other citizens; or if such a common motive exists, it will be more difficult for all who feel it to discover their own strength, and to act in unison with each other. Beside other impediments, it may be remarked that, where there is a consciousness of unjust or dishonorable purposes, communication is always checked by distrust in proportion to the number whose concurrence is necessary.

In *Federalist* number fifty-one he amplifies on this:

In the extended republic of the United States, and among the greater variety of interests, parties, and sects which it embraces, a coalition of a majority of the whole society could seldom take place on any other principles than those of justice and the general good; . . .

We may take this to represent the outline of Madison's answer to the age-old question of how to secure minorities from the tyranny of majorities. His answer seems to rest on the assumption that an extensive republic provides a context in which the people will have sufficient opportunity to deliberate any given course of action and the relative merits of candidates for public office. For this reason, the people are less apt to back for very long those policies that are contrary to their long-term and permanent interests. At the same time, and for essentially the same reason, they are less likely to be swayed by demagogic appeals. Madison comes closest to articulating this assumption in his discussion of the Senate, particularly in *Federalist* number sixty-three.

As the cool and deliberate sense of the community ought, in all governments, and actually will, in all free governments, ultimately prevail over the views of its rulers; so there are particular moments in public affairs when the people, stimulated by some irregular passion, or some illicit advantage, or misled by the artful misrepresentations of interested men, may call for measures which they themselves will afterwards be the most ready to lament and condemn. In these critical moments, how salutary will be the interference of some temperate and respectable body of citizens, in order to check the misguided career, and to suspend the blow meditated by the people against themselves, until reason, justice, and truth can regain their authority over the public mind?

Why, we can well ask, will not those conditions associated with an extensive republic prevent any majority, factious or not, from ruling? That is, why are we to assume that in an extensive republic only factious majorities will be "filtered out," while nonfactious majorities, consistent with republican principles, will be able to rule? A likely answer, thoroughly in keeping with Madisonian theory, is this: A majority of the people, once they have had sufficient time to reflect, to meditate, and in these processes, to "cool off," simply would not back factious proposals. We readily see that this answer involves other assumptions about the basic nature of the American people. (See part I.)

While there is much to be said for this theory, it does contain what can be fairly described as an in-built "tension": a belief that majorities ought to rule along with an equally strong conviction that majorities ought to be controlled so that they cannot tyrannize minorities. We can identify at least four interrelated problems that arise from this basic tension:

(1) What precisely is a faction? Madison's definition certainly leaves room for controversy about whether a given cause or program is factious or not. Moreover, the theory does not answer the following critical questions: Are there specific, invariable, and absolute standards for determining when a majority or minority is promoting a policy contrary to the thoughts of other citizens as the permanent interests of the community? Or is this matter to be settled by the

majority of the community through the deliberative processes associated with an extensive republic?

(2) What changes of an institutional and/or procedural nature would render the government more vulnerable to control by majority factions? When do efforts designed to facilitate rule by the majority actually serve to increase the possibilities of governmental control by majority factions? That is, when do reforms or developments within the system really lead to a breakdown of the deliberative processes essential to preventing rule by factions? On the other hand, when do these processes make it virtually impossible for nonfactious majorities to rule?

(3) If, as Madison and others seemed to believe, representatives are to perform a critical function in preventing rule by factions, to what extent should they reflect the attitudes of their constituents on given issues of public policy? How much independence should they enjoy consistent with the belief that the majority of the people should rule? When, and under what circumstances, should these representatives ignore the majority opinion of their constituents? Conversely, when should they be obliged to recognize and vote in accordance with the will of a majority of their constituents?

(4) To what extent should the Constitution embody specified restraints on the powers of the majority? Is it possible to specify all the things a majority should not do? Is the articulation of such limitations in the Constitution consistent with the republican principle? Would such a specification of restraints serve unduly to restrict subsequent generations that might be confronted with conditions and circumstances necessitating bold action for the preservation of the union? And, of great importance, what should the substance of these restrictions be?

These questions, which have recurred in one form or another throughout our history, were, as the selections in part IV indicate, quite prominent during the formative years. They also, not unexpectedly, engendered heated debate. One of the first decisions that Congress had to make was whether to adopt a Bill of Rights. (See chapter 11.) Here several questions were prominent: Would, as Hamilton maintained in *Federalist* number eighty-four, more harm than good be done by attempting to specify rights? What should the substance of these rights be? What purpose would they serve in a republic designed to allow deliberate majorities to rule? Would they represent little more than "paper barricades" against the thrust of popular majorities? Could they conceivably be interpreted in such a fashion as to benefit factions and render the national government impotent to prevent a take-over by either majority or minority factions? Chapter 12 ("Loyalty, Sedition, and Personal Freedom") highlights these difficulties. What meaning should be attached to the first amendment? Should this amendment be read to prevent the national government from taking steps it feels necessary for its very survival? Would restrictions on speech and publication eventually lead to majority or governmental tyranny by preventing nonfactious majorities from uniting to impress their will on government?

Chapter 11 dealing with the role of the representative and his accountability to his constituents also involves questions of a highly related nature. In specifying the rights of the people in a republican government, should an amendment be added to the Constitution to insure the right of the people to instruct their representatives? Would this serve to eliminate one of the important checks against faction? Or would it tend to preserve and advance the principle of majority control? What rules should a representative assembly adopt in order to insure the degree of deliberation necessary to prevent majority tyranny?

The debates in chapter 9 (particularly selections 9.2 through 9.5) focus on other dimensions of the tension inherent in the notion of "limited" republican government. In these sections certain crucial questions arise: Just what is a faction? Does the development of party spirit expose the system to control by factions? In what ways should our procedures be changed to allow for representation of minority viewpoints in order to temper the will of majorities? What role, if any, should the national government perform to insure that the people are accurately and reliably informed about the activities of their representatives?

While the debates of the formative years do not provide us with any definitive resolution of all the problems arising from this basic tension, they do provide us with greater insight into many of the major controversies, both past and present, within the American political system.

chapter 9

Foundations of popular government

THE REPUBLICAN CHARACTER

9.1 James Hillhouse: "Ours is a free representative Republic, deriving all power from the people. Every branch of our Government, being elective, rests on the public will."*

. . .

I will close my observations with a few general remarks upon the different kinds of Government, including our own.

In a monarchy the powers of Government are concentrated in one man whose will is the supreme law. This is the most energetic and powerful of all Governments for military enterprise or conquest. The whole resources of the nation, being subject to the control of a single chief, are capable of being directed with the greatest energy and effect. In the hands of an able Prince whose measures are directed by wisdom and a supreme regard for the public welfare and

* From a speech by the Senator from Connecticut in the Senate, April 12, 1808, supporting the series of proposed constitutional amendments described in the editors' note preceding selection 9.5. *Annals*, 10th Congress, 1st session, pp. 349-351.

whose aim is to promote the real prosperity and happiness of his subjects (which, unfortunately, too seldom happens) this kind of Government is perhaps as 350 conducive to the tranquility of the nation as any other. But such a Government cannot be elective, as the experience of all ages has demonstrated. It must be hereditary, and is thus liable to all the chances of a weak or wicked succession. And the proportion of such characters is too great to be risked, but in cases of inevitable necessity. In regard to the United States, this form of Government is out of the question. We have neither the materials of which to form such a Government, nor the disposition to introduce it.

Aristocracy is a Government in the hands of nobles. Venice, among others, exhibited an example where the rights and interests of the few were preferred to those of the many. It was a most undesirable Government. To form an aristocracy, privileged orders and hereditary succession are indispensable. The moment you limit the privilege in its duration to any term short of life, or admit the popular voice in its creation by subjecting it at regular periods to a popular election, it ceases to possess the necessary attributes of aristocracy. The United States do not possess the materials for forming an aristocracy. We have no privileged orders; nor should we readily consent to make a selection of men on whom we would confer such privileges, and agree that they should enjoy them as a right of inheritance. It is impossible, therefore, that an aristocracy should grow up or exist in the United States. We have not the means of making even an aristocratic branch to our Government.

A Democracy is a government wholly in the hands of the people, where, in their own proper persons and not by representatives, they manage their own national concerns. Athens, in ancient Greece, nearly answered this description; and, as long as the people preserved their virtue, it was powerful, prosperous, and happy. The great evil to which such a government is exposed is that, in a sudden impulse of passion or of groundless jealousy, the people are excited to some rash and mischievous act which, when their passions subside, they review with the deepest remorse. A popular assembly, inflamed by artful designing men, condemned Socrates, the good and great, to die. After the sentence was executed, their passions subsided; they repented the rash deed, and decreed distinguished honors to his name. When the morals of the people begin to decline,

"Demagogues, the greatest curse of free Governments," make their appearance; and, under the garb of patriotism and love of country, insinuate themselves into the confidence of the people; procure their own elevation to office; and, by their machinations and intrigues, carried on under this specious garb, finally overturn the liberties of their country. Of this melancholy truth, the experience of former republics furnishes abundant proofs, and these ought to serve as a beacon to our country. The people can have no possible interest in supporting such men: but, led into a blind confidence in them by their professions of patriotism, are made the instruments of their own destruction. In ancient republics, the wisest and most virtuous of their citizens were sometimes exclud- 351 ed from office, banished, and even put to death. When a citizen claims to be an exclusive patriot and is very officious in proclaiming his own merit, it is time for the people to be alarmed.

When the three kinds of Government above described are united, as in the Government of Great Britain, it is called a mixed Monarchy. There is always such a spirit of jealousy existing between aristocracy and democracy and between monarchy and democracy, that they cannot long exist together without a third balancing power. As well might a man take up his abode in a tiger's den, as aristocracy with democracy, unless protected by the strong arm of monarchy. Neither can monarchy and democracy dwell together, unless the throne be surrounded by a powerful aristocracy. Singly, democracy is an over-match for either. The reason is obvious —there is the physical force, numbers. Whenever an attempt has been made to oppose either monarchy or aristocracy, singly, as a check on democracy, they have been found too feeble to support themselves. Discord has arisen which has generally terminated in the overthrow of such check, and democracy, remaining master of the field and freed from all restraint or check, has degenerated into faction and paved the way to despotism—despotism of the worst kind, which has entered at the door of discord and civil war. It is a cause of deep regret that it should have been the unhappy lot of most countries where liberty has found an asylum, to lose it by its own excess. And this will be our case unless effectual provision be made to stem the torrent of party spirit and violence.

To superficial observers our Government may seem to be assimilated to the mixed Government before mentioned. But, as the materials necessary to compose such a Government do not and cannot exist among us, whatever attributes of power appropriate to these deficient materials are introduced into our Constitution ought to be taken away; for in practice they are found only to bring evils unmixed with benefits. Ours is a free representative Republic, deriving all power from the people; and, when amended as I propose for the purpose of checking party spirit, Executive influence, and favoritism, will correctly express the public opinion and declare the public will. The people, being numerous and spread over a large extent of territory, cannot meet together and personally manage the public concerns; and are, therefore, obliged to elect a few individuals to represent them in public councils, and confide to them the management of their public affairs. Every branch of our Government, being elective, rests on the public will. And, could the people be left to a fair, uninfluenced exercise of their right of suffrage and our public councils be guided in their deliberations and decisions by an honest zeal for the public good regardless of personal views of elevation to or continuance in office, ours would be the best and happiest Government that does or ever did exist.

. . .

POPULAR ELECTIONS AND PUBLIC INFORMATION

9.2   William Gaston: "In Republican Governments the majority must indeed rule, but it is of vast importance that the majority be compelled to respect not only the rights, but the opinions, feelings, and even the prejudices of the minority."*

. . .

It is well known that no part of the plan of a Federal Government presented greater difficulties to the illustrious men who framed it, than that which relates to the appointment of the Executive. . . .

* From a speech by the Representative from North Carolina in the House of Representatives, January 3, 1814, supporting a proposed constitutional amendment which would require that presidential electors be chosen in separate single-elector districts. *Annals,* 13th Congress, 2nd session, pp. 837-841.

The outlines of their plan were sketched with a masterly hand. Each State was to choose a number of Electors, upon the combined principles of population and State sovereignty, equal to the number of Senators and Representatives. These Electors were to be called into existence for the special purpose of voting for a President, and were to exist only during that special conjuncture. . . . How the electors themselves should be chosen, the Constitution did not provide; it left this part of the process of appointing a Chief Magistrate of the Union to be regulated in each State by its respective Legislature. . . . 838

Is it not desirable, sir, that some uniform mode should obtain? Unless the Constitution should prescribe in definite and imperative terms the process by which Electors shall be taken from the mass of their fellow-citizens, it will be liable to perpetual fluctuation according to the varying notions of eighteen distinct State Legislatures, each of them subject to frequent, in general to annual changes. Nothing can contribute more effectually to the permanence and stability of any institution than that its essential forms should be permanent and stable. The omnipotent force of habit over individuals loses none of its power when extended to communities. Time and custom have an effect upon opinions and feelings and modes of action, which alone can render them distinctive and characteristic. Thus it is that they become intimately associated with the affections, and are converted into what is emphatically called a second nature. It is the part of political wisdom to create and strengthen this union between the affections of the people and the forms of their Government. You thus consecrate these forms in their estimation and establish a solid basis on which the Government itself can rest.
. . . 839

If an uniform and permanent mode of appointing Electors be recommended by these obvious and decided advantages, it remains to be examined which among the different methods that have been essayed has the strongest claims to a preference. In no State has any other mode been thought of, nor have I heard any other suggested, than the three which have been mentioned by my colleague. These are—a choice by the qualified voters of each State in districts, or by a general ticket throughout each State, or an appointment by the State Legislatures. The principle and scope of the proposed amendment is the establishment of the first of these modes. It is very far from my design to enumerate all the advantages which I believe it to possess; many of them have been already stated by my colleague, and it is not my wish to repeat and perhaps thereby weaken any of his arguments. But I will attempt to set forth a few leading considerations which, in my judgment, render it infinitely superior as a permanent and universal rule to either of the others.

Sir, it is recommended to our adoption by a consideration which should endear it to all who feel an attachment to the great and leading principle of Republican Government. It is by this method that the voice of the people of the Union is fairly expressed and fully felt in the selection of their Chief Magistrate. Adopt this mode and it is scarcely practicable that any individual can be chosen for that high office but by the voice of a majority of the people. There may, indeed, be a considerable difference between the relative strength of the minorities in any two districts but, when all the districts are taken into computation, such difference must be equalised. He who obtains the suffrage of more than half of the voters of the two hundred and eighteen districts into which the United States will be parcelled, must in all human probability have a majority of the suffrages of the people. . . . *840*

An eminent advantage which I believe likely to flow from this fair expression of the sentiments of every portion of the people, in the choice of a President, will be found in the security which it affords to the minority in each State, against the intolerance of the majority. In Republican Governments the majority must indeed rule, but it is of vast importance that the majority should be compelled to respect, not only the rights, but the opinions, feelings, and even prejudices of the minority. Unless it feel this sentiment, nature and history prove that it will be unjust and overbearing. When the Electors of President are chosen by States, the minority in each State is utterly without weight. As to this purpose it has no political power. Its opinions are treated with arrogance. The individuals who belong to it are viewed as a class that is arrayed against the cause of the State. They must either forbear from all interference in its concerns, or be subjected to the jealousies and malignant tyranny of intolerant power—never more intolerant than when backed by the physical force of the community, or when exerted upon those who are without the ability to retaliate. Let the voice of every part of the nation be heard in the appointment of the Chief Magistrate, and the minority in each State acquires an importance which insures to them respect and political freedom. If they can give but one vote, it is worth the attention of the majority to conciliate that vote; for, joined with the suffrages of other portions of the people in other States, it may weigh heavily in the balance.

In every Government which is purely of the federative character there is a radical defect arising from the want of an intimate relation between those who administer its powers and those who are subject to its control. Our Government partakes both of the national and federative forms. Without stopping to discuss that great question, which gave rise to the parties that were early seen after its organization, whether it is more likely to encroach upon the State authorities or to be controlled by them in its necessary and proper operations, all will concur, I trust, in the position that it is wise to impart to it every efficiency which abridges not individual liberty nor lessens the useful powers of its component members.

Whatever may be the powers which are in terms delegated, in proportion as you remove the General Government from the people you impair its strength. Wise and reflecting men who are sensible of its infinite value 841 in insuring domestic tranquillity and guarding against external dangers, will venerate and uphold it from principle. But the citizens in general, who have little agency in promoting its operations and who feel not its beneficial influence in their daily concerns, who look elsewhere for the protection of their personal rights, and for redress from individual injuries—who scarcely feel it but in its restraints or in its demand on them for personal services and contributions, will naturally regard it in the light of a foreign Government. It will be scarcely possible to create in them that sentiment of loyal obedience which springs spontaneous in the heart towards the Government which is felt and cherished as their own. Give them an agency as individuals in the appointment of its Chief and they are at once sensible of a participation in the political institution itself. It is brought nearer home to them—a connexion is created between the General Government and themselves, instead of a connexion between the General Government and the State to which they belong. This intimate relation, and the sentiments of loyalty and affection which spring from it, will be a tower of strength to the Federal Government. The vigor which is thus imparted diminishes not one particle of the freedom of the citizen, and deprives not the State governments of a single privilege which is necessary to their support or to the full exercise of their peculiar powers. It impoverishes not those from whom it is taken, while it is invaluable to the institution on which it is conferred.

. . .

9.3 Charles Pinckney and Uriah Tracy: "It is no crime to publish the doings of this body. But are printers at liberty to tell lies about our transactions?"*

[Note by the editors. On February 26, 1800, Senator Uriah Tracy of Connecticut introduced a resolution calling for an inquiry into the editorship of the Philadelphia newspaper *Aurora* and into the grounds for certain assertions printed in that newspaper concerning occurrences in the Senate. The findings of this inquiry were to be reported to the Senate. Senator Pinckney opposes the motion, and Senator Tracy defends it in the extracts of their speeches which are printed here.]

Mr. C. Pinckney: This subject involves the important questions: What are the privileges of Congress and how far are they defined by the Constitution; and what is the liberty of the press as it respects those privileges? . . .

No man who is a friend to order will justify what properly deserves to be termed the licentiousness of the press. When, instead of candidly reviewing the arguments or public conduct of a member of the Legislature or officer of the Government, it meanly descends to private scandal, instead of being defended it should be met with contempt and disdain. Abuse is the price that public men, and frequently those of the most ability, are obliged to pay; and it is seldom, in countries where the press is free and strong political parties are known to exist, that it is much noticed. Men of elevated minds who feel themselves strong in the powers of reasoning will always

* Remarks made in the Senate by Senators Pinckney of South Carolina and Tracy of Connecticut, in debate on a motion to investigate the *Aurora*, March 5, 1800. *Annals*, 6th Congress, 1st session, pp. 69, 75–78 (Pinckney) and pp. 85–87 (Tracy).

yield to their feeble opponents the miserable resort of abuse; it is
the surest test of imbecility and the public, who generally think
right, seldom hesitate to suppose it equally the proof of weakness
and of malice.

. . . 75

It is well known that our Constitution intended the press to be
free; to be the means of communicating the acts of the Government,
and of commenting on them where necessary; that it supposes that
majorities will sometimes exist who may wish to overstep the
boundaries they ought not to pass; and therefore it provides for
them, in the hands of the people, this wholesome correction of the
press which those who resort to must use at their peril. If they use
it properly, animadvert with propriety, and really point out defects
or usurpations in the Government, the people will applaud their
zeal and the laws will support them in their exertions; but if they
falsely or maliciously misrepresent, the law will become the avenger
of the Government and unprejudiced juries be the means of punishing calumniators.

. . . 76

I feel a pride in saying that in no country has the press ever
been as free as in United America; however clouded or interrupted
this freedom has, in my opinion, lately been, I entertain a hope that
in a few months all its shackles will be removed, and that the emo-
tions they have occasioned in the public mind will forever forbid its
being thus fettered again. To no subject have I ever more carefully
applied than what ought in a well regulated Government to be the
freedom of the press. I well know that where the press is not free,
liberty is but a name and Government a mockery. I have therefore
endeavored to form, in my own mind, what ought to be the true
standard of the freedom of the press with us; and I have no doubt
that it consists in this: That the printing press shall be free to every
person who undertakes to examine the proceedings of the Legislature or any branch of the Government, and no law shall ever be
made to restrain the right thereof; that the free communication of
thoughts and opinions is one of the most invaluable rights of man;
and every citizen may freely speak, write, and print on any subject,
being responsible for the abuse of that liberty; that in prosecutions
for the publication of papers investigating the official conduct of
officers or men in a public capacity, or where the matter published is

proper for public information, the truth thereof may be given in evidence; and in all indictments for libels the *Jury* shall have a right to determine the law and the fact, under the direction of the court, as in other cases. . . .

Here the right to investigate the conduct of the Legislature and of official men is not only recognized and established, but the Constitution seems to require it as a duty from the citizens. It says to them, these are men periodically delegated by you to manage your public concerns—to you, and you alone, they 77 are accountable for their conduct; nor can you know whether it is meritorious or otherwise but by having the right to examine into it, and by freely and frequently exercising that right. And would it not be the strangest thing in the world, when the Constitution not only establishes the right but calls upon the citizens to exercise it with alertness and by no means to neglect it, that if they should happen to displease a branch of the Legislature whose conduct they have censured, that they should be delivered immediately into the power of this branch to be dealt with as they please; that the men they had accused, and whom they had by the Constitution a right to accuse, should become their judges? Would not this be a most extraordinary doctrine? Would it not involve an inconsistency, that ought not certainly to be chargeable upon the framers of the Constitution? . . .

And here, sir, let it be asked, why should a Government that means well or is confident in its uprightness and ability ever fear the press? It should be to them a source of great pleasure in reflecting that they had so excellent a mode of diffusing a 78 knowledge of their acts, well knowing, if they were unjustly attacked, it gave them the most ample means of defence; and that if it became immoderate and licentious, the laws were always sufficiently energetic to punish it. How many individuals when attacked or slandered have rejoiced that such a defence has been afforded them; and how indispensable is its free investigation to the removal of doubts which sometimes crowd about the characters of public bodies or men, and which it is necessary to remove! Public bodies are public property; and so indeed are public men who have in any degree rendered themselves conspicuous by their exertions; few of these, if ever there was one, can expect to be without personal enemies; these will be in proportion to the talents of the man they dislike and his consequence with the people. Men who engage in public life or are members of legislative bodies must expect to be exposed to anonymous, and sometimes avowed, attacks on their principles and opinions. Their best shield will be an upright and able conduct. The best informed will sometimes err; but when their intentions are pure, an enlightened nation will easily discover it and ponder the mistake. With the shield of conscious rectitude, a government can never dread the press. . . .

. . .

Mr. Tracy: The gentleman has told us it is no crime to publish the doings of this body. 86 Agreed, but is it nothing to publish untruths concerning the official conduct of the members of this body? [It is] no crime to publish a bill while before this House. But are printers at liberty to tell lies about our transactions?

. . .

The gentlemen had declared themselves the champions of the press; but surely gentlemen will not advocate such liberty as this— the liberty of publishing nothing but lies and falsehood. If by the liberty of the press is meant the publication of truth and just political information, it was proper to be supported; but he was desirous of maintaining, along with the liberty of the press, the liberty of the citizens and the security of the Government; he was not for sacrificing these latter objects to the licentiousness of the press. He was not inclined to enter into a newspaper controversy to maintain the dignity and reputation of the Senate, nor did he think that gentlemen appreciated their own standing in society when they referred the individual members of this body to such a mode of defence against the shafts of calumny 87 which a daring editor might hurl against them individually.

He believed that it was as requisite to maintain the privileges of the Senate as it was to support the liberty of the press; the Constitution secured the first as well as the last; and it became important in considering the subject in this point to ascertain the extent of the privilege on the present occasion. The Constitution declares several privileges to belong to the members of Congress, and these privileges are given in order to secure the execution of the public duties which are enjoined upon us. It is for the interest of the people, and not for our own peculiar advantage, that we enjoy these privileges. It is then proper that we should on their account maintain them. But, in defining what may be privilege, we must govern ourselves according to the original intention, which is the promotion of the general interests of the citizens, and here we can be guided only by sound discretion and common sense.

In this point of view the subject becomes truly important. Will any gentleman contend that our privileges are restrained to this Chamber? No. Are there no other methods by which our deliberations may be interrupted? Certainly there are. Of course, then, our authority must extend to remedy the evil wherever we may meet it, or otherwise our authority is inadequate to protect itself.

On the principle of self-preservation, which results to every public body of necessity and from the nature of the case, the right of self-preservation is vested in the Senate of the United States, as it is in your courts of justice and other public institutions. Suppose a printer was to say that one of the judges had received a bribe in a certain case, would not the court be competent to call him before them and punish him for the slander, if it was one? And shall a printer insinuate that members of this body are guilty of a similar crime, and they have no mode of giving redress? It it not of as much importance that the laws be dictated from pure motives, as that they be executed from pure motives? If it is admitted that we have the right of protecting ourselves within these walls from attacks made on us in our presence, it follows of course that we are not to be slandered and questioned elsewhere. Will gentlemen deny this? then there is no complete remedy; for the defamation and calumny of yesterday, circulated in the newspapers, out-travel the slow and tardy steps of truth; they have spread over the face of the country and entered every cottage, where the contradiction may never penetrate. Or shall the foul aspersions of an editor circulate till you can send to the attorney general to issue a writ, to the marshal to serve it, to the court and jury to bring it, before the contradiction can be published? This also would defeat the object. The Senate, being so long suspected, must have received a deep wound, and some of its members may have to be amputated before a right understanding is acquired.

. . .

POLITICAL ORGANIZATION:
CLUBS, FACTIONS, PARTIES

9.4 Debate on the Democratic Societies:* "A Government that protects property and cherishes virtue will have vice and prodigality for its foes, because it will be compelled to abridge their liberty to prevent their invading the rights of other citizens."

[Note by the editors. In his address to Congress, November 19, 1794, President Washington related the events which we know today as the Whiskey Rebellion of 1794. In his report, he asserted that those who actually resisted efforts to collect federal excises were encouraged to do so by individuals and associations of persons well removed from the scenes of violence. He said: "From a belief that, by a more formal concert [the operation of the laws] might be defeated, certain self-created societies assumed the tone of condemnation." In the course of formulating a reply by the House of Representatives to the President's address, Representative Fitzsimons proposed insertion of the paragraph (quoted immediately below) expressing disapproval of the "self-created societies." This proposal stimulated the debate that is partially presented here. The President's address is in *Annals*, 3d Congress, 2nd session, pp. 787-792.]

Mr. Fitzsimons then rose and said that it would seem somewhat incongruous for the House to present an Address to the President which omitted all notice of so very important an article in his Speech as that referring to the self-created societies. Mr. F. then read an amendment which gave rise to a very interesting debate. The amendment was in these words:

* Representatives Thomas Fitzsimons of Pennsylvania, William B. Giles of Virginia, Fisher Ames of Massachusetts, James Madison of Virginia, and Samuel Dexter of Massachusetts. From debate in the House of Representatives on language to be included in a reply to the President's address to Congress. Fitzsimons and Giles, November 24, 1794; Ames, November 26, 1794; Madison and Dexter, November 27, 1794. *Annals*, 3d Congress, 2nd session, pp. 899-900 (Fitzsimons and Giles); pp. 922-927 (Ames); pp. 934-937 (Madison and Dexter).

"As part of this subject, we cannot withhold our reprobation of the self-created societies, which have risen up in some parts of the Union, misrepresenting the conduct of the Government, and disturbing the operation of the laws, and which, by deceiving and inflaming the ignorant and the weak, may naturally be supposed to have stimulated and urged the insurrection."

These [said Mr. Fitzsimons] are "institutions, not strictly unlawful, yet not less fatal to good order and true liberty; and reprehensible in the degree that our system of government approaches to perfect political freedom."

Mr. Giles said that there was not an individual in America who might not come under the charge of being 900 a member of some one or other self-created society. Associations of this kind, religious, political, and philosophical, were to be found in every quarter of the Continent. The Baptists and Methodists, for example, might be termed self-created societies. The people called the Friends were of the same kind. Every pulpit in the United States might be included in this vote of censure, since from every one of them upon occasion instructions had been delivered, not only for the eternal welfare but likewise for the temporal happiness of the people. There had been other societies in Pennsylvania for several purposes. The venerable Franklin had been at the head of one, entitled a society for political information. They had criminated the conduct of the Governor of this State and of the Governors of other States, yet they were not prosecuted or disturbed. There was, if he mistook not, once a society in this State for the purpose of opposing or subverting the existing Constitution. They also were unmolested. If the House are to censure the Democratic societies, they might do the same by the Cincinnati Society.

It is out of the way of the Legislature to attempt checking or restraining public opinion. If the self-created societies act contrary to law, they are unprotected, and let the law pursue them. That a man is a member of one of these societies will not protect him from an accusation of treason, if the charge is well founded. If the charge is not well founded, if the societies in their proceedings keep within the verge of the law, Mr. G. would be glad to learn what was to be the sequel? If the House undertake to censure particular classes of men, who can tell where they will stop? Perhaps it may be advisable to commence [with] moral philosophers, and compose a new system of ethics for the citizens of America. In that case, there would be many other subjects for censure as well as the self-created societies. . . .

Mr. Ames: . . . Few as the apologists of the clubs have been, the solemnity and perseverance of their appeal to principles demand for it an examination.

The right to form political clubs has been urged as if it had been denied. It is not, however, the right to meet, it is the abuse of the right after they have met that is charged upon them. Town meetings are authorized by law, yet they may be called for seditious or treasonable purposes. The legal right of the voters in that case would be an aggravation, not an excuse, for the offence. But if persons meet in a club with an intent to obstruct the laws, their meeting is no longer innocent or legal; it is a crime.
. . . *923*

Will any reflecting persons suppose for a moment that this great people, so widely extended, so actively employed, could form a common will and make that will law in their individual capacity, and without representation? They could not. Will clubs avail them as a substitute for representation? A few hundred persons only are members of clubs, and if they should act for the others it would be an usurpation, and the power of the few over the many, in every view infinitely worse than sedition itself, will represent this Government.
. . . *924*

Representative Government, therefore, is so far from being a sacrifice of our rights that it is their security; it is the only practicable mode for a great people to exercise or have any rights. It puts them into full possession of the utmost exercise of them. By clubs will they have something more than all? Will such institutions operate to augment, to secure, or to enforce their rights, or just the contrary?

Knowledge and truth will be friendly to such a Government, and that in return will be friendly to them. Is it possible for any to be so deluded as to suppose that the over-zeal for Government on the part of the supporters of this amendment would prompt them to desire or to attempt the obstruction of the liberty of speech or the genuine freedom of the press? Impossible! That would be putting out the eyes of the Government which we are so jealous to maintain.

The abuses of these privileges may embarrass and disturb our present system; but, if they were abolished the Government must be changed. No friend, therefore, of the Constitution could harbor the wish to produce the consequences which it is insituated are intended to ensue.

Mr. A. resuméd the remark that the Government rests on the enlightened patriotism of an orderly and moral body of citizens. Let the advocates of Monarchy boast that ignorance may be made to sleep in chains; that even corruption and vice may be enlisted as auxiliaries of the public order. It is, however, a subject of exultation and confidence that such citizens as we represent, so enlightened, so generally virtuous and uncorrupted, under the present mild Republican system, practically are safe, nay, more, it is evidently the only system that is adapted to the American state of society. But such a system combines within itself two indestructible elements of destruction, two enemies with whom it must conflict forever; whom it may disarm but can never pacify—vice and ignorance. Those who do not understand their rights will despise or confound them with wrongs, and those whose turbulence and licentiousness find restraints in equal laws will seek gratification by evasions or combinations to overawe or resist them.

A Government that protects property and cherishes virtue will of course have vice and prodigality for its foes, because it will be compelled to abridge their liberty to prevent their invading the rights of other citizens. The virtuous and the enlightened will cling to a Republican Government 925 because it is congenial no less with their feelings than their rights. The licentious and the profligate are ever ready for confusion, which might give them everything, while laws and order deny them everything. The ambitious and desperate, by combinations, acquire more power and influence than their fellow-citizens; the credulous, the ignorant, the rash, and violent, are drawn by artifice or led by character to join these confederates. The more free the Government, the more certain they are to grow up, for where there is no liberty at all, this abuse of it will not be seen. Once formed into bodies they have an *esprit du corps*, and are propelled into errors and excesses without shame or reflection. A spirit grows up in their progress, and every disappointment makes them more loose as to the means, and every success more and more immoderate in the objects of their attempt. Calumny is one of those means. Those whom they cannot punish or control, they can vilify; they can make suspicion go where their force could not reach, and by rumors and falsehoods multiply enemies against their enemies. They become formidable, and they retaliate upon the magistrates those fears which the laws have inspired them with. The execution of the laws is not accomplished without effort, without hazard. Instead of mildness, of mutual confidence, instead of the laws almost executing themselves, more rigor is demanded in the framing, more force to secure the operation of the laws. The clubs and turbulent combinations exercising the resisting power, it is obvious that Government will need more force, and more will then be given to it.

Thus it appears that instead of lightening the weight of authority, it will [acquire] a new *momentum* from clubs and combinations formed to resist it. Turbulent men, embodied into hosts, will call for more energy to suppress them than if the discontented remained unembodied. Disturbances, fomented from time to time, may unhappily change the mild principles of the system, and the little finger then may be found heavier than the whole hand of the present Government. For if the clubs and the Government should both subsist, tranquility would be out of the question. The continual contest of one organized body against another would produce the alternate extremes of anarchy and excessive rigor of Government. If the clubs prevail, they will be the Government, and the more secure for having become so by victory over the existing authorities.

In every aspect of the discussion, the societies formed to control and vilify a Republican Government are hateful. They not only of necessity make it more rigorous, but they tend with a fatal energy to make it corrupt. By perverting the truth and spreading jealousy and intrigue through the land, they compel the rulers to depend on new supports. The usurping clubs offer to faction within these doors the means of carrying every point without. A corrupt understanding is produced between them. The power of the clubs will prevail even here, and that of the people will proportionally decline. The clubs echo the language of their protectors here; truth, virtue, and 926 patriotism are no longer principles, but names for electioneering jugglers to deceive with. Calumny will assimilate to itself the objects it falls on. It will persecute the man who does his duty; it will take away the reward of virtue and bestow praise only upon the tools of faction. By betraying his trust, a man may then expect the support of

the powerful combinations opposed to the Government. By faithfully adhering to it, he encounters persecution. He finds neither refuge nor consolation with the public, who become at length so cor-
rupted as to think virtue in a public station incredible because it
would be, in their opinion, folly. The indiscriminate jealousy which
is diffused from the clubs tends no less to corrupt the suspicious than
the suspected. It poisons confidence, which is no less the incitement
than the recompense of public services. It lowers the standard of action.

These observations, which seem to be founded on theory, unfortunately bear the stamp of experience. History abounds with the
proofs. Never was there a wise and free Republic which was exempt
from this inveterate malady. We can find a parallel for the brightest
worthies of Greece, as well as for their calumniators. In that country
as well as in this, the assassins of character abounded. While slander
is credited only by its inventors, it is easy for a man to maintain the
serenity of his contempt for both. But when it is adopted by the public, few are hardy enough to despise opinion; he that pretends to do
so is a hypocrite, and if he really does so, he is a wretch. This precious property is one of the first objects of invasion, and the combinations alluded to are well adapted and actively employed to destroy it.

. . .

It will be asked what remedy for this evil? I answer, no violent
one. The gentle power of opinion, I flatter myself, will prove sufficient among 927 our citizens who have sense, morals, and property.
The hypocrisy of the clubs will be unmasked, and the public scorn,
without touching their persons or property, will frown them into
nothing. . . .

Mr. Madison: . . . If we advert to the nature of Republican Government, we shall find that the censorial power is in the people over the
Government, and not in the Government over the people. As he had
confidence in the good sense and patriotism of the people, he did not
anticipate any lasting evil to 935 result from the publications of these
societies; they will stand or fall by the public opinion; no line can be
drawn in this case. The law is the only rule of right: what is consistent with that, is not punishable; what is not contrary to that, is
innocent, or at least not censurable by the Legislative body.

With respect to the body of the people (whether the outrages have proceeded from weakness or wickedness) what has been done and will be done by the Legislature will have a due effect. If the proceedings of the Government should not have an effect, will this declaration produce it? The people at large are possessed of proper sentiments on the subject of the insurrection; the whole Continent reprobates the conduct of the insurgents; it is not, therefore, necessary to take the extra step. The press, he believed, would not be able to shake the confidence of the people in the Government. In a Republic, light will prevail over darkness, truth over error: he had undoubted confidence in this principle. If it be admitted that the law cannot animadvert on a particular case, neither can we do it. Governments are administered by men; the same degree of purity does not always exist. Honesty of motives may at present prevail, but this affords no assurance that it will always be the case. At a future period, a Legislature may exist of a very different complexion from the present; in this view we ought not, by any vote of ours, to give support to measures which now we do not hesitate to reprobate.

. . .

Mr. Dexter rose in reply to Mr. Madison. He said that, if he viewed the subject as trivial as some gentlemen appeared to, he would not trouble the House with any further remarks after having so long detained them while in Committee. If he viewed the amendment proposed as dangerous to the most perfect freedom of expressing political opinions, as the gentleman seemed to who was last up, he would be the last to support it. He said that the most certain way to destroy this freedom was to encourage an unlimited abuse of it; and the way to render a free press useless, was to prostitute it to the base purposes of party and falsehood until, wearied with constant impositions, the public would reject all information from that source as uncertain and delusive. He said that the most successful weapon used by the enemies of civil freedom ever had been to push the ideas of liberty to such wild extremes as to render it impracticable and ridiculous, and thus to compel the sober part of the community to submit to usurpation, as a less evil than utter insecurity and anarchy. He added, if America loses her liberty, this will be the instrument of her destruction.

We possess, he said, greater equality of property and informa-

tion than any other nation; the means of subsistence are so easily
obtained that no man is necessarily dependent on the will of another; from these circumstances, our country is more fit than any
other for a Republican form of Government. If we fail in maintaining it, we shall be fairly considered to have made an experiment not
only for ourselves but for the world which will prove that the beau-
tiful theory of civil freedom is not practicable by man; that ambition
and envy, aided by ignorance, are naturally too strong for patriotism.

Mr. D. said that the nature of civil freedom is more obscure than
its real friends could wish; that it consists rather in what it forbids
than in what it allows; that man was free before he became a member of society; that the great object of associating was not to obtain
freedom, for that was possessed before, but to guard against the
abuse of it, in violating the rights of others. My liberty, he said, is,
that all other citizens are restrained from violating my rights, and
the liberty of each one of them is, that I and all others are equally
restrained from violating his rights. Restraint, then, is necessary to
constitute civil liberty; and the uniformity of this restraint, as it op-
erates equally on all classes of citizens, is equality.

I know, sir, that a doctrine very different from this has been
holden by some false apostles of liberty, and that the aspiring, the
vicious, the desperate, and the weak, have flocked to this standard.
By them the power to violate the rights of others, and disturb the
public peace with impunity, has been profanely called liberty, and
the universality of this has been called equality. Can I be a freeman,
sir, if the Government, which is my only security for all my rights,
may be invaded with impunity and my reputation, the dearest of all
possessions and the best reward of virtue, blasted by the foul breath
of slander and falsehood? When this shall be admitted as a principle
in the American code, we shall call that freedom which will be our
misery; we shall cease to deserve liberty; we shall need a master.

Let men meet for deliberating on public matters. Let them
freely express their opinions in conversation or in print, but let them
do this with a decent respect for the will of the majority and for the
Government and rulers which the people have appointed. Let them
not become a band of conspirators, to make and propagate falsehood
and slander. Let them not instigate to the highest crimes against society. And, sir, if any have so done, let not us encourage them in

these outrages by calling them the exercise of the inviolable rights
of freemen. 937

To suffer misrepresentations of Government to gain credit
among the people is giving a blow to the weakest part of our Government. It would be a most important political acquisition, if means
could be devised to scatter through the Union true ideas of the
measures of Government. The best intentions cannot now guard the
citizens from being deceived by the cunning and depraved; some
improvement on this subject seems essentially necessary to perfect
the system of political freedom. Scattered, as our countrymen are,
over an immense country and employed in useful industry, perhaps
this is rather to be wished for than expected; but we can at least
take measures to prevent the most fatal effects from misrepresentations and scandal.

. . .

9.5 James Hillhouse: *"Party spirit is the demon which engendered the factions that have destroyed most free governments."**

[Note by the editors. On April 12, 1808, Senator James Hillhouse of Connecticut introduced in the Senate a series of constitutional amendments, arranged in seven aticles, which, if adopted,
would have drastically revised the structure of the national government. The proposed changes included: fix a one-year term for members of the House of Representatives and a three-year term for
members of the Senate; fix a one-year term for the President and fill
that office by selecting for President, by lot, one of the Senators
whose term is expiring; abolish the office of Vice President; and restrict the authority of the President in appointing and removing
officers of the government. These proposals appear not to have been
subjected to debate or vote, but Senator Hillhouse accompanied the
submission of his plan for revision with a speech which thoughtfully
reviewed experience with the form of government established by the
Constitution twenty years before. His address is in *Annals*, 10th
Congress, 1st session, pp. 332-356, and his proposals follow at pp.
356-358.]

* From a speech in the Senate, which is partially printed as selection 9.1
above, by the Senator from Connecticut, April 12, 1808. *Annals*, 10th Congress,
1st session, pp. 334-337, 344-347.

. . . Two evils to be guarded against in a republican government (such as is that of the United States, and such as I hope and trust it ever will be) are *ambition* and *favoritism*. The former induces the most aspiring, artful, and unprincipled men to assume the garb of patriotism for the purpose of obtaining office and power; and when they have obtained it, they extend their patronage and favor 335 to those who have been most active and instrumental in procuring their elevation.

There is no position more generally admitted to be true, than that man is fond of power. When ambition is alive and competitors for office take the field, those means which promise success will be resorted to. None are more powerful or can be used to greater effect than the gift of lucrative and important offices; and none will be more zealous and indefatigable in their exertions than expectants of such offices. A golden eagle will bribe but one man; but an office may operate as a bribe to one hundred expectants. A man who would spurn at a direct offer of money may be induced to believe he may accept an office without dishonor. To an ambitious man, how great must be the self-denial that would not permit him to use such powerful means to obtain an election which alone can raise him to the most dignified office in the nation! . . . 336

It is a sound position that in a republican Government like ours the public will, that is, the sentiment of the majority, when fairly and fully ascertained, should prevail; it will, in most cases comport with the public good. Opinions produced by a sudden impulse of passion, by a feverish, unnatural excitement, or by the intrigues of artful, 337 designing men, are those against which it is necessary to provide. The idea of tying up the hands of the people, who in fact possess the whole power, to prevent the execution of that public will, is chimerical; there are no cords strong enough to hold them.

The most effectual, and indeed the only effectual guard, against popular passion and jealousy is to let the people see clearly and distinctly that there always exists an opportunity for a fair expression and execution of the public will, and that they are in no danger from abuse of power; seeing their public functionaries are obliged frequently to resort to them for a renewal of their authority to exercise their power. No man's jealousy or fears can be excited respecting the exercise of a power which he clearly sees to be subject to his own control. What excites alarm among the people is an accumulation of power in the hands of an individual or of a small body of men which, added to long duration in office and high salaries, they believe may endanger their liberties. To this poison, frequent elections are a complete antidote. Here the people see and understand that there is perfect security; and when an attempt is made to excite their fears or alarm their jealousy they will ask: what possible danger can there be? have we not the power in our own hands? and must not these public functionaries, at short intervals, resort to us for power to act at all? A popular flame cannot be kept alive where there is no fuel to feed it. . . . *344*

Party spirit is the demon which engendered the factions, that have destroyed most free governments. State or local parties will have but a feeble influence on the General Government. Regular, organized parties only, extending from the northern to the southern extremity of the United States and from the Atlantic to the utmost western limits, threaten to shake this Union to its centre. No man can be so blind but he must see, and the fact is too notorious to be denied, that such parties have commenced in this country and are progressing with gigantic strides. The danger is great and demands an early and decisive remedy. There is but one which presents itself to my mind; this is, to cut off the head of the demon. For without a head, without a rallying point, no dangerous party can be formed, no such party can exist.

There is but a single point in the Constitution which can be made to bear upon all the States at one and the same time, and produce a unity of interest and action, and thus serve us as the rallying point of party; and that is the Presidential election. This most dignified and important office of President—made more desirable by having attached to it a high salary, great power, and extensive patronage—cannot fail to bring forth and array all the electioneering artillery of the country, and furnish the most formidable means of organizing, concentrating, and cementing parties. And when a President shall be elected by means of party influence thus powerfully exerted, he cannot avoid party bias and will thence become the chief of a party instead of taking the dignified attitude of a President of the United States.

If some other mode of filling the Presidential chair than that of a general election throughout the United States were devised and adopted, it would be impossible to form national parties. There would in some instances be State and local parties, but they would have a very inconsiderable effect on the General Government; they would be like town or country parties in States, which have a limited operation on the councils of the State. Indeed this Presidential election does more than anything else towards making parties in States —parties dangerous to their ancient institutions and producing an injurious effect upon their most important concerns. In one word, it is now manifest that the present mode of electing a President is producing, and will produce, many and great evils to the Union and to the individual States.

. . . 345

Various modes of election or appointment of a Chief Magistrate have been tried. Sometimes the choice has been confided to the people—sometimes to a Legislature—sometimes to a Senate—sometimes to electors chosen by the people, or the Legislature—and sometimes by electors designated by a complication of lot and ballot. But in no instance of the election of a Chief Magistrate clothed with royal prerogatives, where the votes were permitted to be given directly for the candidate, has it been possible to exclude undue influence, intrigue, and cabal; which have produced serious evils, and sometimes ended in civil war: evils so great and terrible as to induce most nations to prefer an hereditary succession.

If this mode of appointing a President by lot [which I propose] 346 should not be approved, I see but one other shield from the calamities to be apprehended from a popular election of a Chief Magistrate. This is, to strip the office of royal prerogatives and of all power excepting so much as shall enable the President to become the organ of the public will, in such manner as shall be directed by law; to shorten the term of service and lessen the salary. This will moderate the desire of obtaining the office, and paralyze individual exertion. If we mean to preserve both our internal peace and liberties, we must consent to give up the trappings as well as the name of royalty and be content to wear the humble garb of Republicans. If we will not make this sacrifice—if we will have the splendor of royalty—must we not, like the Israelites of old, have a King?

. . .

Of the impropriety and impolicy of the present mode of electing a President, can there be stronger proof, can there be a more convincing evidence, than is now exhibiting in the United States? In whatever direction we turn our eyes, we behold the people arranging themselves under the banners of different candidates for the purpose of commencing the electioneering campaign for the next President and Vice President. All the passions and feelings of the human heart are brought into the most active operation. The electioneering spirit finds its way to every fireside; pervades our domestic circles; and threatens to destroy the enjoyment of social harmony. The seeds of discord will be sown in families, among friends, and throughout the whole community.

In saying this, I do not mean anything to the disadvantage 347 of either of the candidates. They may have no agency in the business; they may be the involuntary objects of such competition, without the power of directing or controlling the storm. The fault is in the mode of election; in setting the people to choose a King. In fact, a popular election, and the exercise of such powers and prerogatives as are by the Constitution vested in the President, are incompatible. The evil is increasing and will increase until it shall terminate in civil war and despotism. The people, suffering under the scourge of party feuds and factions and finding no refuge under the State any more than in the General Government from party persecution and oppression, may become impatient and submit to the first tyrant who can protect them against the thousand tyrants. . . .

chapter **10**

Representation

POPULAR INSTRUCTION OF LEGISLATORS: A CONSTITUTIONAL RIGHT?

10.1 Debate on the Bill of Rights:*   "The People ought to have confidence in the honor and integrity of those they send forward to transact their business; their right to instruct them is a problematical subject."

[Note by the editors. One of the guarantees which Representative James Madison included in his proposed Bill of Rights, to be secured by amending the Constitution, read as follows: "The freedom of speech and of the press, and the right of the people peaceably to assemble and consult for their common good, and to apply to the government for redress of grievances, shall not be infringed." When the House of Representatives took this proposal up for consideration, Representative Thomas Tudor Tucker of South Carolina moved to add to those rights proposed the right of the people "to instruct their representatives." *Annals*, 1st Congress, 1st session, pp. 731, 733

* Representatives Thomas Hartley of Pennsylvania, Elbridge Gerry of Massachusetts, and James Madison of Virginia. Remarks in the House of Representatives on a proposed amendment to the Constitution, April 15, 1789. *Annals*, 1st Congress, 1st session, pp. 733-734 (Hartley); p. 737 (Gerry); pp. 738-739 (Madison).

236

(April 15, 1789). Representative Tucker's motion elicited remarks from several members of the House, the most interesting of which follow.]

Mr. Hartley: . . . Representation is the principle of our Government; the people ought to have confidence in the honor and integrity of those they send forward to transact their business; the right to instruct them is a problematical subject.
. . . 734

It appears to my mind that the principle of representation is distinct from any agency which may require written instructions. The great end of meeting is to consult for the common good; but can the common good be discerned without the object is reflected and shown in every light? A local or partial view does not necessarily enable any man to comprehend it clearly; this can only result from an inspection into the aggregate. Instructions viewed in this light will be found to embarrass the best and wisest men. And were all the members to take their seats in order to obey instructions, and those instructions were as various as it is probable they would be, what possibility would there exist of so accommodating each to the other as to produce any act whatever? Perhaps a majority of the whole might not be instructed to agree to any one point. Is it thus the people of the United States propose to form a more perfect union, provide for the common defence, and promote the general welfare?

Sir, I have known within my own time so many inconveniences and real evils arise from adopting the popular opinions of the moment, that although I respect them as much as any man, I hope this Government will particularly guard against them, at least that they will not bind themselves by a Constitutional act and by oath, to submit to their influence. If they do, the great object which this Government has been established to attain will inevitably elude our grasp on the uncertain and veering winds of popular commotion.

Mr. Gerry: . . . I think the people have a right both to instruct and bind [their representatives]. Do gentlemen conceive that on any occasion instructions would be so general as to proceed from all our constituents? If they do, it is the sovereign will for gentlemen will not contend that the sovereign will presides in the Legislature. The friends and patrons of this Constitution have always declared that the sovereignty resides in the people, and that they do not part with it on any occasion. To say the sovereignty vests in the people, and that they have not a right to instruct and control their representatives, is absurd to the last degree. They must either give up their principle, or grant that the people have a right to exercise their sovereignty to control the whole Government as well as this branch of it. But the amendment does not carry the principle to such an extent. It only declares the right of the people to send instructions; the representative will, if he thinks proper, communicate his instructions to the House, but how far they shall operate on his conduct he will judge for himself.

. . .

Mr. Madison: . . . If we mean nothing more than this, that the people have a right to express and communicate their sentiments and wishes, we have provided for it already. The right of freedom of speech is secured. The liberty of the press is expressly declared to be beyond the reach of this Government. The people may therefore publicly address their representatives, may privately advise them, or declare their sentiments by petition to the whole body. In all these ways they may communicate their will. If gentlemen mean to go further and to say that the people have a right to instruct their representatives in such a sense as that the delegates are obliged to conform to those instructions, the declaration is not true. Suppose they instruct a representative, by his vote, to violate the Constitution; is he at liberty to obey such instructions? Suppose he is instructed to patronize certain measures, and from circumstances known to him but not to his constituents he is convinced that they will endanger the public good; is he obliged to sacrifice his own judgment to them? Is he absolutely bound to perform what he is instructed to do? Suppose he refuses, will his vote be the less valid or the community be disengaged from that obedience which is due to the laws of the Union? If his vote must inevitably have the same effect, what sort of a right is this in the Constitution, to instruct a representative who has a right to disregard the order if he pleases? In this sense the right does not exist; in the other sense it does exist and is provided largely for.

The honorable gentleman from Massachusetts 739 asks if the sovereignty is not with the people at large. Does he infer that the people can, in detached bodies, contravene an act established by the whole people? My idea of the sovereignty of the people is that the people can change the Constitution if they please; but while the Constitution exists, they must conform themselves to its dictates. But I do not believe that the inhabitants of any district can speak the voice of the people; so far from it, their ideas may contradict the sense of the whole people; hence the consequence that instructions are binding on the representative is of a doubtful if not a dangerous nature. . . .

INSTRUCTION OF LEGISLATORS REARGUED: THE VOICE OF THE PEOPLE

[Note by the editors. In 1789 Congress fixed the compensation of members of the House and Senate at six dollars per day of service, with an additional allowance for travel. This provision was not changed until the year 1816 (14th Congress, 1st session) when a new compensation law fixed an annual payment of fifteen hundred dollars per member. The earlier provision for travel costs was continued in effect. It was estimated that the new act fixed a sum approximately one-third greater than members had derived from the per diem allowances of previous years. The act of 1816 met with a storm of adverse criticism, largely because the former per diem payments had been generally regarded as a cost of living allowance and the new act was regarded as having converted membership in Congress to a salaried position. In the election of 1816, a good many Congressmen who had enjoyed the pay increase, if indeed they had not voted for it, were defeated in their campaigns for reelection. These men returned for the final session of the Fourteenth Congress shortly after the election and debated the issue whether the salary act should be repealed and per diem payments restored. This question brought to the front the broader issue of the obligation of legislators to respond to the expectations and preferences of the general population. The salary act was repealed in this session of Congress, and the Fifteenth Congress fixed a per diem payment of eight dollars. The four speeches which are partially reprinted here were delivered during consideration of the repeal bill in the Fourteenth Congress.]

10.2 John C. Calhoun: "Have the people of this country
snatched the power of deliberation from this body? Are we a body
of individual agents and not a deliberate one, without the power
but possessing the form of legislation?"*

. . .

The ear of this House on this subject, said he, is sealed against
truth and reason. What has produced this magic spell? Instructions!
Well, then, has it come to this? Have the people of this country
snatched the power of deliberation from this body? Have they resolved the Government into its original elements, and resumed to
themselves their primitive power of legislation? Are we then a body
of individual agents and not a deliberate one, without the power
but possessing the form of legislation? If such be the fact, let gentlemen produce their instructions, properly authenticated. Let them
name the time and place at which the people assembled and delib-
erated on this question. O no! they have no written, no verbal instructions; but they have implied instructions. The law is unpopular
and they are bound to repeal it in opposition to their conscience and
reason. Have gentlemen reflected on the consequences of this doctrine? Are we bound in all cases to do what is popular? . . .

This doctrine of implied instructions, if I am not mistaken, is a
new one, for the first time broached in this House; and, if I am not
greatly deceived, not more new than dangerous. It is very different
in its character and effects from the old doctrine that the constituents have a right to assemble and formally 577 to instruct the Representative; and though I would not hold myself bound to obey any
such instructions, yet I conceive that the doctrine is not of a very
dangerous character, as the good sense of the people has as yet prevented them from exercising such a right and will, in all probability,
in future prevent them.

But this novel doctrine is of a far different character. Such instructions may exist any day and on any subject. It may be always

* From a speech in the House of Representatives by the Representative
from South Carolina on a bill to repeal the law fixing the compensation of Congressmen, January 17, 1817. *Annals,* 14th Congress, 2nd session, pp. 576-578.

at hand to justify any aberration from political duty. Mr. C. would ask its advocates in what do they differ in their actions from the mere trimmer, the political weathercock? It is true, the one may have in view his own advancement in consulting his popularity and the other may be governed by a mistaken but conscientious regard to duty; yet, how is the country benefitted by this difference, since they equally abandon the plain road of truth and reason to worship at the shrine of this political idol.

It was said by a member from Massachusetts (Mr. Conner) that this right of instruction is only denied in monarchies and, as a proof of it, he cited the opinion of Mr. Burke, whom he called a pensioner, at the Bristol election. So far is he from being correct, that in none of the free Governments of antiquity can he point out the least trace of his doctrine. It originated in the modern Governments of Europe, particularly that of Great Britain. The English Parliament had, at its origin, no other power or duty but granting money to the Crown; and as the members of that body were frequently urgently pressed to enlarge their money grants, it was a pretty convenient excuse to avoid the squeeze, to say they were not instructed. The gentleman was incorrect in calling Burke a pensioner at the time he delivered the celebrated speech at the Bristol polls. Burke at that time, whatever may have been his subsequent character, was a first rate champion in the cause of liberty and of *this* country; and if the gentleman would recur to the points in which he refused to obey the instructions of his constituents, it will not greatly increase his affection for such doctrines. That mind must be greatly different from mine, said Mr. C., who can read that speech and not embrace its doctrines.

I too, said Mr. C., am an advocate for instruction. I am instructed. The Constitution is my letter of instruction. Written by the hand of the people, stamped with their authority, it admits of no doubt as to its obligation. Your very acts in opposition to its authority are null. This is the solemn voice of the people, to which I bow in perfect submission. It is here the *vox populi* is the *vox Dei*. This is the all-powerful creative voice which spoke our Government into existence and made us politically as we are. This body is the first orb in the political creation and stands next in authority to the original creative voice of the people; and any attempt to give a different direction to its movements from what the Constitution and the deliberate consideration of its members point out, I consider as an innovation on the principles of our Government. 578 . . .

You may rely on it, the public wish and expect us to act by the convictions of our mind and will, not to tolerate the idea that either on this or any other important occasion you are acting a part and that you studiously shape your conduct to catch the applause of the audience. Mr. C. said he hoped he would not be misunderstood; that while he combatted the idea that we are bound to do such acts as will render us popular, for such he understood the doctrine, we are to overlook the character of those for whom we were to make laws. This was most studiously to be regarded. The laws ought, in all cases, to fit the permanent and settled character of the community. The state of public feeling, then, is a fact to be reckoned upon and to receive the weight on any particular question to which it may fairly be entitled. But, for his part, he preferred that erectness of mind which in all cases felt disposed to embrace what was in itself just and wise. Such characters he thought more useful, under our form of Government, than any other, and were more certain of the applause of after ages. If he was not mistaken, it constituted the very essence of the admired characters of antiquity such as Cato, Phocian, and Aristides; and if we could conceive them divested of this trait, they would cease to be the objects of our admiration. . . .

10.3 Lewis Williams: "The people are the sovereign power in this country. Hence I lay down the broad principle that they can do nothing wrong and ought to be obeyed."*

. . .

Sir, the people are the sovereign power in this country. Hence, I lay down the broad principle that they must be right; in other words, that they can do nothing wrong and ought to be obeyed. Whenever the sovereign power is lodged in any Government, there must be at least theoretical infallibility. In monarchy the sovereign

* From a speech in the House of Representatives by the Representative from North Carolina on a bill to repeal the law fixing the compensation of Congressmen, January 18, 1817. *Annals*, 14th Congress, 2nd session, pp. 616-618.

power is lodged in a single individual, and hence it is common to say that the King (as in England) can do no wrong. Now, 617 sir, although this may be incorrect or absurd in regard to the practice of England, yet it is theoretically right. . . . If the sovereign of England should do wrong in practice, as has often occurred and will frequently occur again, the people in whom the physical strength resides oppose him and in this way obtain redress.

But, in our Government, the case is widely different. Here, the supposed infallibility of a sovereign and the real physical strength both reside in the people. And if the people should perchance do wrong, how is that wrong to be corrected? The people cannot resist themselves; and if they should even do wrong in practice, there is no power on earth to oppose them. If, in England, the sovereign must be obeyed because he can do no wrong in theory, it appears to me that in our own Government the sovereign must be obeyed because he can do no wrong in theory or practice; and that is the difference between a Republic, constituted like ours, and a monarchy.

That the people are the sovereign power in this country, gentlemen have not pretended, nor will they dare, to deny. This principle is consecrated as the basis of all our political institutions, and long may the people continue to exercise the power which they have thus solemnly guarantied to themselves. Shall I not, then, cheerfully yield obedience to their voice and say this law ought to be repealed? Yes, sir, it would be my duty even if I had previously been in favor of the law; but, as I was opposed to it at the last session, I should now, if it were only in regard to consistency, be for repealing it.

But the gentleman from South Carolina (Mr. Calhoun) will object to this reasoning, because it involves the admission of a right in the constituent to instruct his Representative. Most certainly it does, and for that I contend. We, sir, are no more authorized by the Constitution to suppose the people destitute of intelligence and virtue, than to suppose them destitute of physical strength. The Constitution attaches to them power, wisdom, and goodness, as their attributes of sovereignty. The will of the sovereign, invested with their attributes, must be obeyed, as well from the necessity as the reasonableness of the thing.

It has been urged, on the other hand, that the people are not always sufficiently advised of the circumstances attending a measure, to pronounce upon the policy of its adoption, and that, to practice

upon the presumption that they were sufficiently advised, would
lead to fatal consequences. But I think differently. The people cannot, and never will, speak in a voice audible or directory to their
Representatives, unless they are duly ap- *618* prized of the various
connexions and tendencies of any given measure. I, sir, no more than
the gentleman from South Carolina, would have a Representative
surrender his judgment in obedience to mere passion or caprice. But
if the Repesentative has no rational doubt that the people, in all
their integrity of heart and with all the means of judgment before
them, would decidedly object to a measure or firmly wish its adoption, then I hold that their will should be obligatory upon him. He
should not set at defiance their instructions. He should consider that,
if the people are sufficiently informed to make a wise election, they
ought to be sufficiently informed to give wise instructions; that, if a
supposed want of information would disqualify them from doing the
former, the same want of information ought to have disqualified
them from doing the latter. Such reasoning would at once strike at
the wisdom and policy of the Constitution, and therefore must be
erroneous.

. . .

10.4 Thomas P. Grosvenor: "This is the true theory and spirit
of our representative Government; responsibility for conduct while
in office is the real secret of our safety."*

. . .

Mr. Speaker, I deny, I wholly deny, that in the nature of a representative Government, in the spirit of our system or in our Constitution, one principle, reason, or provision can be found on which
this doctrine of the right to *instruct* in the people and the obligation
of such instruction on the Representative, can rest for a moment. It
matters not to me what form of instructions gentlemen may designate; whether in writing or by parol; whether by the people of districts, of States, or of the whole nation. They have no Constitutional
power to fetter the free will of the Representative or to control his

* From a speech in the House of Representatives by the Representative
from New York on a bill to repeal the law fixing the compensation of Congressmen, January 18, 1817. *Annals,* 14th Congress, 2nd session, pp. 625, 627-628,
630-631, 634-635.

judgment, his conscience, or his independence, in the highest or the lowest act of legislation.

. . . *627*

[It is asked] are not the people the creator, the Representative, the creature? The former the master, the latter the servant? And is the creature independent of the creator—the servant above the master?

. . .

If an answer be necessary, it is to be found in the Constitution. The objection implies that if the people may not instruct with obligatory force the Representative, he is independent of the people. This notion, Mr. Speaker, is founded on a total misconception of the theory and nature of our system. It supposes that the checks upon the abuse of power by their rulers, retained by the people, was a right at all times to interfere with all their acts, and to participate in the exercise of all their powers and duties. Widely and totally distinct from such a system is the actual plan of our Government. . . .

The people well knew the tendency of power to corrupt its possessors—to degenerate *628* into abuse and oppression. Against such corruptions, abuses, and oppressions in their rulers, they resolved to hold in their own hands checks the most effectual, securities the most powerful, which were consistent with the nature of the system. These checks and guards consisted in the direct and indirect responsibility of the rulers continually or periodically to the people themselves. Thus the judges are constantly, though indirectly, responsible to the people for all their judicial conduct—they are subject at all times to impeachment by this House, the immediate representative of the people.

The President is responsible every fourth year directly to the people—for he then descends to their level and depends upon their will for a re-elevation. But as that dependence is not direct, he is also constantly subject to punishment for misconduct by impeachment at the instance of this House.

The members of the Senate are periodically, though indirectly, responsible to the people through their State Legislatures.

The members of this House are every second year responsible directly to the people. At that short period they sink into the great public mass and their official conduct, stripped of all adventitious aids, lies unveiled and naked to the inspection of the people. Can the wisdom of man contrive a more perfect security against all dangerous abuse of power?

The immediate Representatives of the people, biennially brought before the people, stripped of all power and wholly dependent on their will for continued official existence. The Executive, every fourth year, subjected to the same responsibility and the same dependence, while both he and every judge are responsible for their conduct through the right of impeachment vested in this House. This, sir, is the true theory and spirit of our representative Government. Responsibility for conduct, not control over it, while in office, is the real secret of our safety.

This is the great and active principle which pervades our Constitution and, like gravitation in the great solar system, confines each body to its orbit, regulates the whole machinery of our Government, and produces in all its parts that order and harmony, and perfect safety which was the great object of its creation.
. . . 630

When a member enters this Hall, he becomes a Representative of the people of this Republic—he becomes a legislator for the whole American community. What are his duties? Do they constitute him merely the guardian of his district? Are they confined to the little corners of townships and counties? No; they embrace the rights, the interests, and happiness of a great Republic. They "insure domestic tranquility, provide for the common defence, promote the general welfare, and secure the blessings of liberty to ourselves and our posterity"; these are the sublime and comprehensive terms in which the people have taught to all their Representatives the great duties of their stations.
. . . 631

Suppose every Representative instructed at all points on every subject which comes before him, what a babel of legislation would this House present! Local prejudices, narrow feelings, headlong violence must enter this Hall and here, uninformed by discussion, unmitigated by sober reflection, and in their very nature incapable of compromise, would be seen in disgraceful and endless collision.
. . . 634

Do I then disregard the "voice of the people"—the "will of the public"? Oh no. In making up my mind upon almost every subject of legislation that voice would have a powerful influence. I would always view it as a fact, a most important fact, entering into the argument and the reasoning when I was about to decide on any public measure. On many questions it might, on some it certainly would be, conclusive—not because it contains in itself any moral, political, or Constitutional authority to control my judgment or conduct, but because from the nature of the question it might constitute a fact or circumstance so important as to prevail over every other.

To borrow an illustration of my idea from the honorable gentleman from South Carolina (Mr. Calhoun). The question of declaring or not declaring war, however just and necessary I might deem it, would be a question of this kind. I would no more declare even such a war against the general voice and will of the people, than I would declare it with the nation destitute of arms, ammunition, and money —and precisely for the same reason, because the former is as essential to the success of a war as the latter. It is a question solely of expediency, not of Constitutional obligation. But reverse the proposition: suppose the voice of the people distinctly in favor of declaring war, which I in my conscience believed would be unjust and ruinous to the country, should I vote for such a war? No, sir, if the voice of every man in the nation should thunder instructions in my ears, I would still say no—I would struggle for peace against the people themselves; and if I should fall in the struggle, the peace of a good conscience would afford me more real happiness than all the plaudits of the people could bestow on him who might rise on my ruin. Sir, I would not be misunderstood. I am not one of those, if any such there be, who hold the political heresy that the people are their own worst enemies. I believe the people of this 635 Republic to be lovers of honesty, friends of civil order, and as well enlightened in their interests as any people on earth—and I know equally well that they always decide honestly, and when reflection, discussion, and knowledge precede decision, in general correctly.

But I should have read history in vain, I should have lived the last ten years of my life worse than in vain, if I did not know how easy it sometimes is to rouse the popular prejudice and clamor against any measure, and particularly one of the character of the law of last session. . . .

. . .

10.5   Micah Taul: "It is immaterial how I ascertain the wishes
of my constituents; this is a matter altogether between the Representative and the Electors."*

. . .

We are attempted to be arrested at the threshold of this business
by a call for our instructions. Do gentlemen suppose that written instructions are to come into this House, with all those evidences of
authenticity which are required in courts of justice in relation to foreign records and instruments from a foreign country? No gentleman
has pretended that written instructions are necessary. I have only to
observe in relation to myself [that] it is perfectly immaterial to me
how I ascertain the wishes of my constituents; this is a matter altogether between the Representatives and the Electors. Public sentiment can be ascertained in various ways, among others that of personal intercourse with the people. There is another way in which it
is ascertained that is not always very pleasant to the Representative.
If I am sensible of the fact, I shall not except to the evidence of it.
The Representative alone is to be the judge of that evidence. While
I claim for myself the right of giving my vote, by my own conceptions of duty, I am certainly willing to accord the same right to others. If gentlemen choose to disregard the public voice or the wishes
and feelings of their constituents, it is not for me to rise up in my
place and say: Sir, why do you this thing? And I protest against the
right of gentlemen to interfere between my constituents and myself.

The gentleman from New York (Mr. Grosvenor) who addressed
you on Saturday, held up to your view the Constitution of the
United States and, with a triumphant tone and manner, asked in
what part of that instrument this right of the people to instruct their
Representatives is to be found. Here, sir, at the outset, we are at issue. It is not to the scrip of parchment on which the Constitution
was originally enrolled that we are to look for the people's rights.
Instead of looking to that instrument for the people's rights, it is
there you must search for your powers. It is in that instrument the

* From a speech in the House of Representatives by the Representative
from Kentucky on a bill to repeal the law fixing the compensation of Congressmen, January 20, 1817. *Annals,* 14th Congress, 2nd session, pp. 674-677.

people have told you what they have given; and such powers as they have not there given, they have expressly retained. The people have not granted away all their powers, but have made a special grant for purposes particularly defined and enumerated. Previous to the adoption of the Constitution of the United States they were citizens of separate 675 sovereign, and independent States, in the constitutions of which their rights were particularly defined and perfectly understood. Indeed, whether as citizens of the several States, or of the United States, they are at liberty to do that which is not prohibited. If you wish the people not to exercise this right, call upon them to give it up.

. . . 676

I have contended that this right and duty grows out of the very nature of the Government. I am bold to say that it was so understood at the time of the adoption of the several State constitutions, or why is it provided in many of them that the people have a right to assemble together, consult upon the common good, and "instruct the Representatives." Certainly the word "instruct" has a very different meaning from "request"; it implies the power of commanding obedience. The best expositors have it "to teach, to form by precept, to inform authoritatively."

Sir, in the constitutions of Massachusetts, North Carolina, and Vermont, and probably in several others, the right of the people to "instruct the Representatives" is expressly recognized. Certainly the framers of those instruments considered it to be the duty of a Representative to obey such instructions. Would a Representative of the people in the Legislature of North Carolina, sworn to support the constitution, consider himself at liberty to depart from instructions? I would argue that the character given in the different constitutions to the members of the Legis- 677 lative department of their Governments is strongly in favor of my position. In some of them "trustees and servants." In others "trustees and agents." Gentlemen have emphatically asked, shall we be considered as mere "agents." Sir, our fathers were "high-minded" men, but they were not ashamed of the appellation of "agents." I am fearful we will become too much so, too "high-minded."

I beg leave to refer the House, and particularly the honorable gentleman from New York, to the style of the laws in that State. The constitution of the State of New York provides that the style of all laws shall be, "Be it enacted, by the *people* of the State of New York, in Senate and Assembly represented." The convention of that State certainly calculated that the Senate and Assembly, in the enactment of laws in the name of the people, would be governed by the voice of the people. I ask, if a majority of the Senate and Assembly might not as individuals entertain opinions diametrically opposite to nineteen-twentieths of the people? What a mockery of the people to enact laws in their name, for their oppression, or against which they are decidedly opposed. . . .

. . .

EFFICACY OF REPRESENTATION: MAJORITY RULE AND MINORITY OPPOSITION

[Note by the editors. The parliamentary tactic, call for the previous question, is a motion put in this form: "Shall the main question now be put?" The rules adopted by the House of Representatives in its first session in 1789 stipulated that a call for the previous question could be instituted by five members and that during debate on this issue (whether the main question shall now be put) there should be no consideration of the main question. If, in the vote on this issue, a majority of the House voted not to put the previous question, the main question (e.g. to pass or not to pass a bill) was terminated and the House turned to the next item of business; if, on the other hand a majority voted that the previous question shall now be put, a decision was thus made that the main question was still before the chamber for consideration. The original set of House rules contained no provisions restricting debate on the main question subsequent to the decision to keep that main question alive. During the years of bitter controversy excited by the French Revolution and the wars in Europe, minorities in each house of Congress turned more and more to extension of their remarks as a device for delaying the moment when the majority might make a decision which they disliked. The bitterness which prevailed in Congress during this period can be sensed in some of the speeches printed in this book, notably the debate on moral treason presented in selections 12.5, 12.6, and 12.7. A majority of the House decided to terminate these dilatory tactics in a session that adjourned sometime after four o'clock of the morning of February 27, 1811; the House by a vote of sixty-six to thirteen instructed the Speaker to permit no further discussion of the main question after a majority had voted that the previous question shall now be put. In the next session of Congress (12th Congress, 1st session, December 21, 1811) a committee reported to the House a revised set of rules which incorporated the decision of February 27 that after an affirmative vote to put the previous question, there should be no further discussion of the main question. When the committee's report came before the House for consideration, Mr. Nelson made the proposal, quoted in selection 10.6 below, to allow each member who had not already spoken to make one speech on the main question before closing debate and voting on that main question. His motion to amend the proposed new rules was defeated, but the majority compromised with the minority by accepting another alteration of the proposed rules. This alteration provided that one-fifth of the members present (rather than five members) must call for the previous question in order to force a vote on the question: Shall the previous question now be put? This restriction on freedom of debate remained in effect throughout the War of 1812. Soon after the termination of the war, Representative Richard Stanford of North Carolina introduced a motion to expunge from the standing rules and orders of the House the rule relating to the previous question which had been adopted in February of 1811. The speech of Representative Gaston, selection 10.7 below, is in support of Mr. Stanford's motion.]

10.6 Josiah Quincy: "The right of being heard by their Representative is the inherent and absolute right of the people."*

The House resumed the consideration of the . . . amendment proposed by Mr. Nelson . . . :

"That when the previous question is ordered to be taken, upon the main question being put, every member, who has not already spoken, shall have liberty to speak once."

Mr. Quincy: . . . I ask the House to consider what is that principle of civil liberty which is amalgamated and identified with the very

* Representatives Hugh Nelson of Virginia and Josiah Quincy of Massachusetts. From debate in the House of Representatives on a proposed amendment to House rules, December 23, 1811. *Annals*, 12th Congress, 1st session, p. 570 (Nelson's motion); pp. 572-574 (Quincy).

existence of a legislative body. In what does it consist? And what is
its character? It consists in the right of deliberation. And its character is, that it belongs not to the body but the individual members
constituting the body. The body has the power to control and to
regulate its exercise. But it has not the power 573 to take away that
right altogether by the operation of any general principle. An individual member may render himself unworthy of the privilege. He
may be set down; he may be denied the right because he has abused
it. But whenever a legislative body assumes to itself the power of
stopping, at its will, all debate at any stage of deliberation, it assumes a power wholly inconsistent with the essential right of deliberation, and totally destructive of that principle of civil liberty which
exists and is identified with the exercise of that right.

The right of every individual member is, in fact, the right of his
constituents. He is but their Representative. It is in their majesty
that he appears. It is their right that he reflects. The right of being
heard by their Representative is the *inherent* and *absolute* right of
the people. Now it is in the essential character of such a right that
it exists independent and in despite of any man, or body of men,
whatsoever. It is absurd to say that any right is independent, which
depends upon the will of another. It is absurd to say that any right
is absolute, which is wholly relative to the inclination of another;
which lasts only as long as he chooses and terminates at his nod.
Now whether this power be exercised by one or many it matters
not. The principle of civil liberty is gone when the inherent and
absolute nature of the right is gone.

Apply this reasoning to the case before us. It is impossible to
conceal the fact that as our rules and orders stand independent of
the proposition now offered as an amendment, it is in the power of
a majority to preclude all debate, upon any question, and force
every member of the House to vote upon any proposition without
giving him the opportunity of explaining his own reasons, or stating
the interests of his constituents. This is undeniable. Is it not, then,
plain and conclusive that, as our rules and orders now stand according to recent construction, every member of this House holds his
right of speaking, not on the principle of his constituents whose
Representative he is, but upon the will of the majority of this House?
For that which another may at any time take away from me, I hold

not by my own right but at his will. Can anything be more obviously at variance with the spirit of the Constitution and the first principles of civil liberty?

Let not any man say this power will not be abused. In the nature of things it must be abused. This is the favorite argument of every despotism, and of course will not fail to be urged when it is about to plant itself in the very temple of liberty.

I have chosen to consider this subject in relation to the right of the whole body and of one of its individual members, rather than to that of a majority and minority. The right to speak is an individual right. Limit it as you please, consistent with a single exercise of that right. But when this is taken away, or, which is precisely the same thing so far as it respects the principle of civil liberty, when it is in the power of one or many, at its sovereign will and pleasure to take it away, there is no longer any right. We have 574 our tenure of speech as the slave has his—at the will of a master.

But it is said that the Legislature must sometimes "act" and that individuals, by an abuse of this liberty of speech, prevent the whole body from "acting." All I say is, limit the exercise of the right as you please, only do not assume to yourselves the power of taking away the whole right, at your pleasure.

It is in this doctrine of "the necessity of acting" that lies the whole mystery of that error which we are now combating. Strictly speaking, a Legislative body never "acts." Its province is to deliberate and decide. "Action" is, alone, correctly attributable to the Executive. And it will be found that all the cases in which this necessity of "action" has been urged, have been cases in which the Legislative body has departed from its appropriate duties of deliberation and decision and descended to be an instrument or engine of the Executive. I hesitate not to say that this position may be proved by almost every instance in which this necessity of action has been urged. It was an Executive haste to its own purposes which prevailed upon the Legislative body to deny to its own members their privileges.

It has been asserted that "if this amendment passes, this will be the only deliberative body in the world which cannot stop debate." On the other hand I assert that if this amendment does not pass, this will be the only deliberative body in the world pretending to be free in which it is in the power of a majority to force a decision without any deliberation.

. . .

10.7   William Gaston: *"It is your privilege to decide, but the minority have a right to be heard."**

. . .

It is a fundamental principle of civil liberty that no citizen shall be affected in his rights without an opportunity of being heard in support of them. Our Constitution provides "that no citizen shall be deprived of life, liberty, or property, without due process of law." Every freeman is recognised by our Constitution as possessing also the right, either by himself or peaceably assembled with others, to petition the Government for a redress of grievances. The peculiar duties of the Representatives of freemen delegated with authority to bind their constituents by law, constitute these Representatives the agents of the people, to make known their grievances, their wants, and their wishes; that thus, by mutual and free intercommunication, rules of action may be framed fitted "to promote the general welfare."

To refuse to receive the petition of the poorest and meanest member of society alleging a grievance and applying to the competent authority for redress, is an act of tyranny prohibited by the Constitution. To impair by a judicial sentence any one of his rights or restrain him in the exercise of his freedom—to touch either his purse or his person until after regular process to apprize him of the charge brought against him and a full hearing of any defence he may urge by himself or his counsel, is confessedly iniquitous and unconstitutional. Yet by this detested rule he, his neighbors, the whole community, may be mulcted with taxes to an indefinite amount and subjected to obligatory rules of action involving consequences fatal to liberty, property, and life, and their recognised agents, their Constitutional counsel, their Representatives, not suf-

---

° From a speech in the House of Representatives by the Representative from North Carolina, supporting a motion to terminate a rule imposing restrictions on debate by putting the previous question, January 19, 1816. *Annals,* 14th Congress, 1st session, pp. 701-703, 717-718.

fered to allege a grievance or offer a defence! No individual can be condemned unheard—no individual can be refused a hearing of his petition. But thousands petitioning through their Representatives may be commanded into silence and a whole country sentenced without a trial. The people are to be allowed Representatives in the great national council who are forbidden to make known their wants —they are indulged with agents who are refused a hearing!

Sir, such absurdities will not bear examination. They cannot be tolerated by thinking and dispassionate men. It is vain to allege, in the language of the Speaker, that as the House is permitted by the Constitution "to determine the rules of its proceeding," it has a perfect right to forbid discussion, when and as it pleases. It cannot 702 (rightfully cannot) so regulate its proceedings as to annihilate the Constitutional franchise, either of a member or his constituents. They have a right to be heard before their money is voted or their liberty restrained, and he is their delegated agent. The whole Congress cannot, by law, deprive them of their Constitutional franchise to petition for redress of grievances; and this House is not competent to close the mouth through which the petitioners speak.

. . .

The privilege of the Representative to declare the will, to explain the views, to make known the grievances, and to advance the interests of his constituents, was so precious in the estimation of the authors of our Constitution that they have secured to him an irresponsibility elsewhere for whatever may be uttered by him in this House; "for any speech or debate in either House, they (the Senators and Representatives) shall not be questioned in any other place." The liberty of speech is fenced round with a bulwark which renders it secure from external injury—here is its citadel—its impregnable fortress. Yet here, even here, it is to be strangled by the bowstring of the previous question. In vain may its enemies assail it from without; but within, the mutes of despotism can murder it with impunity!

The existence of this arbitrary rule is incompatible with the independence which belongs to the character of a Representative. Called by the voice of a great and free people to the high (and I had almost said sacred) office of making laws for their government, we should all of us feel that our functions and the privileges essential to their discharge, are delegations of sovereignty, not the revocable precarious grants of a courteous majority of our own body; legislating for freemen we should ourselves be free. But what pretensions can he advance to freedom who is indebted for the exercise of his supposed rights to the grace and favor of his associates? Our English ancestors considered those tenures free which were independent of another's will. To hold by the will of another was the tenure of a "villain"—a slave. And has the Constitutional right of a Representative of the people, in the freest of all free countries, become nothing more than a spe- 703 cies of privileged villanage—of splendid servitude? Instead of the legislator being independent of all but God and his country in the exercise of his functions, is he to receive as a favor the permission of his fellows to take a part in legislation? The degradation is not the less because those on whom he depends are equally degraded with himself. Each may be regarded as a slave, in an association of slaves, of which the majority are tyrants. Can it be that to such a body, and so composed, the people of the United States designed by their great Constitutional charter to confide the mighty trust "of securing the blessings of liberty to themselves and their posterity"? Can it be that they should select as guardians of their rights those who should have no right to assert them? That never can be called a right which owes its existence to favor.

. . . 717

"But the majority have a right to govern. It is for them to say when discussion shall end and action begin." . . . That a numerical majority of any society has a perfect right to do as it pleases, is the most impious of political heresies; and a majority acting on such an assumption is the most dreadful of all despotisms. The primary object of law is an association of equals, the fundamental principle of the compact is to restrict the physical sovereignty within moral limits. In a Republican Government this is done by Constitutional charters, by specific delegations of power to distinct and accountable agents, by oaths, by the influence of patriotism, and love of fame. In Governments not republican, it is effected by creating a political distinct from the physical sovereignty; by vesting the power of the Government in a king or an aristocracy. Sir, a majority uncontrolled by rule—unlimited in power—unembarrassed by impediments to action —find it where you may, in a nation, in a village, in a deliberative body—is misrule, tyranny, oppression, caprice, cruelty and confusion; anything but free government. The majority here, like majorities elsewhere where civil and political liberty prevails, have a right to govern according to the prescribed rule; and when a rule is about to be formed for limiting their action, it should be a rule which may indeed protect the rights of which it affects to have a care. Not a nominal rule which imposes no restraint. Not a rule which leaves every right to the mercy of unlimited sway. "Strike," said the illustrious Athenian to his commander, "but hear me." The first may be your right, the second is mine. 718 Such is the language to the majority. It is your privilege to decide, but the minority have a right to be heard.

. . .

chapter **11**

The adoption of a
Bill of Rights

[Note by the editors. On June 8, 1789, Representative James Madison recommended to the House of Representatives that it consider the need for adding to the Constitution a number of provisions which some of the state ratifying conventions had cited as essential but missing from the great charter that they had approved. Mr. Madison had in mind two stipulations concerning the size of the House of Representatives and an alteration of the compensation of Congress, two others relating to the division of authority between the three branches of the national government, and a long series of provisions which would safeguard the American people from abuse of power by their new central government. In August the House examined Madison's proposals, approved a number of them by the necessary two-thirds vote, and sent them to the Senate for consideration. The Senate gave its approval, after having made several changes in the language adopted by the House. In September twelve proposed amendments were sent to the state legislatures for ratification or rejection. Ten of the twelve were ratified by three-fourths of the state legislatures, and they became the first ten amendments to the Constitution, known today as the Bill of Rights.

Debate which occurred in the Senate was not reported. Debate which occurred in the House was reported, and a comparison of the account of this debate with debate reported on other subjects during the first session of Congress gives ground for believing that the *Annals of Congress* contain just about everything of significance which members of the House of Representatives said about the need for a Bill of Rights, what interests ought to be secured, and how specific guarantees ought to be worded. Some of that House debate is presented at other points in this volume: selection 2.6 (on the wisdom of altering the Constitution so early in its existence); selection 2.10 (on the manner in which new language ought to be inserted into or attached to the original document); and selection 10.1 (on the rights of people to assemble and to instruct their representatives).

The statements which are printed in this chapter present almost everything else which the *Annals of Congress* reports as having been said in this debate and which, in the judgment of the editors, is likely to be of interest to our contemporaries who wish to know what members of the First Congress said about need for and content of personal guarantees and safeguards against abuse of governmental authority. Inclusion of additional remarks would serve no useful purpose other than to strengthen two conclusions: (1) that the main reason for considering amendments was a desire to placate a demand from certain groups of the population who thought a Bill of Rights to be necessary; and (2) that many Congressmen considered other legislative business to be in much greater need of attention than the addition of personal guarantees to the Constitution.]

11.1   On the Need for a Bill of Rights:* **"There is a great number of our constituents who are dissatisfied with the Constitution, among whom are many respectable for the jealousy they have for their liberty, which, though mistaken in its object, is laudable in its motive."**

Mr. Madison rose and . . . addressed the Speaker as follows: This day, Mr. Speaker, is the day assigned for taking into consideration the subject of amendments to the Constitution. As I considered myself bound in honor and in duty to do what I have done on this subject, I shall proceed to bring the amendments before you as soon

---

* Representatives James Madison of Virginia, John Vining of Delaware, James Jackson of Georgia, and Roger Sherman of Connecticut. Debate in the House of Representatives, June 8, 1789. *Annals*, 1st Congress, 1st session, pp. 424, 427, 430, 432, 442-443, 447-449.

as possible, and advocate them until they shall be finally adopted or rejected by a Constitutional majority of this House.

. . . 427

It is not now proposed to enter into a full and minute discussion of every part of the subject, but merely to bring it before the House that our constituents may see we pay a proper attention to a subject they have much at heart; and if it does not give that full gratification which is to be wished, they will discover that it proceeds from the urgency of business of a very important nature. But if we continue to postpone from time to time, and refuse to let the subject come into view, it may occasion suspicions which, though not well founded, may tend to inflame or prejudice the public mind against our decisions. They may think we are not sincere in our desire to incorporate such amendments in the Constitution as will secure those rights which they consider as not sufficiently guarded.

. . . 430

Mr. Vining: . . . For my part, I do not see the expediency of proposing amendments. I think, sir, the most likely way to quiet the perturbation of the public mind will be to pass salutary laws; to give permanency and stability to Constitutional regulations, founded on principles of equity and adjusted by wisdom. Although hitherto we have done nothing to tranquillize that agitation which the adoption of the Constitution threw some people into, yet the storm has abated and a calm succeeds. . . . 432

. . .

Mr. Madison: . . . It cannot be a secret to the gentlemen in this House that, notwithstanding the ratification of this system of Government by eleven of the thirteen United States, in some cases unanimously, in others by large majorities, yet still there is a great number of our constituents who are dissatisfied with it, among whom are many respectable for their talents and patriotism and respectable for the jealousy they have for their liberty, which, though mistaken in its object, is laudable in its motive. There is a great body of the people falling under this description who at present feel much inclined to join their support to the cause of Federalism if they were satisfied on this one point. We ought not to disregard their inclination but, on principles of amity and moderation, conform to their wishes and expressly declare the great rights of mankind secured under this Constitution. The acquiescence which our fellow-citizens show under the Government calls upon us for a like return of moderation. But perhaps there is a stronger motive than this for our going into a consideration of the subject. It is to provide those securities for liberty which are required by a part of the community; I allude in a particular manner to those two States that have not thought fit to throw themselves into the bosom of the Confederacy. It is a desirable thing, on our part as well as theirs, that a re-union should take place as soon as possible. I have no doubt, if we proceed to take those steps which would be prudent and requisite at this juncture, that in a short time we should see that disposition prevailing in those States which have not come in, that we have seen prevailing in those states which have embraced the Constitution. *442*

. . .

Mr. Jackson: The more I consider the subject of amendments, the more I am convinced it is improper. I revere the rights of my constituents as much as any gentleman in Congress, yet I am against inserting a declaration of rights in the Constitution, and that for some of the reasons referred to by the gentleman last up. If such an addition is not dangerous or improper, it is at least unnecessary: that is a sufficient reason for not entering into the subject at a time when there are urgent calls for our attention to important business.

Let me ask gentlemen what reason there is for the suspicions which are to be removed by this measure? Who are Congress that such apprehensions should be entertained of them? Do we not belong to the mass of the people? Is there a single right that, if infringed, will not affect us and our connexions as much as any other person? Do we not return at the expiration of two years into private life, and is not this a security against encroachments? Are we not sent here to guard those rights which might be endangered, if the Government was an aristocracy or a despotism? View for a moment the situation of Rhode Island and say whether the people's rights are more safe under State Legislatures than under a Government of limited powers. Their liberty is changed to licentiousness. But do gentlemen suppose bills of rights necessary to secure liberty? If they do, let them look at New York, New Jersey, Virginia, South

Carolina, and Georgia. Those States have no bill of rights, and is the liberty of the citizens less safe in those States than in the other of the United States? I believe it is not.

There is a maxim in law, and it will apply to bills of rights, that when yeu enumerate exceptions the exceptions operate to the exclusion of all circumstances that are omitted; consequently, unless you except every right from the grant of power, those omitted are inferred to be resigned to the discretion of the Government.

The gentleman endeavors to secure the liberty of the press; pray how is this in danger? There is no power given to Congress to regulate this subject as they can [regulate] commerce, or peace, or war. Has any transaction taken place to make us suppose such an amendment necessary? An honor- 443 able gentleman, a member of this House, has been attacked in the public newspapers on account of sentiments delivered on this floor. Have Congress taken any notice of it? Have they ordered the writer before them, even for a breach of privilege, although the Constitution provides that a member shall not be questioned in any place for any speech or debate in the House? No; these things are offered to the public view and held up to the inspection of the world. These are principles which will always prevail. I am not afraid, nor are other members I believe, our conduct should meet the severest scrutiny. Where then is the necessity of taking measures to secure what neither is nor can be in danger?

I hold, Mr. Speaker, that the present is not a proper time for considering of amendments. The States of Rhode Island and North Carolina are not in the Union. As to the latter, we have every presumption that she will come in. But in Rhode Island I think the antifederal interest yet prevails. I am sorry for it, particularly on account of the firm friends of the Union who are kept without the embrace of the Confederacy by their countrymen. These persons are worthy of our patronage; and I wish they would apply to us for protection. They should have my consent to be taken into the Union upon such application. I understand there are some important mercantile and manufacturing towns in that State who ardently wish to live under the laws of the General Government; if they were to come forward and request us to take measures for this purpose, I would give my sanction to any which would be likely to bring about such an event.

But to return to my argument. It being the case that those States

are not yet come into the Union, when they join us we shall have
another list of amendments to consider and another bill of rights to
frame. Now, in my judgment, it is better to make but one work of
it whenever we set about the business. . . . *447*

. . .

Mr. Sherman: I do not suppose the Constitution to be perfect, nor
do I imagine if Congress and all the Legislatures on the continent
were to revise it, that their united labors would make it perfect. I
do not expect any perfection on this side the grave in the works of
man; but my opinion is that we are not at present in circumstances
to make it better. It is a wonder that there has been such unanimity
in adopting it, considering *448* the ordeal it had to undergo. And the
unanimity which prevailed at its formation is equally astonishing.
Amidst all the members from the twelve States present at the Federal Convention, there were only three who did not sign the instrument to attest their opinion of its goodness. Of the eleven States who
have received it, the majority have ratified it without proposing a
single amendment. This circumstance leads me to suppose that we
shall not be able to propose any alterations that are likely to be
adopted by nine States; and gentlemen know, before the alterations
take effect, they must be agreed to by the Legislatures of three-
fourths of the States in the Union. Those States which have not recommended alterations will hardly adopt them unless it is clear that
they tend to make the Constitution better. Now, how this can be
made out to their satisfaction I am yet to learn; they know of no
defect from experience. It seems to be the opinion of gentlemen
generally that this is not the time for entering upon the discussion of
amendments; our only question therefore is how to get rid of the
subject.
. . . *449*

Mr. Vining: . . . He contented himself with saying that a bill of
rights was unnecessary in a Government deriving all its powers from
the people; and the Constitution enforced the principle in the strongest manner by the practical declaration prefixed to that instrument;
he alluded to the words, "We the people do ordain and establish."

There were many things mentioned by some of the State Conventions which he would never agree to on any conditions whatever.

They changed the principles of the Government, and were therefore obnoxious to its friends. The honorable gentleman from Virginia had not touched upon any of them. He was glad of it, because he could by no means bear the idea of an alteration respecting them. He referred to the mode of obtaining direct taxes, judging of elections, &c. . . .

11.2 Madison's Proposals for a Bill of Rights: "The prescriptions in favor of liberty ought to be levelled against that quarter where the greatest danger lies, namely, that which possesses the highest prerogative of power."*

. . .

The amendments which have occurred to me, proper to be recommended by Congress to the State Legislatures, are these:

First. That there be prefixed to the Constitution a declaration, that all power is originally vested in, and consequently derived from, the people.

That Government is instituted and ought to be exercised for the benefit of the people; which consists in the enjoyment of life and liberty, with the right of acquiring and using property, and *434* generally of pursuing and obtaining happiness and safety.

That the people have an indubitable, unalienable, and indefeasible right to reform or change their Government, whenever it be found adverse or inadequate to the purposes of its institution.

Secondly. That in article 1st, section 2, clause 3, these words be struck out, to wit: "The number of Representatives shall not exceed one for every thirty thousand, but each State shall have at least one Representative, and until such enumeration shall be made;" and that in place thereof be inserted these words, to wit: "After the first actual enumeration, there shall be one Representative for every thirty thousand, until the number amounts to _____, after which the proportion shall be so regulated by Congress, that the number shall never be less than _____, nor more than _____, but each State shall, after the first enumeration, have at least two Representa-

---

* From the principal address of Representative James Madison of Virginia in the House of Representatives, recommending a series of additions to the Constitution which would provide a Bill of Rights, April 8, 1789. *Annals*, 1st Congress, 1st session, pp. 433-441.

tives; and prior thereto." [Mr. Madison did not suggest numbers to fill the foregoing blanks.]

Thirdly. That in article 1st, section 6, clause 1, there be added to the end of the first sentence, these words, to wit: "But no law varying the compensation last ascertained shall operate before the next ensuing election of Representatives."

Fourthly. That in article 1st, section 9, between clauses 2 and 4, be inserted these clauses, to wit: The civil rights of none shall be abridged on account of religious belief or worship, nor shall any national religion be established, nor shall the full and equal rights of conscience be in any manner, or on any pretext, infringed.

The people shall not be deprived or abridged of their right to speak, to write, or to publish their sentiments; and the freedom of the press, as one of the great bulwarks of liberty, shall be inviolable.

The people shall not be restrained from peaceably assembling and consulting for their common good; nor from applying to the Legislature by petitions, or remonstrances, for redress of their grievances.

The right of the people to keep and bear arms shall not be infringed; a well armed and well regulated militia being the best security of a free country: but no person religiously scrupulous of bearing arms shall be compelled to render military service in person.

No soldier shall in time of peace be quartered in any house without the consent of the owner; nor at any time, but in a manner warranted by law.

No person shall be subject, except in cases of impeachment, to more than one punishment or one trial for the same offence; nor shall be compelled to be a witness against himself; nor be deprived of life, liberty, or property, without due process of law; nor be obliged to relinquish his property, where it may be necessary for public use, without a just compensation.

Excessive bail shall not be required, nor excessive fines imposed, nor cruel and unusual punishments inflicted.

The rights of the people to be secured in their 435 persons, their houses, their papers, and their other property, from all unreasonable searches and seizures, shall not be violated by warrants issued without probable cause, supported by oath or affirmation, or not particularly describing the places to be searched, or the persons or things to be seized.

In all criminal prosecutions, the accused shall enjoy the right to a speedy and public trial, to be informed of the cause and nature of the accusation, to be confronted with his accusers, and the witnesses against him; to have a compulsory process for obtaining witnesses in his favor; and to have the assistance of counsel for his defence.

The exceptions here or elsewhere in the Constitution, made in favor of particular rights, shall not be so construed as to diminish the just importance of other rights retained by the people, or as to enlarge the powers delegated by the Constitution; but either as actual limitations of such powers, or as inserted merely for greater caution.

Fifthly. That in article 1st, section 10, between clauses 1 and 2, be inserted this clause, to wit:

No State shall violate the equal rights of conscience, or the freedom of the press, or the trial by jury in criminal cases.

Sixthly. That, in article 3d, section 2, be annexed to the end of clause 2d, these words, to wit:

But no appeal to such court shall be allowed where the value in controversy shall not amount to _____ dollars: nor shall any fact triable by jury, according to the course of common law, be otherwise re-examinable than may consist with the principles of common law.

Seventhly. That in article 3d, section 2, the third clause be struck out, and in its place be inserted the clauses following, to wit:

The trial of all crimes (except in cases of impeachments, and cases arising in the land or naval forces, or the militia when on actual service, in time of war or public danger) shall be by an impartial jury of freeholders of the vicinage, with the requisite of unanimity for conviction, of the right of challenge, and other accustomed requisites; and in all crimes punishable with loss of life or member, presentment or indictment by a grand jury shall be an essential preliminary, provided that in cases of crimes committed within any county which may be in possession of an enemy, the trial may by law be authorized in some other county of the same State, as near as may be to the seat of the offence.

In cases of crimes committed not within any county, the trial may by law be in such county as the laws shall have prescribed. In suits at common law, between man and man, the trial by jury, as one of the best securities to the rights of the people, ought to remain inviolate.

Eighthly. That immediately after article 6th, be inserted, as article 7th, the clauses following, to wit:

The powers delegated by this Constitution are appropriated to the departments to which they are respectively distributed: so that the Legisla- *436* tive Department shall never exercise the powers vested in the Executive or Judicial, nor the Executive exercise the powers vested in the Legislative or Judicial, nor the Judicial exercise the powers vested in the Legislative or Executive Departments.

The powers not delegated by this Constitution, nor prohibited by it to the States, are reserved to the States respectively.

Ninthly. That article 7th be numbered as article 8th.

The first of these amendments [which I have now laid before you, said Mr. Madison,] relates to what may be called a bill of rights. I will own that I never considered this provision so essential to the Federal Constitution as to make it improper to ratify it until such an amendment was added; at the same time, I always conceived that in a certain form and to a certain extent, such a provision was neither improper nor altogether useless. I am aware that a great number of the most respectable friends to the Government and champions for republican liberty have thought such a provision not only unnecessary, but even improper; nay, I believe some have gone so far as to think it even dangerous.

Some policy has been made use of, perhaps, by gentlemen on both sides of the question. I acknowledge the ingenuity of those arguments which were drawn against the Constitution by a comparison with the policy of Great Britain in establishing a declaration of rights, but there is too great a difference in the case to warrant the comparison; therefore, the arguments drawn from that source were in a great measure inapplicable. In the declaration of rights which that country has established, the truth is, they have gone no farther than to raise a barrier against the power of the Crown; the power of the Legislature is left altogether indefinite. Although I know whenever the great rights, the trial by jury, freedom of the press, or liberty of conscience, come in question in that body, the invasion of them is resisted by able advocates, yet their Magna Charta does not contain any one provision for the security of those rights respecting which the people of America are most alarmed. The freedom of the press and rights of conscience, those choicest privileges of the people, are unguarded in the British Constitution.

But although the case may be widely different, and it may not be thought necessary to provide limits for the legislative power in that country, yet a different opinion prevails in the United States. The people of many States have thought it necessary to raise barriers against power in all forms and departments of Government, and I am inclined to believe, if once bills of rights are established in all the States as well as the Federal Constitution, we shall find that, although some of them are rather unimportant, yet upon the whole they will have a salutary tendency. It may be said, in some instances, they do no more than state the perfect equality of mankind. This, to be sure, is an absolute truth, yet it is not absolutely necessary to be inserted at the head of a Constitution. 437

In some instances they assert those rights which are exercised by the people in forming and establishing a plan of Government. In other instances, they specify those rights which are retained when particular powers are given up to be exercised by the Legislature. In other instances, they specify positive rights which may seem to result from the nature of the compact. Trial by jury cannot be considered as a natural right, but a right resulting from a social compact which regulates the action of the community, but is as essential to secure the liberty of the people as any one of the pre-existent rights of nature. In other instances, they lay down dogmatic maxims with respect to the construction of the Government, declaring that the Legislative, Executive, and Judicial branches shall be kept separate and distinct. Perhaps the best way of securing this in practice is, to provide such checks as will prevent the encroachment of the one upon the other.

But, whatever may be the form which the several States have adopted in making declarations in favor of particular rights, the great object in view is to limit and qualify the powers of Government, by excepting out of the grant of power those cases in which the Government ought not to act or to act only in a particular mode. They point these exceptions sometimes against the abuse of the Executive power, sometimes against the Legislative, and in some cases against the community itself, or, in other words, against the majority in favor of the minority.

In our Government it is, perhaps, less necessary to guard against the abuse in the Executive Department than any other, because it is not the stronger branch of the system, but the weaker. It therefore must be levelled against the Legislative, for it is the most powerful and most likely to be abused, because it is under the least control. Hence, so far as a declaration of rights can tend to prevent the exercise of undue power, it cannot be doubted but such declaration is proper. But I confess that I do conceive, that in a Government modified like this of the United States, the great danger lies rather in the abuse of the community than in the Legislative body. The prescriptions in favor of liberty ought to be levelled against that quarter where the greatest danger lies, namely, that which possesses the highest prerogative of power. But this is not found in either the Executive or Legislative departments of Government, but in the body of the people, operating by the majority against the minority.

It may be thought that all paper barriers against the power of the community are too weak to be worthy of attention. I am sensible they are not so strong as to satisfy gentlemen of every description who have seen and examined thoroughly the texture of such a defence; yet, as they have a tendency to impress some degree of respect for them, to establish the public opinion in their favor and rouse the attention of the whole community, it may be one means to control the majority from those acts to which they might be otherwise inclined.

It has been said, by way of objection to a bill 438 of rights, by many respectable gentlemen out of doors, and I find opposition on the same principles likely to be made by gentlemen on this floor, that they are unnecessary articles of a Republican Government, upon the presumption that the people have those rights in their own hands and that is the proper place for them to rest. It would be a sufficient answer to say that this objection lies against such provisions under the State Governments as well as under the General Government; and there are, I believe, but few gentlemen who are inclined to push their theory so far as to say that a declaration of rights in those cases is either ineffectual or improper. It has been said that in the Federal Government they are unnecessary because the powers are enumerated, and it follows that all that are not granted by the Constitution are retained; that the Constitution is a bill of powers, the great residuum being the rights of the people; and therefore, a bill of rights cannot be so necessary as if the residuum was thrown into the hands of the Government. I admit that these arguments are not entirely without foundation; but they are not conclusive to the extent which has been supposed. It is true, the powers of the General Government are circumscribed, they are directed to particular objects. But even if Government keeps within those limits, it has certain discretionary powers with respect to the means which may admit of abuse to a certain extent, in the same manner as the powers of the State Governments under their constitutions may [admit of abuse] to an indefinite extent. [This is so] because in the Constitution of the United States there is a clause granting to Congress the power to make all laws which shall be necessary and proper for carrying into execution all the powers vested in the Government of the United States or in any department or officer thereof. This enables them to fulfill every purpose for which the Government was established. Now, may not laws be considered necessary and proper by Congress (for it is for them to judge of the necessity and propriety to accomplish those special purposes which they may have in contemplation), which laws in themselves are neither necessary nor proper, as well as improper laws could be enacted by the State Legislatures for fulfilling the more extended objects of those Governments?

I will state an instance, which I think in point and proves that this might be the case. The General Government has a right to pass all laws which shall be necessary to collect its revenue; the means for enforcing the collection are within the direction of the Legislature. May not general warrants be considered necessary for this purpose, as well as for some purposes which it was supposed at the framing of their constitutions the State Governments had in view? If there was reason for restraining the State Governments from exercising this power, there is like reason for restraining the Federal Government.

It may be said, indeed it has been said, that a bill of rights is not necessary because the establishment of this Government has not repealed those declarations of rights which are added to 439 the several State constitutions; that those rights of the people which had been established by the most solemn act, could not be annihilated by a subsequent act of that people, who meant and declared at the head of the instrument that they ordained and established a new system for the express purpose of securing to themselves and posterity the liberties they had gained by an arduous conflict.

I admit the force of this observation, but I do not look upon it to be conclusive. In the first place, it is too uncertain ground to leave this provision upon, if a provision is at all necessary to secure rights so important as many of those I have mentioned are conceived to be by the public in general as well as [by] those in particular who opposed the adoption of this Constitution. Besides, some States have no bills of rights. There are others provided with very defective ones. And there are others whose bills of rights are not only defective but absolutely improper; instead of securing some in the full extent which republican principles would require, they limit them too much to agree with the common ideas of liberty.

It has been objected also against a bill of rights that, by enumerating particular exceptions to the grant of power, it would disparage those rights which were not placed in that enumeration; and it might follow by implication, that those rights which were not singled out, were intended to be assigned into the hands of the General Government, and were consequently insecure. This is one of the most plausible arguments I have ever heard urged against the admission of a bill of rights into this system; but, I conceive that it may be guarded against. I have attempted it, as gentlemen may see by turning to the last clause of the fourth resolution.

It has been said that it is unnecessary to load the Constitution with this provision, because it was not found effectual in the constitutions of the particular States. It is true, there are a few particular States in which some of the most valuable articles have not, at one time or other, been violated; but it does not follow but they may have, to a certain degree, a salutary effect against the abuse of power.[1] If they are incorporated into the Constitution, independent tribunals of justice will consider themselves in a peculiar manner the guardians of those rights. They will be an impenetrable bulwark against every assumption of power in the Legislative or Executive. They will be naturally led to resist every encroachment upon rights expressly stipulated for in the Constitution by the declaration of rights. Besides this security, there is a great probability that such a declaration in the federal system would be enforced. [This is so] because the State Legislatures will jealously and closely watch the

---

[1] There can be little doubt that the reporter failed to record Madison's remarks correctly at this point. It seems likely that Madison wished to be understood this way: Only a few of the States have escaped having some of their most valuable constitutional safeguards violated at one time or another. But it does not follow that these constitutional guarantees, even though violated on occasions, had no salutary effect against the abuse of power.

operations of this Government, and be able to resist with more effect every assumption of power than any other power on earth can do; and the greatest opponents to a Federal Government admit the State Legislatures to be sure guardians of the people's liberty. I conclude, from this view of the subject, that it will be proper in itself, and highly politic for *440* the tranquility of the public mind and the stability of the Government, that we should offer something in the form I have proposed, to be incorporated in the system of Government as a declaration of the rights of the people.

. . .

I wish also, in revising the Constitution, we may throw into that section which interdicts the abuse of certain powers in the State Legislatures, some other provisions of equal if not greater importance than those already made. The words, "No State shall pass any bill of attainder, *ex post facto* law," &c., were wise and proper restrictions in the Constitution. I think there is more danger of those powers being abused by the State Governments than by the Government of the United States. The same may be said of other powers which they possess, if not controlled by the general principle that laws are unconstitutional which infringe the rights of the community. I should, therefore, wish to extend this interdiction and add, as I have stated in the 5th resolution, that no State shall violate the equal *441* right of conscience, freedom of the press, or trial by jury in criminal cases; because it is proper that every Government should be disarmed of powers which trench upon those particular rights. I know, in some of the State constitutions, the power of the Government is controlled by such a declaration; but others are not. I cannot see any reason against obtaining even a double security on those points. And nothing can give a more sincere proof of the attachment of those who opposed this Constitution to these great and important rights than to see them join in obtaining the security I have now proposed, because it must be admitted on all hands that the State Governments are as liable to attack these invaluable privileges as the General Government is, and therefore ought to be as cautiously guarded against.

. . .

I find from looking into the amendments proposed by the State conventions that several are particularly anxious that it should be declared in the Constitution that the powers not therein delegated should be reserved to the several States. Perhaps other words may define this more precisely than the whole of the instrument now does. I admit they may be deemed unnecessary; but there can be no harm in making such a declaration, if gentlemen will allow the fact is as stated. I am sure I understand it so, and do therefore propose it.

These are the points on which I wish to see a revision of the Constitution take place. How far they will accord with the sense of this body, I cannot take upon me absolutely to determine; but I believe every gentleman will readily admit that nothing is in contemplation, so far as I have mentioned, that can endanger the beauty of the Government in any one important feature, even in the eyes of its most sanguine admirers. I have proposed nothing that does not appear to me as proper in itself, or eligible as patronised by a respectable number of our fellow-citizens; and if we can make the Constitution better in the opinion of those who are opposed to it, without weakening its frame or abridging its usefulness in the judgment of those who are attached to it, we act the part of wise and liberal men to make such alterations as shall produce that effect.

. . .

11.3 The Proposed Amendment Explained: Freedom of Religion and Conscience:*   "The rights of conscience are of peculiar delicacy and will little bear the gentlest touch of governmental hand."

The fourth proposition being under consideration [August 15], as follows:

Article 1. Section 9. Between paragraphs two and three insert "no religion shall be established by law, nor shall the equal rights of conscience be infringed."

Mr. Sylvester had some doubts of the propriety of the mode of expression used in this paragraph. He apprehended that it was liable

* Representatives Peter Sylvester of New York, Daniel Carroll of Maryland, James Madison of Virginia, Benjamin Huntington of Connecticut, Samuel Livermore of New Hampshire, and Thomas Tudor Tucker of South Carolina. Debate in the House of Representatives. *Annals*, 1st Congress, 1st session, pp. 729-731 (August 15, 1789; limitation on national government) and p. 755 (August 17, 1789; limitation on state governments).

to a construction different from what had been made by the committee. He feared it might be thought to have a tendency to abolish religion altogether. *730*

Mr. Carroll: As the rights of conscience are, in their nature, of peculiar delicacy and will little bear the gentlest touch of governmental hand, and as many sects have concurred in opinion that they are not well secured under the present constitution, he said he was much in favor of adopting the words. He thought it would tend more towards conciliating the minds of the people to the Government than almost any other amendment he had heard proposed. He would not contend with gentlemen about the phraseology, his object was to secure the substance in such a manner as to satisfy the wishes of the honest part of the community.

Mr. Madison said he apprehended the meaning of the words to be, that Congress should not establish a religion, and enforce the legal observation of it by law, nor compel men to worship God in any manner contrary to their conscience. Whether the words are necessary or not, he did not mean to say, but they had been required by some of the State Conventions who seemed to entertain an opinion that under the clause of the Constitution which gave power to Congress to make all laws necessary and proper to carry into execution the constitution and the laws made under it, enabled them [i.e., Congress was enabled] to make laws of such a nature as might infringe the rights of conscience and establish a national religion; to prevent these effects he presumed the amendment was intended, and he thought it as well expressed as the nature of the language would admit.

Mr. Huntington said that he feared, with the gentleman first up on this subject, that the words might be taken in such latitude as to be extremely hurtful to the cause of religion. He understood the amendment to mean what had been expressed by the gentleman from Virginia; but others might find it convenient to put another construction upon it. The ministers of their congregations to the Eastward were maintained by the contributions of those who belonged to their society; the expense of building meeting-houses was contributed in the same manner. These things were regulated by by-laws. If an action was brought before a Federal Court on any of these cases, the person who had neglected to perform his engagements could not be compelled to do it; for a support of ministers, or building of places of worship, might be construed into a religious establishment.

By the charter of Rhode Island, no religion could be established by law. He could give a history of the effects of such a regulation; indeed the people were now enjoying the blessed fruits of it. He hoped, therefore, the amendment would be made in such a way as to secure the rights of conscience, and a free exercise to the rights of 731 religion, but not to patronize those who professed no religion at all.

Mr. Madison thought, if the word national was inserted before religion, it would satisfy the minds of honorable gentlemen. He believed that the people feared one sect might obtain a pre-eminence, or two combine together, and establish a religion to which they would compel others to conform. He thought if the word national was introduced, it would point the amendment directly to the object it was intended to prevent.

Mr. Livermore was not satisfied with that amendment; but he did not wish them to dwell long on the subject. He thought it would be better if it was altered and made to read in this manner: that Congress shall make no laws touching religion, or infringing the rights of conscience.

* * * * *

The committee then proceeded [August 17] to the fifth proposition:

Article 1, section 10, between the first and second paragraph, insert "no State shall infringe the equal rights of conscience, nor the freedom of speech, or of the press, nor of the right of trial by jury in criminal cases."

Mr. Tucker: This is offered, I presume, as an amendment to the Constitution of the United States, but it goes only to the alteration of the constitutions of particular States. It will be much better, I apprehend, to leave the State Governments to themselves, and not to interfere with them more than we already do; and that is thought by many to be rather too much. I therefore move, sir, to strike out these words.

Mr. Madison conceived this to be the most valuable amendment in the whole list. If there were any reason to restrain the Government of the United States from infringing upon these essential rights, it was equally necessary that they should be secured against the State Governments. He thought that if they provided against the one, it was as necessary to provide against the other, and was satisfied that it would be equally grateful to the people.

Mr. Livermore had no great objection to the sentiment, but he thought it not well expressed. He wished to make it an affirmative proposition: "the equal rights of conscience, the freedom of speech or of the press, and the right of trial by jury in criminal cases, shall not be infringed by any State."

This transposition being agreed to, and Mr. Tucker's motion being rejected, the clause was adopted.

11.4 The Proposed Amendments Examined: Right to Bear Arms and Quartering of Troops:*   "Whenever Governments mean to invade the rights and liberties of the people, they always attempt to destroy the militia in order to raise an army upon their ruins."

On Right to Bear Arms: August 17.

The third clause in the fourth proposition in the report was taken into consideration, being as follows: "A well regulated militia, composed of the body of the people, being the best security of a free state, the right of the people to keep and bear arms shall not be infringed; but no person religiously scrupulous shall be compelled to bear arms."

Mr. Gerry: This declaration of rights, I take it, is intended to secure the people against the mal-administration of the Government; if we

---

* Representatives Elbridge Gerry of Massachusetts, James Jackson of Georgia, Roger Sherman of Connecticut, Egbert Benson of New York, Thomas Scott and Thomas Hartley of Pennsylvania, Elias Boudinot of New Jersey, and Thomas Sumter of South Carolina. Debate in the House of Representatives. *Annals,* 1st Congress, 1st session, pp. 749-751 (August 17, 1789; on the right to bear arms); pp. 766-767 (August 20, 1789; on the right to bear arms); p. 752 (August 17, 1789; on the quartering of soldiers).

could suppose that in all cases the rights of the people would be attended to, the occasion for guards of this kind would be removed. Now, I am apprehensive, sir, that this clause would give an opportunity to the people in power to destroy the Constitution itself. They can declare who are those religiously scrupulous, and prevent them from bearing arms.

What, sir, is the use of a militia? It is to prevent the establishment of a standing army, the 750 bane of liberty. Now, it must be evident that under this provision, together with their other powers, Congress could take such measures with respect to a militia as to make a standing army necessary. Whenever Governments mean to invade the rights and liberties of the people, they always attempt to destroy the militia in order to raise an army upon their ruins. This was actually done by Great Britain at the commencement of the late Revolution. They used every means in their power to prevent the establishment of an effective militia to the Eastward. The Assembly of Massachusetts, seeing the rapid progress that administration were making to divest them of their inherent privileges, endeavored to counteract them by the organization of the militia; but they were always defeated by the influence of the Crown. . . .

No attempts that they made were successful, until they engaged in the struggle which emancipated them at once from their thraldom. Now, if we give a discretionary power to exclude those from militia duty who have religious scruples, we may as well make no provision on this head. For this reason, he wished the words to be altered so as to be confined to persons belonging to a religious sect scrupulous of bearing arms.

Mr. Jackson did not expect that all the people of the United States would turn Quakers or Moravians; consequently one part would have to defend the other in case of invasion. Now this, in his opinion, was unjust, unless the Constitution secured an equivalent: for this reason, he moved to amend the clause by inserting at the end of it, "upon paying an equivalent, to be established by law."

Mr. Sherman: . . . It is well known that those who are religiously scrupulous of bearing arms, are equally scrupulous of getting substitutes or paying an equivalent. Many of them would rather die than do either one or the other; but he did not see an absolute necessity for a clause of this kind. We do not live under an arbitrary Government, said he, and the States, respectively, will have the government of the militia, unless when called into actual service; besides, it would 751 not do to alter it so as to exclude the whole of any sect, because there are men amongst the Quakers who will turn out, notwithstanding the religious principles of the society, and defend the cause of their country. Certainly it will be improper to prevent the exercise of such favorable dispositions, at least whilst it is the practice of nations to determine their contests by the slaughter of their citizens and subjects.

Mr. Benson moved to have the words "but no person religiously scrupulous shall be compelled to bear arms," struck out. He would always leave it to the benevolence of the Legislature, for, modify it as you please, it will be impossible to express it in such a manner as to clear it from ambiguity. No man can claim this indulgence of right. It may be a religious persuasion, but it is no natural right, and therefore ought to be left to the discretion of the Government. If this stands part of the Constitution, it will be a question before the Judiciary on every regulation you make with respect to the organization of the militia, whether it comports with this declaration or not. It is extremely injudicious to intermix matters of doubt with fundamentals.

I have no reason to believe but the Legislature will always possess humanity enough to indulge this class of citizens in a matter they are so desirous of; but they ought to be left to their discretion.

The motion for striking out the whole clause being seconded, was put, and decided in the negative—22 members voting for it, and 24 against it.

On Right to Bear Arms: August 20.

Mr. Scott objected to the clause in the sixth amendment, "No person religiously scrupulous shall be compelled to bear arms." He observed that if this becomes part of the Constitution, such persons can neither be called upon for their services, nor can an equivalent be demanded; it is also attended with still further difficulties, for a militia can never be depended upon. This would lead to the violation of another article in the Con- 767 stitution which secures to the people the right of keeping arms, and in this case recourse must be had to a standing army. I conceive it, said he, to be a Legislative right altogether. There are many sects I know, who are religiously scrupulous in this respect; I do not mean to deprive them of any indulgence the law affords. My design is to guard against those who are of no religion. It has been urged that religion is on the decline; if so, the argument is more strong in my favor, for when the time comes that religion shall be discarded, the generality of persons will have recourse to these pretexts to get excused from bearing arms.

Mr. Boudinot thought the provision in the clause, or something similar to it, was necessary. Can any dependence, said he, be placed in men who are conscientious in this respect? or what justice can there be in compelling them to bear arms when, according to their religious principles, they would rather die than use them? He adverted to several instances of oppression on this point that occurred during the war. In forming a militia, an effectual defence ought to be calculated, and no characters of this religious description ought to be compelled to take up arms. I hope that in establishing this Government, we may show the world that proper care is taken that the Government may not interfere with the religious sentiments of any person. Now, by striking out the clause, people may be led to believe that there is an intention in the General Government to compel all its citizens to bear arms.

Some further desultory conversation arose, and it was agreed to insert the words "in person," to the end of the clause: after which it was adopted.

On Quartering of Soldiers: August 17.

The fourth clause of the fourth proposition was taken up as follows: "No soldier shall, in time of peace, be quartered in any house, without the consent of the owner, nor in time of war, but in a manner to be prescribed by law."

Mr. Sumter hoped soldiers would never be quartered on the inhabitants, either in time of peace or war, without the consent of the owner. It was a burden, and very oppressive, even in cases where the owner gave his consent; but where this was wanting, it would be a hardship indeed! Their property would lie at the mercy of men irritated by a refusal, and well disposed to destroy the peace of the family.

He moved to strike out all the words from the clause but "no soldier shall be quartered in any house without the consent of the owner."

Mr. Sherman observed that it was absolutely necessary that marching troops should have quarters, whether in time of peace or war, and that it ought not to be put in the power of an individual to obstruct the public service; if quarters were not to be obtained in public barracks, they must be procured elsewhere. In England, where they paid considerable attention to private rights, they billeted the troops upon the keepers of public houses, and upon private houses also, with the consent of the magistracy.

Mr. Sumter's motion being put, was lost by a majority of sixteen.

Mr. Gerry moved to insert between "but" and "in a manner," the words, "by a civil magistrate," observing that there was no part of the Union but where they could have access to such authority.

Mr. Hartley said those things ought to be entrusted to the Legislature; that cases might arise where the public safety would be endangered by putting it in the power of one person to keep a division of troops standing in the inclemency of the weather for many hours; therefore he was against inserting the words.

11.5 The Proposed Amendments Examined: Trials and Punitive Procedures:*   "Villains often deserve whipping, and perhaps having their ears cut off; are we in future to be prevented from inflicting these punishments because they are cruel?"

The fifth clause of the fourth proposition was taken up, viz: "No person shall be subject, in cases of impeachment, to more than one trial or one punishment for the same offence, nor shall be compelled to be a witness against himself, nor be deprived of life, liberty, or

---

* Representatives Thomas Lawrence of New York, William L. Smith of South Carolina, and Samuel Livermore of New Hampshire. Debate in the House of Representatives, August 17, 1789. *Annals,* 1st Congress, 1st session, pp. 753-754.

property, without due process of law; nor shall private property be taken for public use without just compensation."

Mr. Lawrence said this clause contained a general declaration, in some degree contrary to laws passed. He alluded to that part where a person shall not be compelled to give evidence against himself. He thought it ought to be confined to criminal cases, and moved an amendment for that purpose; which amendment being adopted, the clause as amended was unanimously agreed to by the Committee [of the Whole], who then proceeded to the sixth clause of the fourth proposition, in these 754 words, "Excessive bail shall not be required, nor excessive fines imposed, nor cruel and unusual punishments inflicted."

Mr. Smith, of South Carolina, objected to the words "nor cruel and unusual punishments"; the import of them being too indefinite.

Mr. Livermore: The clause seems to express a great deal of humanity, on which account I have no objection to it; but as it seems to have no meaning in it, I do not think it necessary. What is meant by the terms excessive bail? Who are to be the judges? What is understood by excessive fines? It lies with the court to determine. No cruel and unusual punishment is to be inflicted. It is sometimes necessary to hang a man, villains often deserve whipping, and perhaps having their ears cut off; but are we in future to be prevented from inflicting these punishments because they are cruel? If a more lenient mode of correcting vice and deterring others from the commission of it could be invented, it would be very prudent in the Legislature to adopt it; but until we have some security that this will be done, we ought not to be restrained from making necessary laws by any declaration of this kind.

The question was put on the clause, and it was agreed to by a considerable majority.

chapter 12

Loyalty, sedition, and personal freedom

DEBATE ON THE SEDITION ACT OF 1798

[Note by the editors. The Whiskey Rebellion was an early, violent expression of the unease, discontent, and rebellious spirit which disturbed the American scene for two decades before the War of 1812 brought the nation relief from internal tensions. The congressional debates presented at several points in this compilation give one a sense of the strain, impatience, and ill temper which prevailed; selections 3.5 and 10.6 illustrate. In its second session, the Fifth Congress (chosen in the election that made John Adams President) decided by very small majorities to deal with the prospects of increased violence and possible rebellion by enactment of three statutes known today as the Alien and Sedition Acts. Two of the measures authorized the President to expel aliens who might endanger the safety of this country. The third one, applying both to aliens and American citizens, was directed against (1) conspiracies designed to oppose or obstruct the national government, and (2) oral and written statements—false, malicious, and scandalous in character—intended to bring the national government into disrepute, to stir up sedition, or to have certain other consequences which Congress thought the nation ought not have to tolerate. The latter statute, the Sedition Act of 1798, is reprinted in full beginning on the next page and should be read before one reads the speeches in Congress which were made for and against it. This statute was made effective only for the remainder of President Adams' term of office (approximately thirty-two months), but it plagued Congress for years and excited debate on many occasions because of motions to repeal it, to renew it, to print and distribute it, to make restitution to people who were penalized for violating it. First efforts to obtain restitution for injuries suffered by enforcement of the act were unsuccessful, but as remembrance of the cause for enacting the statute dimmed, opposition to restitution diminished. Finally, in 1840, Congress appropriated to the heirs of one of the convicted persons (Matthew Lyon) a sum equal to his fine and costs of prosecution (total $1,060.96) with interest from the time of his conviction. The four speeches that are partially reprinted here were made in debate when the bill was before the House for enactment.]

THE SEDITION ACT
July 14, 1798

(U.S. Statutes at Large, Vol. I, p. 596-7)

An Act in addition to the act, entitled "An act for the punishment of certain crimes against the United States."

Sec. 1. *Be it enacted* . . . , That if any persons shall unlawfully combine or conspire together, with intent to oppose any measure or measures of the government of the United States, which are or shall be directed by proper authority, or to impede the operation of any law of the United States, or to intimidate or prevent any person holding a place or office in or under the government of the United States, from undertaking, performing or executing his trust or duty; and if any person or persons, with intent as aforesaid, shall counsel, advise or attempt to procure any insurrection, riot, unlawful assembly, or combination, whether such conspiracy, threatening, counsel, advice, or attempt shall have the proposed effect or not, he or they shall be deemed guilty of a high misdemeanor, and on conviction, before any court of the United States having jurisdiction thereof, shall be punished by a fine not exceeding five thousand dollars, and by imprisonment during a term not less than six months nor exceeding five years; and further, at the discretion of the court may be holden to find sureties for his good behaviour in such sum, and for such time, as the said court may direct.

Sec. 2. That if any person shall write, print, utter, or publish, or shall cause or procure to be written, printed, uttered or published, or shall knowingly and willingly assist or aid in writing, printing, uttering or publishing any false, scandalous and malicious writing or writings against the government of the United States, or either house of the Congress of the United States, or the President of the United States, with intent to defame the said government, or either house of the said Congress, or the said President, or to bring them, or either of them, into contempt or disrepute; or to excite against them, or either or any of them, the hatred of the good people of the United States, or to stir up sedition within the United States, or to excite any unlawful combinations therein, for opposing or resisting any law of the United States, or any act of the President of the United States, done in pursuance of any such law, or of the powers in him vested by the constitution of the United States, or to resist, oppose, or defeat any such law or act, or to aid, encourage or abet any hostile designs of any foreign nation against the United States, their people or government, then such person, being thereof convicted before any court of the United States having jurisdiction thereof, shall be punished by a fine not exceeding two thousand dollars, and by imprisonment not exceeding two years.

Sec. 3. That if any person shall be prosecuted under this act, for the writing or publishing any libel aforesaid, it shall be lawful for the defendant, upon the trial of the cause, to give in evidence in his defence, the truth of the matter contained in the publication charged as a libel. And the jury who shall try the cause, shall have a right to determine the law and the fact, under the direction of the court, as in other cases.

Sec. 4. That this act shall continue to be in force until March 3, 1801, and no longer: *Provided*, That the expiration of the act shall not prevent or defeat a prosecution and punishment of any offence against the law, during the time it shall be in force.

Approved, July 14, 1798.

12.1   John Nicholas: "The heart and life of a free Government is a free press; take away this and you take away its main support."*

. . .

Mr. Nicholas asked whether this bill did not go to the abridgment of the freedom of speech and of the press? If it did not, he would be glad if gentlemen would define wherein the freedom of speech and of the press consists.

Gentlemen have said that this bill is not to restrict the liberty of the press but its licentiousness. He wished gentlemen to inform

* From a speech in the House of Representatives by the Representative from Virginia, opposing a bill to enact a sedition law, July 10, 1798. *Annals*, 5th Congress, 2nd session, pp. 2140-2144.

him where they drew the line between this liberty and licentiousness of which they speak; he wished to know where the one commenced and the other ended? Will they say the one is truth, and the other falsehood! Gentlemen cannot believe for a moment that such a definition will satisfy the inquiry. The great difficulty which has existed in all free Governments would long since have been done away, if it could have been effected by a simple declaration of this kind. It has been the object of all regulations with respect to the press, to destroy the only means by which the people can examine and become acquainted with the conduct of persons employed in their Government. If there could be safety in adopting the principle that no man should publish what is false, there certainly could be no objection to it. But it was not the intention of the people of this country to place any power of this kind in the hands of the General Government—for this plain reason, the persons who would have to preside in trials of this sort would themselves be parties, or at least they would be so far interested in the issue that the trial of the truth or falsehood of a matter would not be safe in their hands. On this account, the General Government has been forbidden to touch the press. Gentlemen exclaim, what! can anyone be found to advocate the publication of lies and calumny? He would make no answer to inquiries of this sort, because he did not believe he could be suspected of being an advocate for either. But, in his opinion, this was a most serious subject; it is not lying that will be suppressed, but the truth.

If this bill be passed into a law, the people will be deprived of that information on public measures which they have a right to receive, and which is the life and support of a free Government. For, if printers are to be subject to prosecution for every paragraph which appears in their papers that the eye of a jealous Government can torture into an offence against this law, and to the heavy penalties here provided, it cannot be expected that they will exercise that freedom and spirit which it is desirable should actuate them; especially when they would have to be tried by judges appointed by the President, and by juries selected by the Marshal who also receives his appointment from the President, all whose feelings would of course be inclined to commit the offender if possible.

Under such circumstances, *2141* it must be seen that the printers of papers would be deterred from printing anything which should

be in the least offensive to a power which might so greatly harass them. They would not only refrain from publishing anything of the least questionable nature, but they would be afraid of publishing the truth, as, though true, it might not always be in their power to establish the truth to the satisfaction of a court of justice. This bill would, therefore, go to the suppression of every printing press in the country which is not obsequious to the will of Government.
. . . *2142*

In direct opposition to the clause of the Constitution which says, "Congress shall pass no law to abridge the freedom of the press," Congress is now about to pass such a law. For it is vain to talk about the licentiousness of the press; the prohibition is express, "shall pass no law to abridge," &c. And as to what gentlemen called the licentiousness of the press, it was so indefinite a thing that what was deemed licentiousness today by one set of men, might by another set tomorrow be enlarged, and thus the propriety of the information to be given to the public would be arbitrarily controlled. If this bill passed into a law, there could be no doubt it would produce the *2143* effect which he had already mentioned; no man would continue to print a newspaper who could not bring himself to be at least silent as to any impropriety in the conduct of the General Government, which would deprive the people of a great part of its present usefulness.

. . .

Mr. N. said he was as sensible as . . . any other, that some of our printers have abused the liberty of the press, but notwithstanding he saw this, he was far from being convinced of either the propriety or necessity of Legislative interference in the matter. He believed himself to be incapable of promoting or encouraging falsehood; but he was not, because the press may have transgressed in this respect, for taking measures to suppress it. Nor did he think this by any means necessary; because falsehoods issued from a press are not calculated to do any lasting mischief. Falsehoods will always depreciate the press from whence they proceed. He was persuaded that the publication of one falsehood in a paper would do it more mischief than the abuse of its enemies; and he always regretted to see, at any time, a falsehood issue from a press which is generally the organ of truth. He believed, on this account, it would be unnecessary for Government to interfere in this matter, if they had a

right to do it, which he denied, since every publisher of a newspaper who consults his own interest and respectability will, as far as he is able to do it, make it a vehicle of correct information.
. . . *2144*

Mr. N. wished gentlemen, before they give a final vote on this bill, to consider its effects; and, if they do this, he thought they would consent to stop here. He desired them to reflect on the nature of our Government; that all its officers are elective, and that the people have no other means of examining their conduct but by means of the press and an unrestrained investigation through them of the conduct of the Government. Indeed, the heart and life of a free Government is a free press; take away this, and you take away its main support. You might as well say to the people: we, your Representatives, are faithful servants; you need not look into our conduct; we will keep our seats for a little longer time than that for which you have given them to us. To restrict the press would be to destroy the elective principle by taking away the information necessary to election, and there would be no difference between it and a total denial of the right of election, but in the degree of usurpation.
. . .

12.2   Harrison Gray Otis: "Where lies the injury in attempting to check the progress of calumny and falsehood? How is society aided by the gross and monstrous outrages upon truth and honor and public character and private peace which inundate the country?"*

Mr. Otis said the professions of attachment to the Constitution, made by the gentleman from Virginia, are certainly honorable to him; and he could not believe that an attachment so deeply engrafted as he states his to be would be shaken by this bill. The gentleman had caught an alarm on the first suggestion of a sedition bill which had not yet subsided; and though the present bill is perfectly harmless, and contains no provision which is not practised upon under the laws of the several States in which gentlemen had been

* From a speech in the House of Representatives by the Representative from Massachusetts, supporting a bill to enact a sedition law, July 10, 1798. *Annals,* 5th Congress, 2nd session, pp. 2145-2150.

educated, and from which they had drawn most of their ideas of jurisprudence, yet the gentleman continues to be dissatisfied with it.

The objections of the gentleman from Virginia, he believed, might be reduced to two inquiries. In the first place, had the Constitution given Congress cognizance over the offences described in this bill prior to the adoption of the amendments *2146* to the Constitution? and, if Congress had that cognizance before that time, have those amendments taken it away? With respect to the first question, it must be allowed that every independent Government has a right to preserve and defend itself against injuries and outrages which endanger its existence; for unless it has this power, it is unworthy the name of a free Government and must either fall or be subordinate to some other protection. Now some of the offences delineated in the bill are of this description. Unlawful combinations to oppose the measures of Government, to intimidate its officers, and to excite insurrections are acts which tend directly to the destruction of the Constitution, and there could be no doubt that the guardians of that Constitution are bound to provide against them. And if gentlemen would agree that these were acts of a criminal nature, it follows that all means calculated to produce these effects, whether by speaking, writing, or printing, were also criminal.

. . . *2147*

It was . . . most evident to his mind that the Constitution of the United States, prior to the amendments that have been added to it, secured to the National Government that cognizance of all the crimes enumerated in the bill, and it only remained to be considered whether those amendments divested it of this power. The amendment quoted by the gentleman from Virginia is in these words: "Congress shall make no law abridging the freedom of speech and of the press." The terms "freedom of speech and of the press," he supposed, were a phraseology perfectly familiar in the jurisprudence of every State, and of a certain and technical meaning. It was a mode of expression which we had borrowed from the only country in which it had been tolerated, and he pledged himself to prove that the construction which he should give to those terms should be consonant not only to the laws of that country, but to the laws and judicial decisions of many of *2148* the States composing the Union. This freedom, said Mr. O., is nothing more than the liberty of writing, publishing, and speaking one's thoughts, under the condition of being answerable to the injured party, whether it be the Government or an individual, for false, malicious, and seditious expressions, whether spoken or written; and the liberty of the press is merely an exemption from all previous restraints.

In support of this doctrine, he quoted *Blackstone's Commentaries,* under the head of libels, and read an extract to prove that in England, formerly, the press was subject to a licenser; and that this restraint was afterward removed, by which means the freedom of the press was established. He would not, however, dwell upon the law of England, the authority of which it might suit the convenience of gentlemen to question; but he would demonstrate that although in several of the State constitutions the liberty of speech and of the press were guarded by the most express and unequivocal language, the Legislatures and Judicial departments of those States had adopted the definitions of the English law and provided for the punishment of defamatory and seditious libels. To begin with New Hampshire: In the Bill of Rights of that State, it is declared: "That the liberty of the press is essential to the security of freedom in a State; it ought, therefore, to be inviolably preserved." By an act passed in February, 1791, subsequent to the adoption of that Constitution "any person of the age of fourteen and upward, making and publishing a lie or libel, tending to the defamation of any person, is liable on conviction to a fine," &c. The declaration of rights prefixed to the Constitution of Massachusetts contains an article to the same effect with that of New Hampshire; yet in the law establishing the Supreme Court of that State, cognizance is given to it, among other things, over all offences and misdemeanors of a public nature "tending to a breach of the peace, oppression of the subject, raising of faction, controversy or debate, to any manner of misgovernment." By another law, any person aiding in a lottery by printing or publishing a scheme on account of it, was punishable. Another law provided "that if any person by public or private discourse or conversation, or by any ways or means, should dissuade or endeavor to prevent an officer from doing his duty in quelling riots," he is subject to a heavy penalty. In Pennsylvania they carried matters still further. In their Bill of Rights, we find "that the printing presses shall be free to every person who undertakes to examine the proceedings of the Legislature, or any branch of the Government, and no law shall ever be made to restrain the free right thereof. The free com-

munication of thoughts and opinions is one of the invaluable rights
of man, and every citizen may freely write, print or speak, on any
subject, being responsible for the abuse of that liberty." Yet, in
Pennsylvania, a law has been made, and he had heard from the best
authority was still in force, "making it high treason to propose a
new constitution in that State."

Mr. Gallatin denied the existence of any such law. *2149*

Mr. Otis replied that he might, perhaps, have mistaken the precise words, but it was to that effect.

If we go to Virginia, said Mr. O., we shall read in their constitution "that the freedom of the press cannot be restrained, except in
despotic Government"; but, in the act passed December, 1792, it is
provided, "that if any person shall, by writing or speaking, endeavor
to instigate the people to erect or establish any Government, separate or independent of the Government of Virginia, he shall be subject to any punishment not extending to life or member, which the
court may adjudge." They have another act against cursing and
swearing, which is merely using the liberty of speech.

In all these instances, it is clearly understood that to punish
licentiousness and sedition is not a restraint or abridgment of the
freedom of speech or of the press.

. . .

The gentleman from Virginia had inquired how a line could be
drawn between the liberty and licentiousness of the press? He would
inform him that an honest jury was competent to such a discrimination, they could decide upon the falsehood and malice of the intention. How, said he, do they draw a line of discrimination in the case
of a forgery of public security? This crime is effected through the
medium of the press or of the pen. How can they punish the intent
when a man offers a bribe to a Judge, which may be done by words
only? These are offences which the gentlemen would anxiously dis-
countenance. Yet forgery is only the liberty of the press upon his
construction, and an offer of bribery is merely freedom of speech.
Is it not a restraint upon the freedom of speech that the people in
the gallery are not allowed to join in this debate? Yet this *2150*
would hardly be permitted.

Why then, said Mr. O., are gentlemen so feelingly alive on this
subject? Where lies the injury in attempting to check the progress of
calumny and falsehood? Or how is society aided by the gross and

monstrous outrages upon truth and honor and public character and private peace which inundate the country? Can there be any necessity of allowing anonymous and irresponsible accusers to drag before the tribunal of public opinion, magistrates and men in office, upon false and groundless charges? There are sixteen Legislatures in the United States, in which all the measures of Government are open to investigation. There are two Houses of Congress, in which every accusation and suspicion may have free vent, wherein our jealousies and prejudices may be uttered without restraint, and every man will still be at liberty to print and speak at pleasure; but he must be prepared to prove those charges which bring disgrace upon his fellow-citizens. No reasonable being can desire a greater latitude than this. . . .

. . .

12.3 Albert Gallatin: "Laws against writings of this kind have uniformly been one of the most powerful engines used by tyrants to throw a veil on their folly or their crimes and to perpetuate their own tyranny."*

. . .

It had been insisted that Congress had the power, generally, to provide for the punishment of any offences against Government. It is evident that such a power, if it did exist, would embrace the punishment of any offences whatever, or rather of any act which, though not criminal in itself, might be obnoxious to the persons who happened to have Government in their hands; for any such act might, by them, be called an offence against Government and made criminal. But so far from this being the case, it would be found that the Constitution had actually specified the cases in which Congress should have power either to define or to provide for the punishment of offences. . . . *2159*

The only clause of the Constitution which can give a color to the authority now claimed is that . . . which gives Congress authority to make all laws which shall be necessary and proper for

* From a speech in the House of Representatives by the Representative from Pennsylvania, opposing a bill to enact a sedition law, July 10, 1798. *Annals,* 5th Congress, 2nd session, pp. 2158-2159, 2161-2162, 2164.

carrying into execution the power vested by the Constitution in the Government of the United States, or in any department or officer thereof. . . .

In order to claim any authority under this clause, the supporters of this bill must show the specific power given to Congress or to the President, by some other part of the Constitution, which would be carried into effect by a law against libels. They must go further—they must show which of those Constitutional powers it was which could not be carried into effect unless this law was passed. It was in that manner that the authority of Congress had heretofore been exercised; they had passed no penal laws except such as arose from the necessity of carrying into effect some of the specific powers vested in them. Thus, as they had the exclusive power to establish post roads, they had made it penal to rob the mail; and as they were authorized to lay taxes, they had passed laws to punish frauds of revenue officers or evasions of the revenue laws. But until this bill was proposed, Congress had never attempted to define or punish offences generally.

. . . 2161

The advocates of this measure must show to us its necessity for carrying into operation the powers vested in the President or in either branch of the Legislature—who are its objects. They must prove that the President dare not, cannot, will not, execute the laws, unless the abuse poured upon him from certain presses is suppressed. If there be a majority of this House in favor of this law, are that majority ready to declare that that law 2162 is *necessary* in order to enable them to execute the powers vested in them by the Constitution? Are they ready to say that they are prevented from voting according to the dictates of their conscience, for voting is the only power belonging to them, by newspaper paragraphs? Are they ready to say, that unless libels against them shall be punished, that unless they may obtain revenge from the insolence of the printers, they will not or dare not vote as they would otherwise do?

If they are ready to make these declarations, if they do believe this bill *necessary* in order to enable this House to do their duty, they must recollect that this House is composed of individuals, and that, according to their own doctrine, in order to insure a conscientious vote in the whole House, every individual, and not [simply] a majority of the House, ought to be equally sheltered by this law from the abuse of printers. Whilst, therefore, they support the bill in its present shape, do they not avow that the true object of the law is to enable one party to oppress the other; that they mean to have the power to punish printers who may publish against them, whilst their opponents will remain alone and without redress, exposed to the abuse of Ministerial prints? Is it not their object to frighten and suppress all presses which they consider as contrary to their views; to prevent a free circulation of opinion; to suffer the people at large to hear only partial accounts and but one side of the question; to delude and deceive them by partial information and, through those means, to perpetuate themselves in power?

. . .

The bill was intended to punish solely writings of a political nature, libels against the Government, the President, or either branch of the Legislature; and it was well known that writings containing animadversions on public measures almost always contained not only facts but opinions. And how could the truth of opinions be proven by evidence? If an individual, thinking as he himself did, that the present bill was unconstitutional and that it had been intended, not for the public good but solely for party purposes, should avow and publish his opinion, and if the Administration thought fit to prosecute him for that supposed individual offence, would a jury, composed of the friends of that Administration, hesitate much in declaring the opinion ungrounded or, in other words, false and scandalous, and its publication malicious? And by what kind of argument or evidence, in the present temper of parties, could the accused convince them that his opinion was true?

. . . *2164*

Mr. G. said he had intended to make some general remarks on the nature of political libels, or of writings against the measures of the Administration, and on the propriety of interfering at all by law with them. The lateness of the hour prevented him. He would only observe that laws against writings of this kind had uniformly been one of the most powerful engines used by tyrants to prevent the diffusion of knowledge, to throw a veil on their folly or their crimes, to satisfy those mean passions which always denote little minds, and to perpetuate their own tyranny. The principles of the law of political libels were to be found in the rescripts of the worst Emperors of Rome, in the decisions of the Star Chamber. Princes of elevated minds, Governments actuated by pure motives, had ever despised the slanders of malice, and listened to the animadversions made on their conduct. They knew that the proper weapon to combat error was truth, and that to resort to coercion and punishments in order to suppress writings attacking their measures, was to confess that these could not be defended by any other means.

12.4 Robert Goodloe Harper: "He did most firmly believe that France had a party in this country, determined and capable of effecting infinite mischief; to repress the enterprises of this party he wished for a law against sedition and libels, the two great instruments whereby France and her partisans had worked for the destruction of other countries."*

Mr. Harper said that he should hardly expect at so late an hour to be indulged by the House in a detailed answer to the objections urged against this bill, even if he thought it necessary. He did not, however, think it necessary, as most of the arguments which had any appearance of application or force had already been fully refuted. Some few only, which he thought it important to controvert, had remained unanswered, and on them he begged permission to make a few remarks.

In the first place, gentlemen who oppose the bill had said that hitherto the Government of the United States had existed and prospered without a law of this kind, and then exultingly asked: "What change has now taken place to render such a law necessary?" He did not know whether most to wonder at or pity the security of gentlemen who asked this question. They, no doubt, could perceive no change of circumstances, for they had declared that they perceived none. But, to his mind, by the conclusions of which his conduct must be governed, the change was most evident; and he would, for himself, answer the question of the gentleman.

The change, in his opinion, consisted in this: that heretofore we had been at peace, and were now on the point of being driven

* From a speech in the House of Representatives by the Representative from South Carolina, supporting a bill to enact a sedition law, July 10, 1798. *Annals,* 5th Congress, 2nd session, pp. 2164-2165, 2167-2168.

into a war with a nation which openly boasts of 2165 its party among us, and its "diplomatic skill," as the most effectual means of paralyzing our efforts and bringing us to its own terms. Of the operations of this skill among us, by means of corrupt partisans and hired presses, he had no doubt. He was every day furnished with stronger reasons for believing in its existence, and saw stronger indications of its systematic exertion. We knew its effects in other countries, where it had aided the progress of France much more effectually than the force of her arms. He knew no reason why we should not harbor traitors in our bosom as well as other nations; and he did most firmly believe that France had a party in this country, small indeed, and sure to be disgraced and destroyed as soon as its designs should become generally known, but active, artful, and determined, and capable, if it could remain concealed, of effecting infinite mischief. This party was the instrument of her "diplomatic skill." By this party she hoped to stop "the wheels of our Government," enchain our strength, enfeeble our efforts, and finally subdue us. To repress the enterprises of this party, he wished for a law against sedition and libels, the two great instruments whereby France and her partisans had worked for the destruction of other countries, and he had no doubt were now working, he trusted unsuccessfully, for the destruction of this.

He could not, therefore, believe that our safety hitherto ought to lull us into security now; unless gentlemen could convince him that, because a person had existed in health for nine years, he ought to refuse medicine when he at length felt the approach of disease; [or convince him that] when he saw the daggers of assassins everywhere whetted against him, [he] should neglect to put on a coat of mail because for nine years he had not been assailed.
. . . 2167

The gentleman from Pennsylvania (Mr. Gallatin) had gone a step further, Mr. H. said, in his opposition to this bill than the rest of its opposers. They had contended that it was contrary to the third amendment to the Constitution [i.e., the first amendment which was adopted] which provides "that Congress shall pass no law restraining the liberty of speech or the press." The gentleman from Pennsylvania had discovered that, independently of that amendment, Congress had no power to pass a law against sedition and libels, none such being expressly given by the Constitution. But can there, said Mr. H., be so great an absurdity, can such a political monster exist, as a Government which has no power to protect itself against sedition and libels? Has not the Constitution said that "Congress shall have power to make all laws which shall be necessary, or proper, for carrying into execution the foregoing powers, and all other powers vested by this Constitution in the Government of the United States, or in any department or officer thereof." Can the powers of a Government be carried into execution if sedition for opposing its laws and libels against its officers, itself, and its proceedings, are to pass unpunished? The idea, he said, appeared to him so monstrous and absurd that he was astonished that any one should seriously advance it.

In the other objection, he admitted that there was more plausibility; the objection founded on that part of the Constitution which provides that "Congress shall pass no law to abridge the liberty of speech or of the press." He held this to be one of the most sacred parts of the Constitution, one by which he would stand the longest and defend with the greatest zeal. But to what, he asked, did this clause amount? Did this liberty of the press include sedition and licentiousness? Did it authorize persons to throw, with impunity, the most violent abuse upon the President and both Houses of Congress? Was this what gentlemen meant by the liberty of the press?

As well might it be said that the liberty of action implied the liberty of assault, trespass, or assassination. Every man possessed the liberty of action; but if he used this liberty to the detriment of others, by attacking their persons or destroying their property, he became liable to punishment for this licentious abuse of his liberty. The liberty of the press stood on precisely the same footing. Every man might publish what he pleased; but if he abused this liberty so as to publish slanders against his neighbor, or false, scandalous, and malicious 2168 libels against the magistrates, or the Government, he became liable to punishment.

What did this law provide? That if "any person should publish any false, scandalous, and malicious libel against the President or Congress, or either House of Congress, with intent to stir up sedition, or to produce any other of the mischievous and wicked effects particularly described in the bill, he should, on conviction before a jury, be liable to fine and imprisonment. A jury is to try the offence, and they must determine from the evidence and the circumstances of the case, first that the publication is *false,* secondly that it is *scandalous,* thirdly that it is *malicious,* and fourthly that it was made with the *intent* to do some one of the things particularly described in the bill. If in any one of these points the proof should fail, the man must be acquitted; and it is expressly provided that he may give the *truth* of the publication in evidence as a justification. Such is the substance of this law; and yet it is called a law abridging the liberty of the press! That is to say, that the liberty of the press implies the liberty of publishing, with impunity, false, scandalous, and malicious writings, with intent to stir up sedition, &c. As well might it be said that the liberty of *action* implies the liberty to rob and murder with impunity!

Whence was it, Mr. H. asked, that all confidence in the trial by jury was now discarded by those gentlemen who have heretofore so warmly, and so justly, resounded its praises? Why are juries, in whose hands the fortunes, the lives, and the reputations of the citizens had been safely deposited by our laws and Constitutions, no longer to be trusted, when it is in question to punish those who, with wicked intent, publish false, scandalous, and malicious libels against the President and Congress? Is this offence of so sacred a nature, so dear to gentlemen, that the authors of it cannot be trusted in the hands of a jury of their fellow-citizens?

. . .

LIMITS OF OPPOSITION: THE ISSUE
OF MORAL TREASON

[Note by the editors. The War of 1812 seemed unnecessary and unwise to many people in some parts of the country; it was especially unpopular in New England. The speeches that appear below are from debate on two measures to further the prosecution of the war. They boldly face the question, Where is the rightful boundary between right to oppose and obligation to support a declared policy of the nation?]

12.5 Felix Grundy: "I then said and I now repeat that those
who systematically oppose the filling of the loans and the enlistment
of soldiers are, in my opinion, guilty of moral treason."*

. . .

Sir, a sentiment I expressed at the last session, respecting the
conduct of a portion of the Opposition, has been much complained
of. I then said, and I now repeat, that those who systematically
oppose the filling of the loans and the enlistment of soldiers are, in
my opinion, guilty of moral treason. By this, I by no means intend
to censure those who, in the exercise of a Constitutional right, express their opinions freely against the expediency of having declared
the war, or those who, from choice, withhold their own money from
the public service; but those are intended who, after the respective
laws were passed, exerted their influence to prevent others from
carrying them into effect.

I wish gentlemen would discuss this point fairly and coolly with
me. Sir, I challenge them to produce their arguments and ascertain
on which side truth is to be found. Take the case I formerly stated,
and answer it. An individual goes over, joins the ranks of the enemy,
and raises his arms against his country: he is clearly guilty of treason under the Constitution, the overt act being consummated. Suppose the same individual not to go over to the enemy but to remain
in his own neighborhood, and by means of his influence to dissuade
ten men from enlisting; I ask, in which case has he benefitted the
enemy and injured his country most? In the latter, no doubt; because he has weakened his country more than he would have
strengthened the enemy by going over to him. In the fashionable
language of the day, were I to inquire *quo animo* have men organized themselves to prevent the enlistments and filling the loans?
the answer is clear—to weaken the United States, and give to the
enemy the advantage over our arms.

. . .

* From a speech in the House of Representatives by the Representative
from Tennessee on a bill authorizing the President to enlist additional troops,
January 15, 1814. *Annals*, 13th Congress, 2nd session, p. 993.

12.6 John C. Calhoun: "Combined with faction and ambition, opposition bursts those limits within which it may usefully act and becomes the first of political evils."*

. . .

Mr. Calhoun said, it now remained to consider the defence which gentlemen have made for their opposition to the war and the policy of their country; a subject which he conceives is of the greatest importance, not only as affecting the result of the present contest but the lasting peace and prosperity of our country. They assume as a fact that opposition is in its nature harmless, and that the calamities which have afflicted free States have originated in the blunders and folly of the Government, and not from the perverseness of opposition. Opposition, say they, is a very convenient thing; a wicked and foolish Administration never fail to attribute all of their miscarriages to it; and in confirmation of this doctrine, they appeal to Lord North's administration. 998 . . . In England, such is [the] power, patronage, and consequent influence [of the Executive]; such the veneration which its hereditary quality and long descent possess over the subjects of that Empire, that her most enlightened statesmen have ever thought that it endangered the other branches of her Government, and have with much wisdom, ever since the dawn of liberty in that country, strenuously opposed its encroachments.

Very different is the case here, under a Government purely Republican. It presents neither the cause to justify such vehemence of opposition, nor the means of restraining it when excited. But, even as applied to our Government, he would readily acknowledge there was a species of opposition, both innocent and useful. Opposition simply implies contrariety of opinion; and when used in the abstract, it admitted neither censure nor praise. It cannot be said to be either good or bad; useful or pernicious. It is not from itself, but from the connected circumstances, that it derives its character. When it is simply the result of that diversity in the structure of our intellect which conducts to different conclusions on the same subject, and is

* From a speech in the House of Representatives by the Representative from South Carolina on a bill authorizing the President to enlist additional troops, January 15, 1814. *Annals*, 13th Congress, 2nd session, pp. 997-999.

confined within those bounds which love of country and political honesty prescribe, it is one of the most useful guardians of liberty. It excites gentle collision, prompts to due vigilance, a quality so indispensable and at the same time so opposite to our nature, and results in the establishment of an enlightened policy and useful laws. Such are its qualities when united with patriotism and moderation.

But in many instances it assumes a far different character. Combined with faction and ambition, it bursts those limits within which it may usefully act, and becomes the first of political evils. If, sir, the gentlemen on the other side of the House intended to include this last species of opposition, as he was warranted to infer from their expression when they spoke of its harmless character, then have they made an assertion in direct contradiction to reason, experience, and all history. A factious opposition is compounded of such elements that no reflecting man will ever consider it as harmless. The fiercest and most ungovernable passions of our nature, ambition, pride, rivalry, and hate, enter into its dangerous composition—made still more so by its power of delusion, by which its projects against Government are covered in most instances, even to the eyes of its victims, by the 999 specious show of patriotism.

Thus constituted, who can estimate its force? Where can benevolent and social feelings be found sufficiently strong to counteract its progress? In love of country? Alas! the attachment to a party becomes stronger than that to our country. A factious opposition sickens at the sight of the prosperity and success of the country. Common adversity is its life; general prosperity its death. Nor is it only over our virtuous sentiments that this bane of freedom triumphs. Even the selfish passions of our nature, planted in our bosom for our individual safety, afford no obstacle to its progress. It is this opposition which gentlemen call harmless and treat with so much respect; it is this moral treason, to use the language of his friend from Tennessee (Mr. Grundy), which has in all ages and countries ever proved the most deadly foe to freedom. Nor is it then only dangerous when it breaks forth into open treason and rebellion. Without resort to violence, it is capable in a thousand ways to counteract and deaden all the motions of Government; to render its policy wavering and to compel it to submit to schemes of aggrandizement on the part of other Governments; or, if resistance is determined on, to render it feeble and ineffectual.

. . .

12.7   Zebulon R. Shipherd: "In the whole of the Constitution there is not a word, by reasonable exposition, that imposes upon the citizen the least obligation to aid the Government in the prosecution of a war beyond our territorial jurisdiction."*

. . .

Before I make any remarks directly to the bill on your table, Mr. Chairman, I feel constrained to notice the old subject of moral treason, renewed by the honorable gentleman from Tennessee (Mr. Grundy) in a speech in support of the bill. He has condescended to treat us with a definition of the crime in so enlarged a manner that even the minority on this floor, which the gentleman last session in the plenitude of his clemency saw fit to spare, will be fortunate if they escape being enmeshed in his net.

. . .

One cannot be guilty of treason in law, without lifting his arm against the Government. To commit this crime, he must set at defiance the sovereignty and power of the State; and as such acts constitute the crime legally, it may easily be supposed the moral traitor must set at defiance the authority and obligation of moral principles, the moral law not only [must] be infringed, but something more—its validity, its sovereignty over the heart and conscience must be denied, and all the feelings and passions be armed in hostile phalanx against the whole moral kingdom. If moral treason can exist, which is doubtful, certain I am that the sin of differing in opinion from the majority will not constitute the crime.

The gentleman's doctrine shall be tested by the Constitution; by the genuine principles of civil and religious liberty; by the purest laws of our nature; and the still more imposing laws of the Creator. And if on this trial it shall appear that we are wrong, then there can be no doubt but we must confess, repent, and reform; but if otherwise, we shall claim to be exempted from any further charges of the kind.

First. The Constitution, letter and spirit, is at the gentleman's service to prove us guilty, and when examined with care and can-

* From a speech in the House of Representatives by the Representative from New York on a bill authorizing the President to enlist additional troops, January 17, 1814. *Annals,* 13th Congress, 2nd session, pp. 1019-1022.

dor, placing a fair interpretation to every syllable, it will be found, instead of supporting him, to overthrow not only his superstructure but tear away his foundation. Sir, in the whole of this instrument there is not a word, by reasonable exposition, that imposes upon the citizen the least obligation to aid the Government in the prosecution of a war beyond our territorial jurisdiction, nor has the Government any power over its citizens in this respect, except the levying of taxes.

It is left to the feelings, discretion, and volition of every man whether, when solicited to lend his assistance, he will accept the invitation to engage in the war. Why this omission in the Constitu-
1020 tion? It was undoubtedly omitted by design for two reasons:

1st. To prevent the prosecution of foreign wars.

2nd. Because the power to drag forth the reluctant unconsenting citizen to a war of conquest is wholly inconsistent with the principles of civil and religious liberty.

Where would be the benefit to your countrymen, Mr. Chairman, in possessing a Constitutional right to aid, or refuse to aid, the Government in such a war, if there existed at the same time in the breast of the conscientious man a paramount obligation to become the auxiliary of the Government in the prosecution of such a war? This boasted privilege of our citizens would be but a shadow that never could be realized. Strange, too, that we should commend our Government, that leaves us free to choose or refuse, when the higher laws of morality take away all that liberty and leave us but one course to pursue.

. . .

The silence of the Constitution amounts to demonstration that our wise men believed such a power in Government was incompatible with the liberty intended to be secured by that instrument, and by such silence left that power as denied. If such were their views, they bespeak the soundness of their minds and goodness of their hearts; for it is folly to speak of a free government so long as the whole, or any part of the male population of the country, are compelled to embark in any ambitious project at the nod of a proud Executive or corrupt majority of the Legislature. Never let your country be mocked with the title of free, if the enjoyments and employments of domestic life are ever placed in the hands of any group of erring and perhaps wicked men. 1021

. . .

Secondly. A practice, under the creed of the honorable gentleman, would be an alarming encroachment upon the prerogatives of religion, and thereby blot another feature of liberty from the Constitution.

A man really pious, believing that offensive wars originate in the vilest passions of the depraved human heart, and that he shall incur guilt of a serious kind if he contributes to their prosecution, would suffer martyrdom before he would stain his soul with the blood of a slaughtered fellow-being. Shall it then be justified that such a man shall stand condemned as guilty of an odious violation of moral obligation because he obeys the dictates of conscience? Shall he have the liberty of judging for himself, from the lights of reason and revelation, or shall he be compelled to submit his conscience, his religion, and soul, to the arbitrament of a majority, who may scout the ties and obligations of the two former and deny the existence of the latter?

That there are people whose religious feelings are opposed to a war of revenge cannot be denied. Indeed, there is a set of Christians who deny the right of man to shed blood for any cause, . . . This society of Friends, not excelled if equalled for purity of morals, industry, and the practice of the most amiable virtues by any class of citizens, would not contribute to the prosecution of any war to save their lives. And those who know them will not doubt their sincerity, unless charity is frozen from their hearts. Yet this whole society, notwithstanding their high deserts, must all be subject to the gentleman's brand—"Moral Traitor."

Sir, will it be said that a majority is the best judge of what is morally right and wrong on the subject; and that those who are conscientiously opposed to a war of retaliation are squeamish, that they are deluded by education, that they have erroneous notions and opinions, and that an act of Congress can absolve them from guilt, and justify their conduct?

The good man never can be made easy in this way. The crime of a multitude is no less heinous in his sight than that of an individual —of men in office than men out of office. In his breast the laws of God are superior to the laws of men, and when he finds them opposed he obeys the former and disregards the latter. He reads— "Thou shalt not kill," in the former, and "Thou shalt kill," in the latter. He views the former as sacred, the latter as impious, and feels that he would rather wrap his soul in a single leaf of that book which says "Blessed is the peacemaker," than to be shielded against the vengeance of insulted Omnipotence with all the statutes that were ever made by man.

Sir, it is mocking such a man to tell him he is *1022* safe to shed his brother's blood if he has a statute to plead in justification. For the universe he will not believe you. He will believe that the voice of that blood will be heard, and that dreadful retribution will be awarded for the horrid deed. The right to tax—to take our property —is admitted, but a dominion over my conscience I deny. It does not exist—it must not exist. Take my property, rob me of my interest in this world, but attempt not to blast my hopes of Heaven.

. . .

Sir, permit me to say, if this is moral treason let me be the traitor. It will be pleasant while I live—it will console me when I die.

. . .

APPENDIX:
BIOGRAPHICAL SKETCHES

Biographical sketches are provided for all persons whose remarks are printed in this volume. The number (or numbers) in brackets following a sketch indicates the selection (or selections) in which that person's remarks are presented. An asterisk (*) following a name indicates that that person was a member of the Constitutional Convention of 1787. Nine persons are so marked.

ADAMS, JOHN. Born in Braintree, Massachusetts, 1735. Graduated from Harvard College in 1755; practiced law in Suffolk County; joined the Sons of Liberty and appeared before Governor Hutchinson, with Otis and Gridley, to argue against the Stamp Act; was elected to represent Boston in the general court in 1768; member of the First Continental Congress 1774-78; signed the Declaration of Independence; appointed commissioner to the Court of France; later made minister plenipotentiary to Holland to negotiate a loan in 1782; was the first minister to England 1785-88; elected in 1788 as the first Vice President of the United States, reelected in 1792 and served 1789-97; elected President of the United States and served 1797-1801. Died, 1826. [1.1]

ALLEN, JOHN. Born in Great Barrington, Massachusetts, 1763. Attended the common schools; studied law at the Litchfield (Connecticut) Law School; practiced law in Litchfield; member of the Connecticut House of Representatives 1793-96; served in U.S. House of Representatives 1797-99; was not a candidate for reelection; member of the state council and the state supreme court of errors 1800-06. Died, 1812. [3.4]

AMES, FISHER. Born in Dedham, Massachusetts, 1758. Graduated from Harvard College in 1774; practiced law in Dedham; served in the state house of representatives in 1788; member of the Massachusetts convention called for the ratification of the federal Constitution in 1788; served in the U.S. House of Representatives 1789-97; was not a candidate for reelection; resumed practice of law in Dedham;

member of the governor's council 1799-1800; chosen president of Harvard College but declined because of ill health. Died, 1808. [1.6, 5.4, 7.1, 7.2, 9.4]

ANDERSON, JOSEPH. Born near Philadelphia, 1757. Served throughout the Revolutionary War and attained the rank of brevet major; practiced law in Delaware; appointed U.S. judge of the Territory South of the River Ohio in 1791; member of the first constitutional convention of Tennessee; served in the U.S. Senate 1797-1815; was appointed first Comptroller of the Treasury and served in this capacity 1815-36. Died, 1837. [1.4]

BACON, JOHN. Born in Canterbury, Connecticut, 1738. Graduated from Princeton College in 1765; studied theology and had charge of the Old South Church, Boston, but was dismissed owing to differences of opinion; subsequently practiced law in Stockbridge, Massachusetts; served on the committee of correspondence, inspection, and safety in 1777; member of the state constitutional convention 1779-80; member of both the state house of representatives and senate between 1780 and 1806, serving as president of the senate in 1806; served in U.S. House of Representatives 1801-03; presiding judge of the court of common pleas; chief justice of the state supreme court in 1809. Died, 1820. [3.9]

BALDWIN, ABRAHAM.* Born in North Guilford, Connecticut, 1754. Moved with his father to New Haven in 1769; graduated from Yale College in 1772; studied theology and served as a chaplain in the Revolutionary Army 1777-1783; subsequently practiced law in Fairfield, Connecticut; moved to Augusta, Georgia, in 1784 and continued practice of law; served as a member of the state house of representatives in 1785; originator of the plan for and author of the charter of the University of Georgia and served as its president for a number of years; member of the Continental Congress 1785-88; member of the federal Constitutional Convention in 1787; served in the U.S. House of Representatives 1789-99; elected to the U.S. Senate in 1799 and served until his death in 1807. [7.2]

BARBOUR, PHILIP P. Born near Gordonsville, Virginia, 1783. Graduated from William and Mary College in 1799; practiced law in Bardstown, Kentucky; returned to Gordonsville in 1801 and continued practice of law; served as a member of the Virginia House of Representatives 1812-14; served as a Democrat in U.S. House of Representatives 1814-25 and as Speaker of the House, 1821-23; was not a candidate for reelection; appointed a judge of the General Court of Virginia and served for two years, resigning in 1827; again served in the U.S. House of Representatives 1827-30; president of the Virginia constitutional convention in 1829; appointed in 1830 judge of the United States Circuit Court for the Eastern District of Virginia; refused nomination for a judgeship of the state court of appeals, for governor, and for U.S. Senator; appointed Associate Justice of the U.S. Supreme Court in 1836. Died, 1841. [4.2]

BAYARD, JAMES ASHETON, SR. Born in Philadelphia, 1767. Graduated from Princeton College in 1784; practiced law in Wilmington, Delaware; declined appointment as minister to France tendered by President John Adams; served in the U.S. House of Representatives 1797-1803; unsuccessful candidate for reelection; served in the U.S. Senate 1804-13, resigned; appointed one of the members of the commission to negotiate peace with Great Britain in 1813; aided in negotiating the Treaty of Ghent; declined appointment as minister to Russia tendered by President Madison in 1815. Died, 1815. [3.10, 4.4, 6.2]

BENSON, EGBERT. Born in New York City, 1746. Graduated from Kings College (now Columbia University) in 1765; practiced law in New York City; deputy to the Provincial Convention in 1775; member of the council of safety in 1777 and 1778; in 1777 was appointed the first attorney general of New York and served until 1789; member of the state assembly 1777-81 and again in 1788; in 1783 was appointed one of the three commissioners to direct the embarkation of the Tory refugees for the loyal British Provinces; associate judge of the Supreme Court of New York 1784-88; member of the state constitutional convention which ratified the federal Constitution; served in the U.S. House of Representatives 1789-93; regent of New York University 1789-1802; appointed judge of the United States Circuit Court 1801; served as the first president of the New York Historical Society 1804-16; again served in the U.S. House of Representatives from March to August, 1813, when he resigned. Died, 1833. [11.4]

BOUDINOT, ELIAS. Born in Philadelphia, 1740. Practiced law in Elizabethtown, New Jersey; member of the board of trustees of Princeton College 1772-1821; member of the committee of safety in 1775; commissary general of prisoners in the Revolutionary Army 1776-79; member of the Continental Congress, 1777, 1778, and 1781-84; President of the Congress 1782-83 and signed the treaty of peace with England; served in the U.S. House of Representatives 1789-95; was not a candidate for reelection; Director of the Mint 1785-1805, resigned; elected first president of the American Bible Society in 1816. Died, 1821. [11.4]

BRECKENRIDGE, JOHN. Born near Staunton, Virginia, 1760. Educated at Augusta Academy (now Washington and Lee University) and at William and Mary College; elected a member of the house of burgesses in 1780 at the age of nineteen but, being under age, was not allowed to take his seat until elected the third time; served as subaltern in the Virginia militia in the latter part of the Revolutionary War; subsequently practiced law in Charlottesville, Virginia, in 1785; elected as a Democrat to the Third U.S. Congress, but resigned in 1792 before the commencement of the term; moved to Kentucky in 1793 and resumed practice of law in Lexington; unsuccessful candidate for election to the U.S. Senate in 1794; appointed attorney general of Kentucky in 1795; elected to the state house of representatives in 1798 and served as speaker in 1799 and 1800; member of the state constitutional convention in 1799; served in the U.S. Senate 1801-05, when he resigned to accept the position of Attorney General of the United States; served in this capacity until his death in 1806. [3.8]

BUCK, DANIEL. Born in Hebron, Connecticut, 1753. Studied law and commenced practice in Thetford, Vermont; prosecuting attorney of Orange County 1783-85; clerk of the court 1783-84; moved to Norwich, Vermont, in 1785; delegate to the state constitutional convention in 1791; member of the state house of representatives 1793-94 and served as speaker; served in the U.S. House of Representatives 1795-97; unsuccessful candidate for reelection; attorney general of Vermont 1802-03; moved to Chelsea, Vermont, and served in the state house of representatives 1806-07. Died, 1816. [1.5]

BURKE, AEDANUS. Born in Galway, Ireland, 1743. Attended the theological college at St. Omer, France; emigrated to the United States and settled in Charles Town (now Charleston), South Carolina; member of the South Carolina House of Representatives 1779-82; served in the Revolutionary War; was appointed one of three commissioners to prepare a digest of the state laws; member of the state convention to consider ratification of the federal Constitution; served in U.S. House of Representatives 1789-91; did not seek reelection; elected a chancellor of the courts of equity in 1799 and served until his death in 1802. [1.7]

CALHOUN, JOHN CALDWELL. Born near Calhoun Mills, South Carolina, 1782. Graduated from Yale College in 1804 and from Litchfield Law School in 1806; practiced law in Abbeville, South Carolina; member of the state house of representatives 1808-09; elected as "War Democrat" and served in U.S. House of Representatives 1811-17, resigned; appointed Secretary of War and served 1817-25; elected Vice President of the United States in 1824; reelected in 1828 on the Jackson ticket and served until December, 1832, when he resigned, having been elected to the U.S. Senate; reelected to the Senate in 1834 and 1840; resigned from Senate in 1843; appointed Secretary of State and served in this capacity April, 1844-March, 1845; again elected to the U.S. Senate and served from November, 1845, until his death in 1850. [5.2, 6.4, 10.2, 12.6]

CAMPBELL, GEORGE WASHINGTON. Born in parish on Tongue, Sutherlandshire, Scotland, 1769. Emigrated with parents to North Carolina in 1772; graduated from Princeton College in 1794; practiced law in Knoxville, Tennessee; served as a Democrat in U.S. House of Representatives 1803-09; judge of the state supreme court of errors and appeals 1809-11; elected to the U.S. Senate and served 1811-14, resigned; appointed Secretary of the Treasury and served from February to October, 1814; resigned due to ill health; again elected to the U.S. Senate and served 1815-18, resigned; minister to Russia 1818-21; member of the French Spoliation Claims Commission in 1831. Died, 1848. [2.5]

CARROLL, DANIEL.* Born in Upper Marlboro, Maryland, 1730. Member of the Continental Congress 1780-84; delegate to the convention that framed the federal Constitution; served in U.S. House of Representatives 1789-91; member of the first State Senate of Maryland; took an active part in fixing the seat of government; appointed a commissioner for surveying the District of Columbia by President Washington in 1791; engaged in agricultural pursuits, his farm being the site of the present city of Washington. Died, 1796. [11.3]

CHIPMAN, NATHANIEL. Born in Salisbury, Connecticut, 1752. Graduated from Yale College in 1777; served in the Revolutionary War; practiced law in Tinmouth, Vermont; member of the state house of representatives 1784-85; elected judge of the state supreme court in 1786 and chosen chief justice in 1789; appointed judge of the U.S. district court in 1791 and served until 1794; again elected chief justice of the state supreme court in 1796; served in U.S. Senate 1797-

1803; unsuccessful candidate for reelection; again a member of the state house of representatives 1806-11; chief justice of Vermont 1813-15. Died, 1843. [8.4]

CLAY, HENRY. Born in Hanover County, Virginia, 1777. Practiced law in Lexington, Kentucky; member of the state house of representatives in 1803; elected to U.S. Senate and served November, 1806-March, 1807, in contravention of the thirty-year age requirement of the Constitution; again a member of the state house of representatives 1808-09, serving as speaker in 1809; elected to the U.S. Senate and served January, 1810-March, 1811; elected to the U.S. House of Representatives and served 1811-1814, resigned; served as Speaker of the House from November, 1811, until his resignation; appointed one of the commissioners to negotiate the treaty of peace with Great Britain in 1814; reelected to the U.S. House of Representatives and served 1815-21; served as Speaker of the House December, 1815-October, 1820, when he resigned the office; once again elected to the U.S. House of Representatives and served 1823-25, resigned; again served as Speaker of the House December, 1823-March, 1825; appointed Secretary of State and served 1825-29; served in U.S. Senate 1831-42, resigned; unsuccessful candidate on the Whig ticket for President of the United States in 1832 and again in 1844; again elected to the United States Senate and served from 1849 until his death in 1852. [3.2, 3.7]

CRAWFORD, WILLIAM H. Born in Nelson County, Virginia, 1772. Attended Richmond Academy, Augusta, Georgia; practiced law in Lexington, Georgia; appointed to prepare a digest of the laws of Georgia in 1799; member of the state house of representatives 1803-07; served in the U.S. Senate 1807-13, resigned; declined the portfolio of Secretary of War tendered in 1813; minister to France 1813-15; appointed Secretary of War in 1815; was transferred to the Treasury in 1816 and served until 1825; unsuccessful Democrat candidate for President of the United States in 1824; because of illness refused the tender to remain as Secretary of the Treasury; returned to Georgia and was appointed judge of the northern circuit court in 1827, serving in this capacity until his death in 1834. [5.5]

DEXTER, SAMUEL. Born in Boston, 1761. Graduated from Harvard College in 1781; practiced law in Lunenberg, Massachusetts; member of the state house of representatives 1788-90; served in the U.S. House of Representatives 1793-95; served in the U.S. Senate 1799-

1800, resigning to become Secretary of War; served in this capacity May, 1800-January, 1801; served as Secretary of the Treasury January, 1801-May, 1801; resumed practice of law in Washington, D.C.; moved to Boston and continued practice of law; declined the appointment of minister to Spain; unsuccessful candidate for governor in 1816. Died, 1816. [9.4]

DUVAL, WILLIAM. Born in Mount Comfort, Virginia, 1784. Moved to Kentucky and commenced practice of law; elected as a Democrat to the U.S. House of Representatives and served 1813-15; appointed in 1821 United States judge for the East Florida District; Governor of the Territory of Florida 1822-34; appointed law agent in Florida 1841; moved to Texas in 1848; was the original of "Ralph Ringwood" of Washington Irving and "Nimrod Wildfire" of James K. Paulding. Died, 1854. [3.6]

FITZSIMONS, THOMAS.* Born in County Tubber, Wicklow, Ireland, 1741. Emigrated to the United States and entered a countinghouse in Philadelphia as a clerk; served in the Revolutionary War; member of the Continental Congress in 1782 and 1783; member of the Pennsylvania House of Representatives in 1786-87; delegate to the federal Constitutional Convention in 1787; served in the U.S. House of Representatives 1789-95; unsuccessful candidate for reelection in 1794; president of the Philadelphia Chamber of Commerce; trustee of the University of Pennsylvania; founder and director of the Bank of North America. Died, 1811. [7.2, 9.4]

GALLATIN, ALBERT. Born in Geneva, Switzerland, 1761. Graduated from the University of Geneva in 1779; emigrated to the United States and settled in Boston; served in the Revolutionary War; settled in Fayette County, Pennsylvania; member of the Pennsylvania constitutional convention of 1789; member of the state house or representatives 1790-92; presented credentials as a U.S. Senator elect in 1793, but the Senate ruled his election void because he had not been a citizen of the United States the term of years required by the Constitution; elected a member of the state house of representatives, but declined; served in the U.S. House of Representatives 1795-1801; was not a candidate for renomination; served as Secretary of the Treasury 1802-14; appointed one of the commissioners to negotiate the Treaty of Ghent; one of the commissioners which negotiated a commercial convention with Great Britain in 1816; served as U.S. envoy extraordinary and minister plenipotentiary to France 1815-23; minister plenipotentiary to Great Britain 1826-27; returned to New York City and became president of the National Bank of New York. Died, 1849. [3.4, 6.5, 12.2, 12.3]

GASTON, WILLIAM. Born in New Bern, North Carolina, 1778. Graduated from Princeton College in 1796; practiced law in New Bern; member of the state senate in 1800; served in the state house of representatives 1807-09 and as speaker in 1808; again a member of the state senate in 1812, 1818, and 1819; served as a Federalist in the U.S. House of Representatives 1813-17; was not a candidate for renomination; again served in the state house of representatives in 1824, 1827, 1828, 1829 and 1831; appointed judge of the Supreme Court of North Carolina in 1833, holding this position until his death; member of the state constitutional convention in 1835; declined a nomination for election to the U.S. Senate in 1840. Died, 1844. [9.2, 10.7]

GERRY, ELBRIDGE.* Born in Marblehead, Massachusetts, 1714. Graduated from Harvard College in 1762; engaged in commercial pursuits; member of the colonial house of representatives 1772-75; member of the Continental Congress 1776-81 and 1782-85; a signer of the Declaration of Independence; delegate to the federal Constitutional Convention in 1787; refused to sign the document but subsequently gave it his support; served in the U.S. House of Representatives 1789-93; sent to France with Marshall and Pinckney on a diplomatic mission in 1797; unsuccessful Democratic candidate for Governor of Massachusetts in 1801 and again in 1812; Governor of Massachusetts 1810-11; elected Vice President of the United States as a Democrat on the ticket with James Madison in 1812 and served from March, 1813, until his death in 1814. [10.1, 11.4]

GILES, WILLIAM BRANCH. Born in Amelia County, Virginia, 1762. Graduated from Princeton College in 1781; practiced law in Petersburg, Virginia; served in the U.S. House of Representatives 1790-98, resigned; member of the state house of delegates 1798-1800; served as a Democrat in the U.S. House of Representatives 1801-03; served in the U.S. Senate 1804-15, resigned; again a member of the state house of delegates in 1816-17 and 1826-27; unsuccessful candidate for election to the U.S. Senate in 1825; Governor of Virginia 1827-30; member of the state constitutional convention 1829-30; again elected governor in 1830 but declined. Died, 1830. [5.5, 8.1, 9.4]

GRISWOLD, ROGER. Born in Lyme, New London County, Connecticut, 1762. Graduated from Yale College in 1780; practiced law in both Norwich and Lyme, Connecticut; served in the U.S. House of Representatives 1795-1805, resigned; declined the portfolio of Secretary of War tendered in 1801; judge of the Supreme Court of Connecticut in 1807; Lieutenant Governor of Connecticut 1809-11; governor of the state from 1811 until his death in 1812. [4.1]

GROSVENOR, THOMAS P. Born in Pomfret, Windham County, Connecticut, 1778. Graduated from Yale College in 1800; practiced law in Hudson, New York; member of the state assembly 1810-12; district attorney of Essex County 1810-11; served as a Federalist in the U.S. House of Representatives 1813-17; engaged in the practice of law in Baltimore. Died, 1817. [10.4]

GRUNDY, FELIX. Born in Berkeley County, Virginia, 1777. Moved with parents to Kentucky; practiced law in Bardstown, Kentucky; member of the Kentucky constitutional convention in 1799; member of the state house of representatives 1800-05; chosen judge of the Supreme Court of Kentucky in 1806 and became chief justice in 1807; moved to Nashville, Tennessee, in 1807 and resumed practice of law; served as a "War Democrat" in the U.S. House of Representatives 1811-14, resigned in 1814; member of the Tennessee House of Representatives 1815-19; served in the U.S. Senate 1829-38, resigned; appointed Attorney General of the United States in 1838, resigning this position in 1839 to return to the U.S. Senate, where he served until his death in 1840. [12.5]

HARPER, ROBERT GOODLOE. Born near Fredericksburg, Virginia, 1765. Moved with his parents to Granville, North Carolina; served in Revolutionary War; graduated from Princeton College in 1785; practiced law in Ninety-Six District, South Carolina; member of the state house of representatives 1790-95; served in the U.S. House of Representatives 1795-1801; was an unsuccessful candidate for reelection; moved to Baltimore, Maryland, and resumed practice of law; served in the War of 1812, attaining the rank of major general; member of the State Senate of Maryland; served as a U.S. Senator from Maryland 1815-16, resigned. Died, 1825. [6.6, 6.7, 12.4]

HARTLEY, THOMAS. Born in Reading, Pennsylvania, 1748. Practiced law in Yorktown (now York), Pennsylvania; member of the Provincial Convention in Philadelphia in 1775; served in the Revolutionary War, attaining the rank of colonel; member of the state house of representatives in 1778; member of the council of censors in 1783; member of the state convention which adopted the Constitution of the United States in 1787; served in the U.S. House of Representatives from 1789 until his death in 1800. [1.7, 10.1, 11.4]

HILLHOUSE, JAMES. Born in Montville, Connecticut, 1754. Graduated from Yale College in 1773; practiced law in New Haven; served in the Revolutionary War; member of the state house of representatives 1780-85; member of the council in 1789 and 1790; served in U.S. House of Representatives 1791-96, resigned, having been elected to the U.S. Senate; served in Senate 1796-1810, resigning to become commissioner of the school fund, a capacity in which he served until 1825; member of the Hartford Convention; treasurer of Yale College 1782-1832. Died, 1832. [9.1, 9.5]

HUGER, BENJAMIN. Born at or near Charleston, South Carolina, 1768. Engaged in agricultural activities; member of the state house of representatives 1798-99; served in the U.S. House of Representatives 1799-1805; again a member of the state house of representatives 1808-12; again served in U.S. House of Representatives, 1815-17; member of the state senate 1818-23 and served as president 1819-22. Died, 1823. [2.4]

HUNTINGTON, BENJAMIN. Born in Norwich, Connecticut, 1736. Graduated from Yale College in 1761; practiced law in Norwich; member of the state house of representatives 1771-1780, serving as speaker in 1778 and 1779; clerk of the state house of representatives in 1776 and 1777; delegate to the Provincial Congress at New Haven in 1778; member of the Continental Congress 1780-1784, 1787, and 1788; member of the state senate 1781-90 and 1791-93; mayor of Norwich 1784-1796, resigned; elected to the U.S. House of Representatives and served 1789-91; judge of the superior court of the state 1793-98. Died, 1800. [11.3]

JACKSON, JAMES. Born in Moreton-Hampstead, Devonshire, England, 1757. Emigrated to the United States in 1772 and located in Savannah, Georgia; clerk of the court, by election of the Provincial Congress, in 1776 and 1777; member of the first constitutional convention of Georgia 1777; elected govenor in 1778, but declined; served in Revolutionary War; served in U.S. House of Representatives

1789-91; contested the election of Anthony Wayne in the Second Congress, and the seat was declared vacant by the House of Representatives in 1792; served in the U.S. Senate 1793-95, resigned; Governor of Georgia 1798-1801; was again elected to the U.S. Senate, and served from 1801 until his death in 1806. [1.7, 2.6, 6.1, 7.1, 11.1, 11.4]

LAWRENCE, THOMAS. [Correct spelling: Laurence]. Born in Cornwall, England, 1750. Emigrated to the United States and settled in New York City; practiced law in New York City; served in the Revolutionary War and became aide-de-camp to General Washington; regent of the University of the State of New York; trustee of Columbia College 1784-1810; member of the Continental Congress 1785-87; member of the state senate in 1789; served in the U.S. House of Representatives 1789-93; United States judge of the District of New York 1794-96, resigned; served in U.S. Senate 1796-1800, resigned. Died, 1810. [11.5]

LEE, RICHARD BLAND. Born in Prince William County, Virginia, 1761. Attended William and Mary College; member of the state house of delegates 1784-88; served in the U.S. House of Representatives 1789-95; unsuccessful candidate for reelection; again a member of the state house of delegates 1796 and 1799-1806; moved to Washington, D.C., about 1815; appointed in 1816 commissioner to adjudicate claims arising out of the loss or destruction of property during the War of 1812; appointed in 1819 judge of the Orphans Court of the District of Columbia and served until his death in 1827. [1.2, 6.1]

LIVERMORE, SAMUEL. Born in Waltham, Middlesex County, Massachusetts, 1732. Graduated from Nassau Hall (now Princeton University) in 1752; practiced law in Waltham, Massachusetts; moved to Portsmouth, New Hampshire, and later to Londonderry; member of the general court from Londonderry 1768-70; moved to Holderness in 1775; state's attorney for three years; elected a member of the Continental Congress in 1780; chief justice of the state supreme court 1782-89; member of the state constitutional convention, 1788; served in the U.S. House of Representatives 1789-93; president of the state constitutional convention in 1791; served in the U.S. Senate 1792-1801, resigned. Died, 1803. [8.2, 11.3, 11.5]

LIVINGSTON, EDWARD. Born in Clermont, New York, 1764. Graduated from Princeton College in 1781; practiced law in New York City;

served in the U.S. House of Representatives 1795-1801; United States district attorney 1801-03; mayor of New York City 1801-03; moved to New Orleans in 1804; engaged in the practice of law and in the real estate business; author of a legal code for Louisiana; served at the Battle of New Orleans on the staff of General Jackson; member of the state house of representatives, 1820; served as a Democrat in the U.S. House of Representatives 1823-29; served in the U.S. Senate 1829-1831, when he resigned, having been appointed to the Cabinet; Secretary of State 1831-33; minister plenipotentiary to France 1833-35. Died, 1836. [3.4]

LLOYD, JAMES. Born in Boston, Massachusetts, 1769. Graduated from Harvard College in 1787; engaged in merchandizing and foreign trade; member of Massachusetts Senate 1804; elected to U.S. Senate in 1808 to complete the unexpired term of John Quincy Adams; reelected in 1808 and served until he resigned in 1813; later reelected and served in the same body 1822-26 when he again resigned; took up permanent residence in Philadelphia in 1826. Died, 1831. [5.5]

McDUFFIE, GEORGE. Born in Columbia County, Georgia, 1790. Graduated from South Carolina College (now the University of South Carolina) in 1813; practiced law in Pendleton, South Carolina; member of the state house of representatives 1818-20; elected as a Democrat to the U.S. House of Representatives and served 1821-34, resigned; Governor of South Carolina 1834-36; president of the board of trustees of South Carolina College; served in the U.S. Senate 1842-46, resigned. Died, 1851. [2.8]

MADISON, JAMES.* Born in Port Conway, King George County, Virginia, 1751. Graduated from Princeton College in 1771; studied law at Princeton College one year; returned to Virginia and was admitted to the bar; member of the committee of safety from Orange County in 1774; delegate in the Williamsburg Convention in 1776; member of the first General Assembly of Virginia in 1776, and was unanimously elected a member of the executive council in 1778; member of the Continental Congress 1780-83 and 1786-88; prominent delegate in the federal Constitutional Convention 1787; served in U.S. House of Representatives 1789-97; declined a mission to France and also the position of Secretary of State, both tendered in 1794; again a member of the Virginia Assembly from Orange County in 1799; served as Secretary of State 1801-09; elected President of the United States as a Democrat, and served 1809-17; delegate in the

Virginia constitutional convention in 1829; rector of the University of Virginia. Died, 1836. [1.7, 2.6, 2.9, 3.1, 5.1, 5.4, 7.1, 9.4, 10.1, 11.1, 11.2, 11.3]

MASON, STEVENS THOMSON. Born in Stafford County, Virginia, 1760. Attended William and Mary College; practiced law in Dumfries, Prince William County, Virginia; served in the Revolutionary Army as an aide to General Washington at Yorktown; brigadier general in the Virginia militia; member of the state house of delegates 1783 and 1794; served in the state senate 1786-90; delegate to the state constitutional convention in 1788; served as a Democrat in the U.S. Senate 1794 until his death in 1803. [8.4]

MILLER, MORRIS SMITH. Born in New York City, 1780. Graduated from Union College in 1798; served as private secretary to Governor Jay and, subsequently, commenced the practice of law in Utica, New York; judge of the Court of Common Pleas of Oneida County from 1810 until his death; served as a Federalist in U.S. House of Representatives 1813-15; represented the United States government at the negotiation of a treaty between the Seneca Indians and the proprietors of the Seneca Reservation in 1819. Died, 1824. [3.6]

MORRIS, GOUVERNEUR.* Born in Morrisania (now a part of New York City), 1752. Graduated from Kings College (now Columbia University) in 1768; practiced law in New York City; member of the New York Provincial Congress 1775-77; signer of the Articles of Confederation in 1775; member of the committee to prepare a form of government for the state of New York in 1776; member of the first state council of safety in 1777; member of the first state assembly 1777-78; member of the Continental Congress 1777-78; appointed assistant minister of finance in 1781 and served for four years; member of federal Constitutional Convention in 1787; commissioner to England in 1789; minister plenipotentiary to France 1792-94; returned to the U.S. in 1798; served in the U.S. Senate 1800-03; chairman of the Erie Canal Commission, 1810-13. Died, 1816. [8.4]

MURRAY, WILLIAM VANS. Born in Cambridge, Dorchester County, Maryland, 1760. Studied law at the Temple, London; returned to the United States and practiced law in Cambridge; member of the state house of delegates in 1791; served in U.S. House of Representatives 1791-97; minister resident to the Netherlands 1797-1801; while holding this post was appointed in 1799 a member of a diplomatic mission to France. Died, 1803. [1.5]

NELSON, ROGER. Born near Frederick, Maryland, 1759. Attended William and Mary College; served in the Revolutionary War, attaining the rank of brigadier general; practiced law in Taneytown and Frederick; held several local offices; member of the state house of delegates in 1795, 1801, and 1802; served as a Democrat in U.S. House of Representatives 1804-10, resigned; associate justice of the Maryland District Court. Died, 1815. [2.1, 10.6]

NICHOLAS, JOHN. Born in Williamsburg, Virginia, about 1757. Graduated from William and Mary College; practiced law in Williamsburg; served in the U.S. House of Representatives 1793-1801; moved to Geneva, Ontario County, New York; member of the New York State Senate 1806-09; judge of the court of common pleas 1806-19; engaged in agricultural pursuits. Died, 1819. [12.1]

NICHOLSON, JOSEPH HOPPER. Born in Chestertown, Kent County, Maryland, 1770. Practiced law; member of the state house of delegates 1796-98; served in the U.S. House of Representatives 1799-1806, resigned; participated in the defense of Fort McHenry during the War of 1812; served as associate justice of the Maryland Court of Appeals from 1806 until his death in 1817. [8.4]

OTIS, HARRISON GRAY. Born in Boston, Massachusetts, 1765. Graduated from Harvard College in 1783; practiced law in Boston; member of the state house of representatives in 1796; appointed district attorney for the district of Massachusetts, May, 1796, and served until December, 1796; served in U.S. House of Representatives 1797-1801; was not a candidate for reelection; appointed U.S. district attorney for Massachusetts 1801-02; member and speaker of the state house of representatives 1802-04; served in the state senate 1805-16, serving as president in 1805 and 1808-10; overseer of Harvard College 1810-23; delegate to the Hartford Convention in 1814; judge of the court of common pleas 1814-1818; served in the U.S. Senate 1817-22, resigned; unsuccessful candidate for Governor of Massachusetts 1823; fellow of Harvard College 1823-25; mayor of Boston 1829-32. Died, 1848. [12.2]

PAGE, JOHN. Born in Gloucester County, Virginia, 1744. Graduated from William and Mary College in 1763; served under Washington in an expedition against the French and Indians; delegate to the state constitutional convention in 1776; Lieutenant Governor of Virginia when the Revolution started; served in the Revolutionary War and attained the rank of colonel; member of the state house of delegates 1781-83 and 1785-88; elected to the U.S. House of Representatives and served 1789-97; again a member of the state house of delegates in 1797, 1798, 1800, and 1801; Governor of Virginia 1802-05; appointed United States commissioner of loans for Virginia and held office until his death in Richmond, Virginia, 1808. [1.7, 2.3]

PARKER, JOSIAH. Born in "Macclesfield," Isle of Wight County, Virginia, 1751. Member of the committee of safety in 1775 and of the Virginia Convention that held sessions in March, July, and December of that year; served in the Revolutionary War and attained the rank of colonel; member of the Virginia House of Delegates in 1780 and 1781; naval officer at Portsmouth, Virginia, 1786; unsuccessful candidate for delegate to the Virginia Convention in 1788; served in the U.S. House of Representatives 1789-1801. Died, 1810. [1.6]

PINCKNEY, CHARLES.* Born in Charleston, South Carolina, 1757. Practiced law in 1779; member of the state house of representatives 1779-84, 1786-89, 1792-96, 1805, 1806, and 1810-14; taken prisoner by the British in 1780; member of the Continental Congress 1784-87; also a member of the federal Constitutional Convention in 1787; member of the state constitutional conventions in 1788 and 1790 and served as president; Governor of South Carolina 1789-92 and 1796-98; elected as a Democrat to the U.S. Senate and served 1798-1801, resigned; minister to Spain 1801-05; again Governor of South Carolina 1806-08; served as a Democrat in U.S. House of Representatives 1819-21; resumed practice of law and also engaged in agricultural pursuits. Died, 1824. [7.5, 8.3, 9.3]

POPE, JOHN. Born in Prince William County, Virginia, 1770. Moved to Springfield, Kentucky; practiced law in Washington, Shelby, and Fayette Counties; member of the state house of representatives in 1802, 1806, and 1807; served as a Democrat in U.S. Senate 1807-13; member of the Kentucky State Senate 1825-29; Territorial Governor of Arkansas 1829-35; resumed practice of law in Springfield, Kentucky; elected as a Democrat to the U.S. House of Representatives 1837-43; unsuccessful candidate for reelection in 1842. Died, 1845. [2.2]

PORTER, PETER B. Born in Salisbury, Connecticut, 1773. Graduated from Yale College in 1791; practiced law in Canandaigua, New York; clerk of Ontario County 1797-1804; member of the state assembly in 1802 and again in 1828; moved to Buffalo; served as a Democrat in

U.S. House of Representatives 1809-13; declined to be a candidate for renomination; appointed a canal commissioner in 1811; served in the War of 1812, attaining the rank of major general, New York Volunteers; presented a gold medal by joint resolution of Congress for gallantry; again elected to the U.S. House of Representatives 1815-16, resigned; secretary of state of New York in 1815 and 1816; unsuccessful candidate for Governor of the State of New York 1817; regent of the University of the State of New York 1824-30; Secretary of War 1828-29; moved to Niagara Falls, where he died, 1844. [3.3, 5.5]

QUINCY, JOSIAH. Born in Boston, Massachusetts, 1772. Graduated from Harvard College in 1790; practiced law in Boston; served in the state senate in 1804 and 1805; served as a Federalist in U.S. House of Representatives 1805-13; was not a candidate for reelection; again served in the state senate 1813-20; member of the state house of representatives in 1821-22; served as speaker of the state house of representatives in 1822; delegate to the state constitutional convention in 1820; judge of the Boston municipal court in 1822; mayor of Boston, 1823-29; president of Harvard College 1829-1845. Died, 1864. [3.5, 7.4, 10.6]

RANDOLPH, JOHN. Born in Prince George County, Virginia, 1773. Studied at the College of New Jersey (now Princeton University) and Columbia College; studied law in Philadelphia but never practiced; member of U.S. House of Representatives 1799-1813 and served as a manager for the House in impeachment preceedings of 1804 against U.S. District Judge John Pickering and U.S. Supreme Court Justice Samuel Chase; defeated for reelection in 1812 but was again elected and served 1815-17; defeated for reelection in 1816 but was elected in 1818 and four times thereafter, serving until he resigned in 1825; appointed to U.S. Senate in 1825 to complete an unexpired term ending March 3, 1827, and during that period fought a duel with Henry Clay without damage to either; failed to win reelection to the Senate but was elected to the U.S. House of Representatives and served 1827-29; did not seek election for the next two Congresses but in 1832 was again elected to the House and had served less than three months when he died; during 1829-30 served in the Virginia constitutional convention and as minister to Russia. Died, 1833. [4.4]

SCOTT, THOMAS. Born in Chester County, Pennsylvania, 1739. Practiced law in Lancaster County, Pennsylvania; moved to Westmoreland County, Pennsylvania, in 1770; justice of the peace in 1773; member of the first Pennsylvania Assembly in 1776; member of the supreme council in 1777; member of the state convention that ratified the federal Constitution; served in U.S. House of Representatives 1789-91; again a member of the Pennsylvania Assembly in 1791; again served in U.S. House of Representatives 1793-95. Died, 1796. [11.4]

SEDGWICK, THEODORE. Born in West Hartford, Connecticut, 1746. Attended Yale College; practiced law in Great Barrington, Massachusetts; served in the Revolutionary War; member of the Massachusetts House of Representatives in 1780, 1782, and 1783; served in the state senate in 1784 and 1785; member of the Continental Congress 1785-88; again a member of the state house of representatives in 1787 and 1788 and served as speaker; delegate to the state convention that adopted the federal Constitution in 1788; served in U.S. House of Representatives 1789-96, resigned; served in the U.S. Senate 1796-99; again served in the House of Representatives 1799-1801; served as Speaker of the House of Representatives; judge of the Supreme Court of Massachusetts 1802-13. Died, 1813. [1.8]

SHERMAN, ROGER.* Born in Newton, Massachusetts, 1721. Moved to New Milford, Connecticut, in 1743; practiced law; member of the Connecticut Assembly 1755, 1756, 1758-61, and 1764-66; justice of the peace Litchfield County 1755-61, and of the quorum 1759-61; served in the state senate 1766-85; judge of the superior court 1766, 1767, and 1773-88; member of the council of safety 1777-79; member of the Continental Congress 1774-81, 1783, and 1784; a signer of the Declaration of Independence and a member of the committee which drafted it; member of the committee to prepare the Articles of Confederation; mayor of New Haven from 1784 until his death; delegate to the federal Constitutional Convention in 1787; served in U.S. House of Representatives 1789-91; elected to the U.S. Senate and served from 1791 until his death in 1793. [2.9, 4.3, 11.1, 11.4]

SHIPHERD, ZEBULON. Born in Granville, Washington County, New York, 1768. Practiced law in Granville, New York; served as a Federalist in the U.S. House of Representatives 1813-15; resumed practice of law in Granville; trustee of Middlebury College, Vermont, 1819-41; moved to Moriah, Essex County, about 1830, where he died in 1841. [12.7]

SMITH, WILLIAM L. Born in Charleston, South Carolina, 1758. Studied law in Middle Temple in London, England; pursued higher studies in Geneva, 1774-78; returned to Charleston and practiced law; member of the privy council in 1784; member of the state house of representatives 1784-88; warden of the city of Charleston in 1786; served in the U.S. House of Representatives 1789-97, resigned; served as U.S. minister to Portugal 1797-1801, took leave of absence; returned to Charleston; unsuccessful Federalist candidate for election to the U.S. House of Representatives in 1804, 1806, and 1808; again a member of the state house of representatives in 1808; president of the Santee Canal Company. Died, 1812. [8.2, 11.5]

SMYTH, ALEXANDER. Born on the Island of Rathlin, Ireland, 1765. Emigrated to the United States and settled in Botetourt County, Virginia, in 1775; practiced law in Abingdon, Virginia; member of the state house of delegates in 1792, 1796, 1801, 1802, and 1804-08; served in the state senate in 1808 and 1809; served in the U.S. army as a colonel 1798-1812, and as Inspector General with rank of brigadier general 1812-13; again a member of the state house of delegates in 1816, 1817, 1826, and 1827; served in the U.S. House of Representatives 1817-25; again elected to U.S. House of Representatives and served from 1827 until his death in 1830. [5.3]

STONE, MICHAEL JENIFER. Born near Tobacco, Charles County, Maryland, 1747. Member of the state house of delegates 1781-83; member of the state convention that ratified the federal Constitution in 1788; served in the U.S. House of Representatives 1789-91; appointed judge of the First Judicial District of Maryland in 1791. Died, 1812. [2.9, 4.3, 8.2]

SUMTER, THOMAS. Born in Hanover County, Virginia, 1734. Engaged in surveying; moved to South Carolina about 1760 and settled near Stateburg; served in the Revolutionary War, attaining the rank of brigadier general; member of the South Carolina Senate in 1781 and 1782; elected a delegate to the Continental Congress in 1783, but declined to accept; delegate to the state convention that ratified the federal Constitution; served in the U.S. House of Representatives 1789-93; did not seek reelection; again served in U.S. House of Representatives 1797-1801, resigned; served in U.S. Senate 1801-10, resigned. Died, 1832. [11.4]

SYLVESTER, PETER. (Correct spelling: Silvester). Born at Shelter Island, Long Island, New York, 1734; practiced law in Albany; member of the Albany Common Council in 1772; member of the committee of safety in 1774; served in the First and Second Provincial Congresses in 1775 and 1776; moved to Kinderhook, New York, and practiced law; appointed judge of the Court of Common Pleas of Columbia County in 1786; regent of the University of the State of New York 1787-1808; served in the U.S. House of Representatives 1789-93; served in the state assembly in 1788; member of the state senate 1796-1800; again served in the state assembly 1803-06. Died, 1808. [11.3]

TAUL, MICAH. Born in Bladensburg, Maryland, 1785. Moved to Kentucky with his parents in 1787; practiced law in Monticello, Kentucky; clerk of Wayne County courts in 1801; served as a colonel of Wayne County Volunteers in the War of 1812; served as a Democrat in the U.S. House of Representatives fom 1815-17; did not seek re-election; moved to Winchester, Tennessee, and then to Mardisville, Alabama, where he died in 1850. [10.5]

TAYLOR, JOHN. Born at Mill Farm, Caroline County, Virginia, 1754. Graduated from William and Mary College in 1770; practiced law in Caroline County in 1774; served in the Revolutionary War, attaining rank of colonel; member of the state house of delegates 1779-85 and 1796-1800; served in the U.S. Senate 1792-94, resigned; appointed to U.S. Senate to fill a vacancy and served from June to December, 1803; was not a candidate for reelection; served in the U.S. Senate from 1822 until his death in 1824. [4.7]

TRACY, URIAH. Born in Franklin, Connecticut, 1755. Graduated from Yale College in 1778; practiced law in Litchfield, Connecticut; member of state house of representatives 1788-93, serving as speaker in 1793; state's attorney for Litchfield County 1794-99; served in the U.S. House of Representatives 1793-96, resigned; elected to the U.S. Senate and served from 1796 until his death in 1807. [4.6, 9.3]

TUCKER, HENRY ST. GEORGE. Born in Williamsburg, Virginia, 1780. Graduated from William and Mary College in 1798; practiced law in Winchester, Virginia; Captain of Cavalry in the War of 1812; served in the U.S. House of Representatives 1815-19; was not a candidate for renomination; chancellor of the Fourth Judicial District of Virginia 1824-31; during this period he maintained a private law school from which many of the most distinguished lawyers in the state came; president of the Court of Appeals of Virginia 1831-41; professor of law at the University of Virginia from 1841-45; author of the honor system adopted at the university; author of *Tucker's Commentaries* and also of works dealing with the formation of the Constitution. Died, 1848. [2.7]

TUCKER, THOMAS TUDOR. Born in Port Royal, Bermuda, 1745. Studied medicine at the University of Edinburgh, Scotland; practiced medicine in South Carolina; served as a surgeon in the Revolutionary War; member of the Continental Congress in 1787 and 1788; served in the U.S. House of Representatives 1789-93; appointed U.S. Treasurer and served from 1801 until his death in 1828. [11.3]

VINING, JOHN. Born in Dover, Kent County, Delaware, 1758. Practiced law in New Castle County; member of the Continental Congress 1784-86; member of the state house of representatives in 1787 and 1788; served in the U.S. House of Representatives 1789-93; was not a candidate for renomination; served in the U.S. Senate 1793-98, resigned. Died, 1802. [11.1]

WASHINGTON, GEORGE.* Born at "Wakefield," near Popes Creek, Westmoreland County, Virginia, 1732. Attended private schools; engaged in the surveying of lands; in 1751 appointed adjutant general of a military district in Virginia with the rank of major; served in the French and Indian War, becoming aide-de-camp to General Braddock; appointed Commander-in-Chief of colonial forces, and from 1755 to 1758 engaged in recruiting and organizing troops for colonial defense; commanded a successful expedition to Fort Duquesne in 1758; served as a magistrate and as a member of the colonial house of burgesses 1758-74; delegate to the Williamsburg Convention of August, 1773; member of the First and Second Continental Congresses in 1774 and 1775; unanimously chosen in 1775 as Commander-in-Chief of all the colonial forces raised or to be raised and commanded the colonial armies throughout the war for independence; was a delegate to, and president of, the federal Constitutional Convention in Philadelphia; unanimously elected the first President of the United States in 1788; reelected in 1792 and served until 1797. Died, 1799. [1.3]

WHITE, ALEXANDER. Born in Frederick County, Virginia, 1738. Studied law at the Inner Temple, London, in 1762 and attended Gray's in 1763; member of the state house of delegates 1782-86 and in 1788; delegate to the state convention in 1788; served in the U.S. House of Representatives 1789-93; again a member of the state house of delegates 1789-1801; appointed by President Washington as one of three commissioners to lay out the city of Washington, D.C., and erect the public buildings; served until May, 1802. Died, 1804. [3.1, 7.1]

WHITE, SAMUEL. Born near Dover, Kent County, Delaware 1770. Attended Cokesbury College, Maryland; practiced law in Dover, Delaware; served two years as a captain in the U.S. Army; adjutant general of Delaware 1803; served in the U.S. Senate from 1801 until his death in 1809. [4.5]

WILLIAMS, LEWIS. Born in Surry County, North Carolina, 1786. Graduated from the University of North Carolina in 1808; member of the state house of commons in 1813 and 1814; served in the U.S. House of Representatives from March, 1815, until his death; received the title of "father of the House." Died, 1842. [10.3]

3 1543 50084 3109

342.73
U58s

724675

DATE DUE

AP 5'78

WITHDRAWN

Cressman Library
Cedar Crest College
Allentown, Pa. 18104

DEMCO